The International Political Economy of New Regionalisms Series

The International Political Economy of New Regionalisms series presents innovative analyses of a range of novel regional relations and institutions. Going beyond established, formal, interstate economic organizations, this essential series provides informed interdisciplinary and international research and debate about myriad heterogeneous intermediate level interactions.

Reflective of its cosmopolitan and creative orientation, this series is developed by an international editorial team of established and emerging scholars in both the South and North. It reinforces ongoing networks of analysts in both academia and think-tanks as well as international agencies concerned with micro-, meso- and macro-level regionalisms.

Recent titles in the series

Governing Regional Integration for Development
Monitoring Experiences, Methods and Prospects
Edited by Philippe De Lombaerde, Antoni Estevadeordal and Kati Suominen

Beyond Regionalism?
Regional Cooperation, Regionalism and Regionalization in the Middle East
Edited by Cilja Harders and Matteo Legrenzi

The EU-Russian Energy Dialogue
Europe's Future Energy Security
Edited by Pami Aalto

Regionalism, Globalisation and International Order
Europe and Southeast Asia
Jens-Uwe Wunderlich

Published by
Ashgate Publishing Limited
Gower House
Croft Road
Aldershot
Hampshire GU11 3HR
England

Ashgate Publishing Company
Suite 420
101 Cherry Street
Burlington, VT 05401-4405
USA

Ashgate website: http://www.ashgate.com

British Library Cataloguing in Publication Data
Chin, Christine B.N., 1963-
    Cruising in the global economy : profits, pleasure and work
    at sea. - (The international political economy of new
    regionalisms series)
    1. Cruise lines 2. Cruise ships - Economic aspects
    I. Title
    387.5'42

Library of Congress Cataloging-in-Publication Data
Chin, Christine B. N., 1963-
    Cruising in the global economy : profits, pleasure, and work at sea / by Christine B.N.
Chin.
        p. cm. -- (The international political economy of new regionalisms series)
    Includes bibliographical references and index.
    ISBN-13: 978-0-7546-7242-5
    1. Ocean travel--Economic aspects. 2. Cruise lines. I. Title.

G550.C55 2008
338.4'791045--dc22

2007034131

ISBN 978 0 7546 7242 5

Printed and bound in Great Britain by MPG Books Ltd, Bodmin, Cornwall.

Contents

Acknowledgements

As an academic who specializes in the cross-border movements of peoples, and as a self-professed 'land-lubber', I dared venture and immerse myself in another world; one with which I was barely familiar save for fond memories and yearnings for the occasional underwater adventure and/or boat-ride. For the past several years, I experienced a deep sense of intellectual excitement and frustration as I explored the maritime world and its inhabitants, wanting to understand the ways in which life at sea is changing in relation to life on land. I had to be able to identify and draw from the contributions of different academic fields for the construction of a framework on which I could arrange the puzzle pieces into a coherent albeit complicated picture of changes in the maritime world. Although this book is the culmination of my integrative efforts on the topic, it could not have come about without the contributions of many individuals.

I am deeply grateful to undergraduates in the honours program, as well as graduate students at American University for their intellectual curiosity, and especially their courage to explore and debate the relevance of theory to the conduct of social life. By their incessant questions on the nature and status of my research, they provided the extra fuel to sustain my intellectual stamina. Graduate research assistants, Emily Morris and Joyce Tam, were indispensable to the research process for this book. I learned much from the many hours of intellectual conversations and wish them the very best as they now pursue their respective careers.

Thank you much to my colleagues within and beyond the School of International Service at American University: Fanta Aw, Robin Broad, Hamid Mowlana, Fantu Cheru, Mary Kennard, Peter Lewis (now at Johns Hopkins University), Michael Mass, James Mittelman, Randolph Persaud, John Richardson, Vidyamali Samarasinghe, Paula Warrick and Gary Wright. They supported this project directly and indirectly in their own ways, e.g., from intellectual discussions on conceptual issues, to sharing their experiences and love of travel on cruise ships. I am indebted especially to Fanta Aw for patiently listening to the development of key arguments as they unfolded in these past years, asking questions that I did not like (read: ones that I could not answer), and to be sure, encouraging me not to give up on completing the puzzle. To Gary Wright and Cynthia McClintock (George Washington University), I extend a heart-felt 'thank you' as well for helping me with a very important piece of the puzzle.

Many thanks to colleagues in the larger profession of International Studies with whom I have had conversations over the past few years on different aspects of the framework: Anna Agathangelou, Robert W. Cox, Cynthia Enloe, Lily H. M. Ling, Timothy M. Shaw, J. Ann Tickner, Cynthia Enloe and Sandra Whitworth. An earlier version of Chapter 5 was presented at the 2006 International Studies Association

Annual Convention. Thank you to the discussant Carrie Currie, as well as fellow panellists and members of the audience who offered their constructive criticisms.

My gratitude to the anonymous reviewers who provided incisive comments that could only make for a clearer and stronger manuscript. Thank you to the editorial team at Ashgate, especially to Kirstin Howgate, publisher of the Politics and International Relations titles; Margaret Younger, Assistant Editor and Pam Bertram, Senior Desk Editor. It is my honour and privilege to work with Tim Shaw, who serves also as editor of the International Political Economy of New Regionalisms series. He continues to be unswerving in his encouragement and support of my work in general, and this book's road to publication in particular.

To the women and men seafarers who took the time to speak with me about their shipboard lives, please know that I am immensely appreciative of your efforts. My gratitude to the individuals listed below as well who not only patiently answered my questions but took the time to educate me on complex dimensions of the maritime world: Bro. Ed. Munro, Chaplain of the Baltimore International Seafarers' Center; Mary H. T. Davisson who eventually succeeded Bro. Munro as chaplain; Douglas B. Stevenson, Director of Policy, Advocacy and Law at the Seamen's Church Institute of New York and New Jersey; Arthur Petitpas, ITF Inspector based in Baltimore; Rev. James D. Von Dreele, Director of the Seamen's Church Institute in Philadelphia, PA; and Johan Oyen, Director of the Norwegian Seafarers' Union in Miami, Florida.

The following publishers have generously given permission to reproduce material from the respective works: From the website (and related webpages) of *Cruise Critic* (http://www.cruisecritic.com), All Rights Reserved by *The Independent Traveler, Inc.* 1995-2007; from *Cruise Industry News*, All Rights Reserved by *Cruise Industry News*, Inc; from *The 2006 Overview* by Cruise Lines International Association, All Rights Reserved by *Cruise Lines International Association*; from *The Honolulu Advertiser,* All Rights Reserved by *Gannett Pacific Corporation*; from *The Star-Bulletin*, All Rights Reserved by *Oahu Publications, Inc.* Thank you as well to the following journals for permission to draw from my earlier essays, that first appeared in the *Journal of International Communication* vol. 10, no. 2 (2004); and the *International Feminist Journal of Politics* vol 10, no 1 (2008).

Above all else, I am indebted to my family particularly my father, K.V. Chin; my siblings Sandra, B.Y. and Beek See; and my life-long Buddhist teacher, Wong Soon Kin who continue to support me unconditionally in my quest to generate and disseminate knowledge. We suffered a heartbreaking loss with the unexpected passing of my youngest sister, Beek Yin in 2003. She had an incisive, inquisitive mind laced with humour and fuelled by a compassionate heart. Time, however, denied me the opportunity to show her how much I had learned from our conversations, especially on the need to balance a passion for travel with that of social responsibility. Wherever she may be, I hope she is proud of this book.

Christine B.N. Chin
Washington D.C.

List of Abbreviations

CARICOM	Caribbean Community
CBA	Collective Bargaining Agreement
CCL	Carnival Corporation & Carnival plc
CLIA	Cruise Lines International Association
CTO	Caribbean Tourism Organization
EUSC	(Under) Effective US Control
FBI	Federal Bureau of Investigation
FCCA	Florida-Caribbean Cruise Association
FOC	Flag of Convenience
GRT	Gross Registered Tonnage
HAL	Holland America Lines
ICCL	International Council of Cruise Lines
ICONS	International Commission on Shipping
ICV	International Cruise Victims Association
ILO	International Labour Organization
IMF	International Monetary Fund
IMO	International Maritime Organization
INS	Immigration and Naturalization Service
IRS	Internal Revenue Service
ISPS	International Ship and Port Facility Security
ITF	International Transport Workers' Federation
LISCR	Liberian Ship & Corporate Registry
MARPOL	International Convention for the Prevention of Pollution from Ships
MOU	Memorandum of Understanding
NCL	Norwegian Cruise Line
NSU	Norwegian Seafarers' Union
OECD	Organisation for Economic Co-operation and Development
OECS	Organisation of Eastern Caribbean States
POEA	Philippine Overseas Employment Administration
PRC	People's Republic of China
PSC	Port State Control
RCL	Royal Caribbean Cruises Ltd
SCL	Star Cruises Ltd
SCTW	International Convention on Standards, Training, Certification and Watchkeeping for Seafarers
SIRC	Seafarers International Research Centre
SOLAS	International Convention for the Safety of Life at Sea
TMS	Theory of Moral Sentiments

Chapter 1

Making the Connection: Profits, Pleasure and Work on the Open Seas

A tree so big it can fill the span of a man's arm grows from a tiny sprout. A terrace nine stories high rises from a shovelful of earth. A journey of a thousand miles begins with a single step.

Lao Tzu, circa 600 B.C.E (trans. by Ni 1997, 83)

A society's reactions to the events of the day, to the pressure upon it, to the decisions it must face, are less a matter of logic or even self-interest than the response to an unexpressed and often inexpressible compulsion arising from the collective unconscious.

Fernand Braudel (1987, 22)

The large cruise ship's horn blows to announce its arrival in Sint Maarten waters as a warm breeze makes it seem as if its flag is waving hello to all. Many may or may not notice the flag, but if they do, it becomes apparent quickly that it is not the national flag of the US, even though the ship set sail carrying over 1,000 passengers from a US embarkation port. The flag could belong to countries such as Panama, Bahamas or even Italy.

Shore-side businesses (tour operators, restaurants, taxis, car rentals and retail shops) prepare for the onslaught of throngs of potential customers as passenger debarkation will be followed shortly by seafarers, some in uniform and others in civilian clothing. They may come from as close by as the US, Canada, Honduras and Venezuela, to as far away as Bulgaria, Greece, South Africa, India, Indonesia and the People's Republic of China. If two or more large cruise ships arrive at the same time, then the port of call will host thousands of visitors that day.

The sheer number of cruise passengers, young and old, immediately leads to massive congestion on Philipsburg's roads and sidewalks as they go in search of new sights, food, ground transportation and/or duty-free items for purchase. Seafarers who have visited this port many times over the course of a few months may be more interested in replenishing personal supplies and/or searching for seafarer-friends from ships that have arrived at the same time. For the next few hours, a cacophony of spoken languages will permeate the public spaces of Philipsburg.

Meanwhile job schedules keep some seafarers shipboard cleaning cabins and public areas, preparing meal service or, in general, catering to passengers who chose to remain onboard. Toward the end of the day, traffic will reverse direction as passengers and crew members embark the ship to set sail for its next port of call that may include a 'private island' owned/leased by the cruise line exclusively for passenger recreation.

To a large degree, organized chaos of this kind will be repeated elsewhere in the Caribbean basin (including Southern ports of the US and Mexico's Yucatan peninsular), and along North America's west coast from Alaska all the way south to Ixtapa in the 'Mexican Riviera'. Aptly named in the industry as 'mass market' cruising, large cruise ships that carry anywhere from approximately one thousand to several thousand passengers are calling also at destination ports in other regions such as South America, Southeast Asia and the Mediterranean, with new itineraries planned for East and South Asia. Deep ocean pleasure cruising is enjoying a renaissance that transcends its elitist origins in transatlantic voyages.

Since the last decades of the twentieth century, the numbers of passenger-tourists worldwide have grown steadily as cruise tourism is made affordable for many more people. In 1989, a total of four million passengers travelled on cruise ships in all regions of the world. By 2005, the number had risen to over 11 million passengers (CLIA 2006b; Mathisen 2005). Some destinations within the Caribbean basin have been experiencing exponential growth, e.g., the percentage of cruise passengers in Belize increased by 80 per cent to 575, 196 in 2003 (CTO 2004, 132). One year later, the percentage increased again by 48 per cent to 851, 436 (CTO 2004, 14).

Straddling the global shipping and tourism sectors, the business of deep ocean pleasure cruising averages an annual growth rate of eight to nine per cent. This is remarkable especially given the slower or even negative growth rates of other sea-based transportation, and land-based tourism industries.[1] There are new ship-build orders for large or larger/mega-ships (with the carrying capacity of over three thousand passengers, excluding seafarers) to be delivered in the next few years; improvements in or new constructions of port facilities in the US and elsewhere; the proliferation of internet sites specializing in all aspects of cruise vacations; and sustained demands for seafarers from all over the world. There may be as many as 80-90 nationalities of seafarers on board cruise ships today.

The attraction of mass market cruise tourism perhaps is captured nicely in recent years by Princess Cruises' media advertising campaign (e.g., in newspapers and magazines) built on the motto, '*Escape Completely*'. Cruise vacations offer passenger-tourists opportunities to leave behind the 'hassles' of their everyday life in return for extraordinary experiences. They are able to visit a succession of foreign destinations without the hassles of coordinating point to point flight schedules with hotel reservations, packing and unpacking suitcases, searching for good local restaurants as well as tourist sites and having to make their own way there. On the ship, they will be pampered by seafarers, e.g., passenger-tourists can enjoy a variety of entertainment programming and cuisine, spa treatments, twice-a-day cabin service, and so forth.

---

1 From 1988-98, while other categories of ships (e.g., bulk, oil tankers, general cargo) averaged annual growth rates of less than five per cent, cruise/passenger ships experienced the highest average annual growth rate of approximately eight to nine per cent (see especially ILO 2001).

Mass market cruise tourism's popularity today is a testament of cruise lines' success in catering to different market segments as prospective vacationers (from retirees to young couples and families with a variety of interests and greater disposable incomes and/or access to credit) select from a range of packages and destinations. The more people desire and are able to afford cruise vacation packages, the more profits cruise lines will make and reinvest to increase berth capacity, offer more itineraries as well as shipboard amenities that, in turn, attract more passengers, subsequently increase employment opportunities to seafarers from all over the world.

Punctuating the positive growth picture, however, are controversies surrounding certain cruise line practices. They have been accused of deploying bully tactics to reverse proposed legislation in some port communities; polluting coastal and deep waters; failing to ensure passengers' personal safety; and operating 'sweatships' of low wage foreign seafarers. In recent years for example, cases of alleged criminal activities affecting passengers on cruise ships have garnered global media attention (e.g., a female passenger who was assaulted on an Australian cruise, and a male passenger who went missing on a Mediterranean cruise).[2]

This begs a very important question, 'Why and how do the interrelated processes of cruise lines' pursuit of profits, passengers' consumption of pleasure, and seafarers' performance of work that occur in an arena said to "belong to all and to no one", generate an underside of loss, pain and servility respectively for some communities, passengers and seafarers?' To frame the question in this way is not to deny that cruise line profits come from selling vacation packages to consumers while controlling operating costs. Rather, it is to facilitate analytic clarity of why and how the whole cannot exist without each part, as well as the relationship between specific parts to one another and to the whole. Cast in this way, we can better grasp the complexities of, and contradictions emanating from, these interrelationships.

Despite or perhaps because of the fact that cruise lines are headquartered on land, their ship operations represent a unique mode of business conducted, pleasure experienced and work carried out primarily on international waters with brief interregnums at home ports and foreign ports of call. The story of mass market cruise tourism's phenomenal growth since the late twentieth century appreciatively is complicated because its plot takes place on terra firma *and* at sea linking communities on the local, national, regional and global levels, as well as blurring what are considered the distinct realms of leisure and work.

To answer the question then, we first need to unpack it. How have cruise ships come to fly national flags that have no correspondence with their home ports or cruise lines' headquarters? What is the nature of states' relationship to promoting and/or regulating profits, pleasure and work at sea? To what extent are existing national

---

2 Some might argue that personal safety includes protection of passengers against disease especially since in recent years there have been many instances of shipboard outbreaks of noroviruses. This topic is not discussed here because cruise lines cannot and have not been held responsible for a naturally occurring disease. Noroviruses are commonly found in contexts characterized by close living quarters (e.g., hospitals, retirement homes, restaurants and so forth). One key way in which cruise lines continue to mitigate outbreaks is by having their ships disinfected (e.g., wiping down railings) on a daily basis.

and international legal instruments, mechanisms or regulations effective or not in governing ocean-based industries that transport people and/or goods? For whom and how do cruise lines produce pleasure? In what ways does the production of pleasure affect passenger safety, and/or social and physical environments? Are most passengers aware of contradictions arising from the production-consumption nexus, and if so how do they respond? Why have seafarers from all over the world come to work on cruise ships? Who gets to perform which jobs and under what conditions?

By examining states' relationship to the maritime structure regulating ownership, management and operations of oceanic vessels; mass market cruise lines' business strategies of generating profits from the production of pleasure; passengers' expectations and experiences of consuming pleasure; and foreign seafarers' work on cruise ships, we can ascertain more clearly why and how the contradictions of loss, pain and servility accompany that of profits, pleasure and work at sea. Mass market cruise tourism's sustained popularity offers us the unparalleled opportunity to conduct an inter-disciplinary study that draws from, as well as contribute to integrating knowledge of states' relationship to capital in an era of global free markets, the production-consumption nexus in tourism, and the migration of foreign workers. It is pertinent to stress that existing stocks of knowledge on the state, tourism and migrant labour have life on land as their common referent point, e.g., state policies of regionalism as a key response to regulating capital flows freed from restrictive national regulations;[3] collaboration between state, tourist firms and communities in developing sustainable modes of tourism;[4] consumers' motivations and identities in leisure travel at home and abroad;[5] and cross-border movements of men and women for work in labour-receiving countries.[6] Hence, while we know much of the ways

---

3 Even though literature on the state acknowledges the importance of space, in addition to place, it is surprising that in the main, major texts on International Relations and International Political Economy have examined mostly the causes and effects of land-based as opposed to ocean-based transformations. One outcome is emphasis paid to emerging 'regional' modes of political-economic governance. See, for example, Kahler and Lake 2003; and Webber 2005. The importance and use of maritime space, then, are comparatively unexplored leaving studies of maritime governance largely dominated by legal analyses of the United Nations Convention on the Law of the Sea (UNCLOS) and related issues of contestation over marine resources and territorial waters (see especially Borgese 1998; Vidas and Ostreng 1999; and Wilson and Sherwood 2000).

4 Studies of tourism development, to be sure, have been concerned with the economic dimension (for example, Mowforth and Munt 1998; and Tisdell 1999). Nonetheless, there have been calls to examine the economic-culture nexus (see especially Azarya 2004; Hannam 2002; Pearce 1999; and Picard and Wood 1997). Still, landed tourism remains the key referent point, leaving ocean-based tourism relatively unexamined. Some exceptions to the rule are Duval 2004; and Pattullo 2005, 1996. Their focus on the Caribbean basin makes sense especially given its importance to cruise tourism.

5 For example, the observed shift from mass to niche tourism has been paralleled by a shift in conceptualizing the passive waiting-to-be-acted upon tourist to one who actively interprets meanings in leisure travel. Representative literature are Aitchison 1999; Bruner 1991; McCannell 1996; Pred 1996; Selwyn 1996; and Urry, 2002.

6 For international migration policies see, for example, Massey et al. 1998; and Messina and Lahav 2005. For women and international migration, see for example Arya and Roy 2006; and Sharpe 2001.

in which landed life and activities are being reconfigured within a global political economy of constructing and integrating free markets, we know comparatively little of what is happening on the open seas.

This study's conceptual framework, designed to cut across different levels of analysis and realms of social life, encourages a comprehensive examination of the relationship between state regulation of oceanic capital, cruise lines' pursuit of profits, passengers' consumption of pleasure and foreign seafarer's performance of work. We will find that processes arising from, and affirming the overall structure of free markets cannot but generate an underside connection of loss, pain and servility that comes with the pursuit of profits, pleasure and work at sea in mass market cruise tourism. These contradictions will persist so long as they are explained away either as by-products of a fledgling global industry, and/or miscalculations of costs and benefits in free market exchange, instead of inherent structural tendencies being shaped by and shaping the conduct of states, cruise lines, port communities, passengers and seafarers. Notably, such explanations tend to minimize or ignore a relationship between morality and conduct in the free market, hence mitigate serious considerations of why and how it is important to assuage the underside connection of loss, pain and servility.

Regulating a Borderless Maritime World

Since the mid-late twentieth century, states have embarked on a gradual retreat from intervening in their economies. Instead of owning-managing industries and/or distributing subsidies, state agencies increasingly are expected to maintain the context for free market operations that render economic life more efficient, productive and competitive, with the objective of improving the human condition for all.

The justificatory context for removing state intervention came in the midst of structural crises (as seen in inflation and unemployment rates, growing deficits and so forth) experienced by major Organisation for Economic Co-operation and Development (OECD) economies that, by the early 1980s, affected countries of the Global South as well. A key outcome was the 'liberation' of distinct territorially-based capital from highly restrictive home and host country regulations. Derived from, and informed by neoliberal policies of economic liberalization, privatization and deregulation, the operative vision would be that of a borderless world for capital. Paradoxically, the logic of free market's global or 'transplanetary' reach and outcome is to be affirmed by, and within, an existing political system of states (Scholte 2000).[7]

Particularly in the US and Western Europe, responses to structural crises initiated highly contested processes of dismantling state-mediated Fordist pacts between capital and labour, most notably the weakening of regulations governing labour

---

7 Depending on the perspective, this kind of structural transformation has been called 'globalization,' 'economic globalization,' or 'neoliberal globalization' (see especially Castells 2000; Duménil and Lévy 2004; George 1999; Rapley 2004; Robinson 2003; and Watson 2004). I deliberately do not invoke the concept 'globalization' because its contested nature within and between academic disciplines is not the primary focus of this study.

rights and benefits. At the very same time for land-based industries, new production technologies first aided in parcelling out of the mass production process (from parts to whole assembly) to different countries in the world, eventually followed by the adoption of niche-based production. Mass production and its corollary of mass consumption under the Fordist system gave way to niche production and consumption characterizing the present post-Fordist system. Meanwhile, economies of the Global South gradually came under International Monetary Fund (IMF) and World Bank mandated structural adjustment programs (e.g., currency devaluation and drastic cuts in public expenditure) with a similar overall intent of commanding the state's retreat from the economy.

In the Fordist era, states were conceptualized either as autonomous from, or able to balance competing interests while functioning to provide public goods; a tool serving corporations; or a protector of the capitalist system even at the expense of alienating the owners of capital (Dahl 1971; Domhoff 1979; Miliband 1983; Poulantzas 1973). The shift to post-Fordism, however, called for different conceptualizations of the state especially since multi-national corporations became transnational in their operations: corporations no longer were restricted to domestic sources of capital, bound by traditional domestic chains of raw material supplies and labour, nor subject to mandated benefit packages for workers, all of which were seen to have undermined economic efficiency, productivity and competitiveness, hence potential profits. Bolstered by applications of new technologies, corporations have and continue to parcel-out the production process to different parts of the world, i.e., more freely move capital while scouring the world for low wage material and labour resources.

Drawing on empirical evidence from land-based industries, scholars argue that state regulatory power in the context of capital's 'hypermobility' (Beck 2000; Harvey 1989) is considerably weakened, leaving a hollowed out 'defective' state evinced from implementations of economic liberalization, privatization and deregulation policies (Boggs 2000; Strange 1996). At the very same time, states can and do enter into partnership with, or in the service of transnational capital, hence becoming 'competition' or 'efficient capitalist' states (Cerny 1997; Hirst and Thompson 1999; Panitch 1996; Opello and Rosow 1999). As a result, states increasingly confront the contradictory pressures of facilitating transnational capital flows while maintaining domestic legitimacy at the same time (Sassen 2001). One key response to these pressures can be discerned from the move to construct new or to strengthen existing regional groupings (Farrell, Hettne and van Langehove 2005; Stubbs and Underhill 2005). In spite of state efforts at regional integration to better coordinate regulation of capital across place and space, the maritime world remains largely separate from, or peripheral to, a primary focus on landed activities.

However, the phenomenon of 'offshore tax havens' most often associated with firms' and individuals' attempts to shelter capital, offers a conceptual window through which to better understand and integrate the pursuit of profits with state regulatory power on land and at sea (Blum 1984; Diamond and Diamond 1998; Gilmore 1992). At the outset, offshore tax havens may seem merely as capital's response to restrictive home state regulations by 'relocating to relatively unregulated realms that present themselves as external to the state' (Palan 2003, 3).[8] Yet, Palan's analysis of their historical origins demonstrates that offshore tax havens should not be understood primarily as the outcome of resistance to state regulatory power per se since they are the creation of states. Rather, offshore tax havens are integral to the 'continuing process of state formation in a period of intensified capital mobility' (Palan 2002, 153). In other words, capitalism's gradual worldwide expansion does not occur in spite of the state, but changing modes of state regulation are deeply implicated in the process.

Since 'the rise of offshore is an inherent tendency of an internationalizing economy operating within a particularistic political system' (Palan 2003, 9) the state then has not lost its regulatory power as much as reconfigured it. Increasingly, states today are encouraged to 'lease' their regulatory power in the form of offshore tax havens:

> [states accrue] 'rent' or license fees in return for granting firms a right to incorporate in their jurisdictions ... *The principal attraction of tax haven* and the main cause for their spectacular success lie in their ability to provide protection from national regulation and taxation *without* the need to physically relocate to the host country [my emphasis] (Palan 2002, 163).

An inescapable observation is the commercialization of state sovereignty.

Offshore tax havens, to be sure, are located still in place, i.e., on physical territory of host states. Yet, tax havens are constituted to operate mainly in space given the electronic set up and management of accounts. In this way, tax havens can be considered 'purely juridical residences', or as Palan further clarified, they are 'fictional' juridical residences created by host states to shelter capital: foreign corporations and individuals need never physically relocate there.

In this new global political economy, state establishment of offshore tax havens begins to foreground an emerging 'shadow' state system and mode of regulation that operates in space more so than place. One consequence of this space-place bifurcation is that the offshore tax haven '[helps produce] an economy that is serving to destabilize established concepts of place, territory and identity' (Palan 2003, 162).

What, then, is the link between offshore tax havens and the maritime world? The adjective 'offshore' already connotes locations beyond contiguous land mass, e.g., the more commonly known tax havens of island states such as the Bahamas and Jamaica, or island territories/possessions such as the Netherlands Antilles and Gibraltar. Nonetheless, this still does not explain how offshore tax havens facilitate state regulation of capital operating in what is a 'borderless' environment of the open seas. The answer lies in a historicized practice of assigning nationality to ships, and how a particular form of offshore tax haven continues this practice in the present day even as it legitimizes the denationalization-deterritorialization of maritime capital.

---

8 Palan describes clearly the different classes of tax havens as well as their advantages (2003, 36-45).

Vessels transporting goods and people do so in what have been considered for a few hundred years as the 'global commons' of the oceans.[9] Beyond the United Nations Convention on the Law of the Seas (UNCLOS) that delimits nautical mile extensions for countries with coastlines, as well as delineating access to marine resources, the open seas belong to all and to no one. Given this, it has been claimed that neoliberal restructuring in the maritime world cannot but offer 'a glimpse into a possible future in which government has receded almost entirely into the background and society in nearly every aspect is governed by markets alone' (Garin 2005, 11). States, nevertheless, have not retreated entirely from regulating maritime operations as much as reconfigured their regulatory power. The purely juridical residences symbolizing commercialized state sovereignty encompasses a specific way in which reconfiguration has taken place.

Despite and because of open seas' inherently borderless environment, the assignment of nationalities to ships was and continues to be accepted as *the* way of inscribing order by assigning oversight to corresponding home states. In the past, primary or national ship registries were responsible for regulating their citizens' construction, ownership-management and operation of vessels as well as seafarer education and training. Maritime capital, thus, had a unique national base and character evinced from national flags flown by ships.

Particularly since the late twentieth century, this mode of state regulation remains in practice but with a unique twist. Ship owners may elect to register their vessels in open or international ship registries created by non-traditional maritime states. For example, ships owned by United Kingdom citizens now may be registered in, and fly the flag of, Panama as opposed to the 'Union Jack'. By the century's end, many ships had been reflagged or flagged-out to open registries. The top three open registries regulating over 50 per cent of the world's fleet belong respectively to Panama, Liberia and the Bahamas (ITF 2005a, 8). What is particularly striking about the top three open registries is that they challenge and affirm at the same time the meaning of 'offshore' tax havens. While the open registries operate in space, the space finds its physical expression in offices established throughout capital cities in the world, e.g., the Liberian registry has offices in Hong Kong, Zurich and other cities, the Bahamian registry has offices in New York and London, and the Panamian registry operates out of its consulates.

These three and other flag states with open registries compete in the global business of flagging oceanic vessels: '[a]n international register is one that has been set up with the specific aim of offering ship owners internationally competitive terms, often as a means of earning revenue for the flag state' (Stopford 1988, 160). This system of open registries is known commonly as 'flags of convenience' (FOC) because of the convenience accorded to flag states and ship owners: flag states oversee foreign

---

9 As an imperial power during the nineteenth century, Great Britain first implemented the Plimsoll Act of 1876 to regulate the construction and operations of ships. Approximately two decades later, the US organized an international maritime conference to standardize international regulations. The United Nations Law of the Sea Conference 1958 would produce four treaties respectively governing the high seas, territorial waters, continental shelf and conservation of fisheries (see especially Boczek 1962; Stopford 1998).

ship owners' compliance with domestic and international regulations such as those governing ship and worker safety, in return for minimal registration fees and tonnage taxes from ship owners. Ship construction, ownership, management, operations and crewing sources no longer need be unified and regulated under the national umbrella of a primary registry. Instead, oceanic vessels for transporting goods and people now can be built in one country, owned by those living in another country, registered and flagged in a third country, possibly managed by a company in a fourth country and crewed by seafarers from all over the world. In a competitive global milieu, even the land-locked state of Bolivia has established an open registry to compete with those created by Panama, Liberia, Bahamas, Sri Lanka, Honduras, Belize and others for the business of flagging foreign ships.

Underwritten by an expanding system of open registries, this maritime version of parcelling-out ship construction, ownership, management, operations and crewing sources all over the world facilitates a degree and level of denationalizing-deterritorializing capital not previously observed in landed industries. From ship owners' perspective, open registries' main advantage is the minimal regulatory power of FOC states. By permitting the fragmentation of ship ownership and registration, for example, open registries facilitate obfuscation of ship owners' legal and financial accountability and liability. Further, even though ship owners pay registration and tonnage taxes, they are not taxed on revenue from activities at sea nor are they subject to citizenship requirements for employing seafarers. Meanwhile in the face of heightened competition from FOC states, some traditional maritime states have created 'second' registries paralleling their primary registries: second registries generally offer more relaxed regulations particularly those concerning the percentage of foreign ownership and/or foreign seafaring labour.

The ease with which ships may flag-out to FOC states has a paradoxical effect of affirming nationality as the maritime world's central organizing principle, while stripping it of meaning. It is in this way there now exists a unique maritime regulatory structure shaped by the co-existence of primary, second and open registries. Significantly, this co-existence exposes the centrality and ensuing contradiction of maintaining a borderless maritime environment for the free flow of capital because of, and despite, the existing framework of an interstate system.

Chapter Two reconstructs the larger maritime context from which to locate and understand modern cruise lines' emergence, growth and conduct. We begin by discussing open registries' particularistic origins and eventual widespread adoption toward the end of the twentieth century. In the early decades of that century, Panama with the assistance of the US established the world's first open registry. The latter state's support of this registry (despite earlier vehement objections from European states, and continued objections from labour organizations) offered a solution to the two-fold challenge of maintaining a competitive merchant marine that also could be requisitioned by the military during national emergencies. Since then, many more states have established open registries as a politically viable way to generate revenue.

Open registries are based on, and validate two main characteristics associated with neoliberal economic restructuring on land, i.e., the denationalization-deterritorialization of capital in concert with the deregulation of labour. The second section specifically examines how FOC states underwrite deregulation of the seafaring workforce. Ship owners no longer are subject to primary registries' citizenship requirements and labour regulation: they can employ non-citizen seafarers whose terms of work are governed by the often weak or watered down regulations of FOC states. Significantly, the analysis also will show that labour deregulation is not a straightforward process concerned with cutting labour costs per se. Integral to the process are labour recruitment and employment practices based on persistent stereotypes of seafarers leading to a global phenomenon of crew stratification according to intersections of nationality, race/ethnicity, class and gender.

In light of FOC states' minimal regulatory power, enforcement of national and international maritime regulations presently are shifting from flag states to ports state as issues of ship safety, health of the oceans, seafarer rights and the present 'war on terrorism' not only can and do affect port communities but potentially threaten to undermine the legitimacy of open registries. Chapter Two concludes with a discussion on the aftermath of the 'September 11th 2001' terrorist attacks on the US (hereafter called '9/11'). Growing concerns with maritime security have produced measures designed not so much to better regulate global shipping, but to protect oceanic trade and port communities from possible terrorist disruptions. In light of international organizations' (International Maritime Organization [IMO] and International Labour Organization [ILO]) lack of enforcement powers, key responsibilities for ensuring compliance with environmental regulations in addition to ship and seafarer safety are relegated largely to the purview of port states as well as informal alliances made with non-governmental organizations. As responsibility shifts to port states, contradictions emanating from an overall uneven state-based structure regulating the maritime world cannot but persist.

Processes of denationalizing-deterritorializing capital, deregulating labour and manipulating identities are well underway on the open seas. State responses to late twentieth century economic downturn removed restrictive national regulations governing not just capital flows but also the seafaring labour-force, and in ways that (re)produce nationality-race/ethnic, gender and class hierarchies at sea. Modern cruise lines would surface from, and expand within this larger context.

Producing Pleasure for Profit

Cruise lines are distinctive in the maritime world because they straddle the oceanic transportation and tourism sectors:

> Developing in parallel business mobility, the mobility of leisure-time activities has given tourism a leading role in the movement of peoples, the point where the recreational sector has become a fully-fledged player in economic deployment. In this respect, transport subtends both trade and tourism in upholding the new international economic system (Wackermann 1997, 23).

As a mode of oceanic transportation, cruise ships are governed by maritime regulations. Many mass market cruise ships fly the flags of Panama and Bahamas, the two leading FOC states. By doing so, cruise lines enjoy the advantages as outlined previously.

While FOC states offer the important minimal regulatory framework for cruise lines' pursuit of profits at sea, they nevertheless do not guarantee profits per se. The question then concerns specific ways in which cruise lines are able to do so. For this, we turn to the core business of cruise tourism: cruise lines pursue ocean-based profits by way of producing pleasure for cruise passenger-tourists. Chapter Three presents an analysis of cruise lines' major business strategies that can and do have the effect of destabilizing the concepts of place, territory and identity. It is appropriate here to stress that seafarers, indeed, are essential to the production of pleasure. Detailed analysis of their recruitment and employment conditions is offered separately in Chapter Five.

We first examine the origins of mass market cruise lines as located primarily in the US, followed by a period of late twentieth century consolidation and expansion. Cruise line ownership and operations increasingly reflect some of what characterize land-based firms that execute horizontal integration strategies in a competitive environment.[10] Foreign-flagged cruise lines' major advantage, however, is that they operate in a mainly income tax-free oceanic environment created and legitimized by open registries. Toward the end of the century, some cruise lines' access to new funding sources (e.g., equity markets) led to a series of buy-outs and mergers producing the world's top three cruise corporations, i.e., Carnival Corporation and Carnival plc (operating as one business enterprise, hereafter referred as CCL), Royal Caribbean Cruises Ltd. (RCL) and Star Cruises Ltd. (SCL) that together control roughly 80 per cent of the global market. They are able to build new ships, develop itineraries and attract market segments without much threat from smaller lines.

Horizontal integration encourages the construction of 'niche brands' of cruise lines. Take, for example, CCL that owns Carnival Cruise Lines (Carnival) alongside other lines including Holland America Line (HAL) and Cunard. Younger passengers interested in more boisterous, fun-loving cruise vacations may opt for Carnival cruises whereas older passengers with more financial means who are interested in formal-styled cruises can opt to travel on HAL ships.

Emerging from a period of intra-industry competition, the three cruise corporations now have begun to position their respective cruise lines to compete effectively with land-based hospitality firms. To do so, they implement vertical integration strategies of owning, managing or entering into profit-sharing arrangements with select tour operators, lodging, transportation and excursion firms. In this way, cruise corporations and their holdings of cruise lines can rationalize operating costs, control quality of services and when necessary, reduce profit-sharing with landed firms. Passengers benefit from the 'total package', if you may, because their needs and wants are anticipated and addressed from pre- to post-cruise phases: 'the logic of commodification which applies to production also applies to consumption, as in effect, tourists are eliminating risk and uncertainty by "subcontracting" their travel arrangements', hence experiences of pleasure directly to cruise lines (Meethan 2001, 75).

---

10 For examples of discussions on horizontal integration and vertical integration strategies in other industries, please see Ensign 1998; Fan and Goyal 2006 and Goshal and Patton 2002.

At first glance, integration strategies in the business of deep ocean pleasure cruising appear to mirror the shift from Fordist to post-Fordist modes of production and consumption in the larger tourism sector: '[t]he logical outcome of post-Fordism is niche marketing in which the mass markets of Fordism are disaggregated into segments or niches or lifestyle segments' (Meethan 2001, 70. See also Ioannides and Debbage 1997). Cruise vacation packages targeting niche market segments from teen cruising to gay cruising and other identities and lifestyle preferences (e.g., cuisine, music and so forth) abound today. Consumers also can pick and choose from a range of sites and activities for the land-based portion of their vacations. Post-Fordism's distinguishing characteristic of niche production-consumption does seem to characterize cruise tourism: 'a situation where the satisfaction of consumer needs is governed by an apparently limitless splitting of markets into ever small segments and niches' (Meethan 2001, 70).

Nonetheless there is an important difference. Analysis in Chapter Three demonstrates that with the exception of smaller cruise lines catering to the wealthy, niche segments generally are created within mass market cruise tourism designed to appeal to the middle classes. This relates not so much to the variety of consumers' lifestyles and interests per se, but their successful articulation in, and by, calculated business strategies. As Meethan writes on tourism development in general, '[t]his generation of difference [niche segments], while appearing on the surface to be admirably postmodern, may actually only be the application of an instrumental rationality by the producers' (2001, 72). Cruise corporations' horizontal and vertical integration strategies indicate that niche markets are not supplanting mass markets. Instead, niche markets are nested within mass market cruising: this is not a transitional state but a necessary condition for pursuing profits more efficiently, and from many more peoples at the same time in cruise tourism.

Of special note is that even though mass market cruise tourism is becoming a worldwide middle class phenomenon with increasing numbers of European and Southeast Asian passengers, the majority of cruise passengers continue to come from North America, and in particular the US. Cruise ship design and itineraries especially to the world's top destination sites in the Caribbean basin, then, not only are dependent on increasing US passenger yields but in ways commensurate with their expectations and preferences. Some cruise lines are planning to, or have deployed larger/mega-sized cruise ships built to compete with all-inclusive landed resorts. These mass market cruise ships achieve economies of scale in their operations by offering thousands of passengers at any one time the experience of affordable 'dream' vacations involving a wide variety of pleasure-producing ship venues and activities from entertainment and sports, to casinos and spas, and twenty-four hour service by seafarers from all over the world. On a single cruise itinerary, passengers will get to visit several foreign ports and subsequently delimit their exposure to real or perceived dangers (e.g., crime, poverty, harassment and so forth) of the locales.

Emanating from cruise lines' production of dream vacations for the middle classes are key challenges faced by some port communities. The last section of Chapter Three discusses cruise lines' exercise of political economic power. Flagged in the main by open and second registries, cruise ships are the physical manifestations of denationalized-deterritorialized capital operating mostly and legally beyond the juridical reach of ports of call. Still, cruise lines have formed regional and national associations to protect their interests. Conflicts between cruise lines and ports over proposed taxation (especially those designed to alleviate infrastructural stress on small island communities) are 'resolved' easily in some cases by threatening or actually removing such ports from, and adding new ones to cruise itineraries. Experiences of various Caribbean and Alaskan port communities hosting mass market cruise ships reveal that many tourist-dependent port communities give in to cruise line demands in order to continue earning revenue from tourist expenditures. Uneven negotiating power between cruise lines and port communities amplifies earlier arguments of international tourism as a form of 'leisure imperialism' that persists despite the adoption of sustainable modes of land-based niche tourism such as eco-tourism projects in which local communities participate in decision-making processes and revenue sharing arrangements.[11]

Endorsed by a global political economy grounded in the construction and integration of free markets, the cruise line-port community relationship parallels that of the cruise line-FOC state relationship. Both sets of dyadic relationships validate free market 'willing' buyer-seller transactions, i.e., ship registration fees and tonnage taxes in return for minimal flag state regulation, and cruise ship-related expenditures and landed employment opportunities in return low port taxes. Contradictions emanating from the intersection of these dyads bring to light a mostly hidden relationship between ship regulation and tourism development.

Consuming 'Pleasure' in Pleasure Cruising

The focus on cruise lines' production of pleasure for profits crucially raises an important related topic of pleasure consumption. Who are consumers of mass market cruises, and to what extent do free market transactions shape consumers' relationship with cruise lines, as well as their responses to cruise line practices? Do cruise passenger-tourists uncritically accept dominant meanings constructed by cruise lines to sell vacations and to justify their conduct or, do cruise passengers actively interpret, question or even resist such meanings and if so, in what ways and with what consequences?

Since the late twentieth century, applications of new communication and information technologies that inhere in post-Fordist production and consumption are nurturing the new middle or 'service' classes in which consumption, as opposed to production, has become a central organizing principle of everyday life. Consumption-oriented middle classes have been discerned in countries of the Global North as well as those of the Global South. As an extension of the increasing commodification of life, the consumption of tourism or leisure travel parallels that of material goods in identity construction of and for new middle classes-in-the-making.[12]

---

11 Studies of Caribbean tourism especially during the late twentieth century strengthened the concept of 'leisure imperialism' (Crick 1989; Davis 1978; Hannam 2002; Nash 1978; Young 1977).

12 For detailed analyses of the middle classes and consumption in Western Europe and North America, see especially Brown 2005; Gershuny and Miles 1983; Gottdiener 2000;

Although scholars may agree that niche tourism is related to changing consumer lifestyles and interests, there is disagreement on conceptualizing tourist motivations per se. For instance, MacCannell asserts that tourists are driven by the search for authentic experiences even though they may not always be successful in doing so because of the extent to which authenticity can be 'staged' in tourism (1989). Urry, on the other hand, argues that tourists in the post-Fordist era are not driven by authenticity or lack thereof, but by what may simply be the search for 'extraordinary' experiences (2002). In their examination of landed resorts such as those in Las Vegas and Florida, Ritzer and Liska emphasize the power of structural forces in influencing tourist motivations (1997). Categorized respectively as 'voluntarism', 'postmodernism' and 'structuralism', these major perspectives conceptualize tourist motivations primarily as shaped either by human agency or social structure (Rojek 2000, 51-70).

In spite of their differences, all three perspectives inhere in the consumption of mass market cruise tourism, i.e., tourist motivations are shaped by the social structure-human agency nexus. The fact that US passengers dominate mass market cruising is not lost at all on cruise lines for the latter depend inordinately on the former for revenue generation. Mass market cruise ships are designed to offer passengers extraordinary experiences without sacrificing many amenities to which they are accustomed. Such amenities already are evident in land-based leisure travel:

> It is crucial to add, however, that most people who wish to broaden their search for the different and to observe other peoples, culture and landscapes are still unwilling to part with the daily amenities of their familiar surroundings and lifestyle. They want the food and drink they like, their hot showers and the instant news from back home. Some amenities are, therefore, transported with them to their places of destinations (Azarya 2004, 952-3).

Gradually, a host of amenities associated with 'home' and with landed vacation sites increasingly can be found also on large cruise ships especially since the latter are being marketed as floating resort destinations in mass market cruising. Further, when cruise ships call at foreign ports, cruise passengers can experience new sights and activities on land that already have been vetted previously by cruise lines (although some passengers may and do elect to transcend pre-constituted 'tourist bubbles' at these ports). Thus, the production of cruise vacations may be read as integrated oceanic and landed forms of 'institutionalized leisure' to be consumed by passenger-tourists (Britton 1991; MacCannell 1989; Urry 2002). In this way, mass market cruise tourism appeals to, and reinforces what Ritzer and Liska identify as the four principles of predictability, efficiency, calculability and controllability that similarly order ordinary everyday life especially of the US middle classes. Succinctly put, cruise passenger-tourists are able to consume new sights and experiences from the comfort and security of a structured 'home' away from home.

Martin 1998; Rojek 1995; and Urry 1995. For detailed analyses of the new middle classes and consumption in another region such as Southeast Asia, please see Chin 1998; Chua 2000; and Sen and Stivens 1998.

Cruise lines' strategies of producing pleasure in dream vacations necessarily must be able to draw on intersubjective meanings and knowledge, i.e., leisure travel reflects the sense and knowledge of what consumers would think, know and/or expect from their vacations. Much importance is attached by cruise lines to market-consumer surveys that help inform their business strategies and practices: many even have established e-pages within official websites to facilitate consumer feedback. It can be said that there is a mutually dependent relationship between the production and consumption of mass market cruise vacations. This implies that the distinction between producer and consumer may not be as clearly delineated in cruise tourism: under certain conditions, consumers can and do participate as producers when they (re)enter the production process (Ateljevic 2000; du Gay 1997; Meethan 2001). Why, when and how does this occur?

Consumer knowledge of tourism today no longer is restricted to 'traditional' sources of print brochures, television programs, travel agents, and/or existing social networks. Many observers and scholars acknowledge that tourism is being 'mediatized' by applications of new communication and information technologies (Jansson 2002). However, despite the potential for consumers to engage in 'virtual touring' (Ritzer and Liska 1997, 101) or travel in cyberspace, published research demonstrates that many consumers tend to rely on the internet to gather information in preparation for physical travel (see, for example, Buhalis 1998; L. Klein 1998).

Chapter Four examines self-styled 'cruisers'' participation in e-discussion threads of message boards on Cruise Critic, a popular website that disseminates information on all aspects of cruise vacations. Millions of posts on a variety of topics indicate an active presence of a 'virtual community' of consumers seeking and sharing information on deep ocean pleasure cruising (Wang, Yu and Fesenmaier 2002, 411. See also Smith and Kollock 1999). Consumers or 'posters' who relate their experiences and/or share photographs on-line, in effect, re-enter the cruise vacation production process by taking on informal advisory and educational roles within the virtual community.

In this chapter, we analyze e-discussion threads from 2004-2006 namely those on large ships, Caribbean destination sites, private islands, seafarer gratuities/ tips, romance and environmental degradation to ascertain the manner and extent to which posters in the virtual community support or not cruise lines' business strategies, together with their responses to controversial allegations of shipboard labour exploitation, sexual assault of passengers and cruise ship pollution. We will find that the consumption of 'pleasure' in mass market cruise tourism is centred on 'extraordinary' gazes and experiences arising from the use of shipboard amenities, participation in shipboard activities and/or shore-side excursions. For some, the meaning of 'pleasure' can take on a more heightened sensual experience in the form of intimate shipboard relationships with fellow passengers or seafarers.

Posters' focus on, and experiences of pleasure do not mean that they are unaware of cruise line efforts to generate more shipboard revenue over the course of a voyage. Some posters make it a point to share their strategies for mitigating these efforts. For example, first-time cruisers are warned to keep tabs on their shipboard identity-credit cards, and not to purchase too many photographs or specialty drinks. There are even posts identifying the many ways to smuggle alcohol on board a ship (e.g., in miniature liquor bottles, water bottles, or in one case, empty baby milk bottles), or to share 'soda cards' meant for unlimited individual consumption. Nevertheless, posters who do so are criticized by others for 'cheating' or 'stealing' from cruise lines.

Even though a few posts are critical of cruise line practices, many do not question cruise lines' official explanations especially with regard to seafarer exploitation, personal safety of passengers and disposal of cruise ship waste. Posters then tend to privilege the human agency rather than social structure perspective, i.e. they do not consider allegations of labour exploitation, assault and pollution as built into cruise lines' profit-seeking activities within a minimally regulated maritime structure. Take, for instance, the topic of seafarer gratuities. Many posters acknowledge that although seafarers work very long hours, they willingly sell their labour in return for wages: the implication is that seafarers can and will stop working on cruise ships if they believe that they have been exploited by cruise lines. In discussions of passenger safety, some posters comment that cases of assault or missing persons are rare when compared to what happens on land, and they occur when passengers fail to ensure their own personal safety (such as when they are too friendly with, or too trusting of strangers; or, when they imbibe too much alcohol). The same can be said of cruise ship pollution. Posters argue that when pollution does occur, it is only because of human error: cruise ships would not willingly pollute the oceans on which they operate, and from which they derive profits.

Particularly noteworthy is the subtext of, and on a few occasions, direct references in discussion threads to 'common sense': the lack of common sense on the part of some passengers and/or seafarers is seen as a main cause of controversial issues. This in no way implies that posters have been 'duped' by cruise lines. The combination of posters' social positioning and their privileging of pleasure on cruise vacations encourage what Hall, in a different context, called the 'preferred' reading/interpretation of dominant meanings encoded by, and arising from cruise line practices in free market contexts (1992).

Of significance is that a legitimating function inheres in their narratives on e-discussion threads because many posters have had extensive cruise vacation experiences. By participating in discussions, posters re-enter the production phase of the production-consumption cycle as producers or 'expert' cruisers. This kind of preferred reading is expressed, in some instances, in response to the few posters who exhibit a 'negotiated' reading, i.e., awareness and subsequent critique of select cruise line practices. Those who express 'oppositional' readings directly challenging the dominant meanings, however, are not found in this virtual community. While the internet democratizes access to travel related resources, it does not mean that virtual communities will make space for in-depth articulation of oppositional views. In recent years, former cruise passengers providing information highly critical of cruise line practices have set up alternative virtual communities to share and disseminate knowledge for consumers, activists and researchers.

Overall, majority of posters in the virtual community perceive and rationalize incidences ranging from the smuggling of alcohol and sharing of soda cards, to seafarer gratuities and cruise ship pollution as 'anomalies' that arise when social actors fail to exercise common sense, take responsibility for their actions or simply, the outcome of human error. Given the larger framework of free market operations grounded on the basic premise that buyers and sellers willingly enter into or opt out of transactions, then posters' emphasis on individual choice and action as opposed to inherent structural tendencies and constraints in the production-consumption of pleasure at sea should not come as a surprise.

Performing Work at Sea

Located at the conjuncture of cruise lines' production and passengers' consumption of pleasure are seafarers from all over the world. Similar to workers in landed tourism firms, seafarers' workplace is unique: on-going expansion of capitalist modes of production and consumption since the late twentieth century has collapsed boundaries separating the realms of leisure and work. In cruise tourism, the cruise ship represents a site of leisure for passengers as well as a site of work for seafarers. And, while some seafarers may want to work on cruise ships as a way to see the world at the same time, others need to do so to provide for their families back home. As 'migrant tourist-workers', the former group blurs the separate categories of tourist and worker (Bianchi 2000). In any case, commodification processes most often associated with domestic service, sales and hospitality work (see, for instance, Chin 1998; Hochschild 1983; Romero 1992; Taylor 1998) similarly are discernible in cruise tourism: seafarers exchange not only their physical but also their emotional labour for wages.

Cruise ships flagged by open registries are not required to employ the latter's citizen seafarers. Consequently, there can be as many as 90 nationalities of seafarers working on board mass market cruise ships. This kind of multinational-multicultural shipboard workforce often is referred by cruise directors as 'mini U[nited] N[ations] crew'. The moniker, however, neither explains why or how foreign workers are recruited as seafarers.

Cruise ship crew diversity results from the interplay of labour deregulation on land and at sea. In the past two decades, the field of international/transnational migration studies has generated a wealth of knowledge on how labour deregulation unfolds on land: the movement of low wage transnational migrant workers is a key cause and effect of economic deregulation, privatization and liberalization policies in labour-sending and receiving countries.[13]

As discussed in the earlier section on pursuing profits, capital's relationship to labour cannot but be transformed as the former is liberated to move from one site

---

13 The academic field is multidisciplinary in nature. Ferment in the field can be discerned readily from contributions of scholars based in International Relations, International Political Economy, Sociology, Anthropology, Geography and so forth (see, for example, *International Migration Review* and *International Migration*). Debates on which adjective to employ, i.e., 'international' or 'transnational' migration come on the heels of empirical research revealing different ways in which migrant workers maintain material and symbolic ties to their countries of birth, e.g., setting up and managing businesses in home and host countries, sending children home during school vacations as a way to socialize them in familial and group cultures, and so forth.

to another with few restrictions. 'Labour flexibilization' is the euphemistic phrase frequently deployed in business and economic parlance referring to a different relationship between capital/management and labour/workers. Labour flexibilization concerns the processes of socially reconstructing labour, i.e., to render labour less demanding or more flexible in relation to capital. States facilitate labour flexibilization via policies and legislation such as those pertaining to the establishment (or not) of minimum wage levels, the ability of firms to out-source or off-shore jobs (hence shielding themselves from accountability and responsibility to workers) and the right of workers to collective action that seek to 'naturalize' new meanings and conditions of work. For the credentialed classes or 'core' workers, internal labour flexibilization may be experienced as the need to learn additional skills (e.g., to be 'certified' to perform a variety of new tasks/responsibilities), to adapt to new work environments and schedules, and/or to have to work more for the same level of wages and benefits (Bax 1996; Wilthagen 2002).[14] For the working classes or 'peripheral' workers, external labour flexibilization processes (e.g., sub-contracting or out-sourcing jobs to third parties) elicit greater job insecurity, declining opportunities for seeking legal recourse in many cases of work-related disputes and so forth (Atkinson 1984; Douglas 2000; Standing 1999). In other words, flexible labour is needed for the post-Fordist system of flexible accumulation.

On-going implementations of economic restructuring policies persist in compelling under- or unemployed workers in countries of the Global South to seek employment opportunities elsewhere, and many can only do so increasingly as undocumented low wage workers on temporary contracts in secondary and tertiary labour markets of receiving countries. These transnational migrant workers are exemplars of flexibilized labour: they are relatively 'cheap' to employ and easily retrenched (albeit not as easily repatriated) at a moment's notice.

While capital may be liberated as never before to flow freely around the world, this is not the case for all land-based transnational migrants despite alarmist public discourse on illegal immigration in major labour-receiving countries. Depending on the labour-receiving country, specific intersections workers' nationality, race/ethnicity, class, gender and increasingly religion, may and can be seen to threaten the existing social-cultural fabric of society. Viewed from this perspective, labour flexibilization processes are not as simple as rendering labour less demanding to capital per se: the social reconstruction of land-based labour is mediated through, or grounded in, specific intersections of identity modalities.

Given the unique system of states with their corresponding geopolitical identities, landed activities and life then can reproduce and further stratify social identities according to a host of identity modalities.[15] While states welcome the in-flow of capital, they will engage in selective regulation of foreign workers giving rise to,

---

14 For a rich theoretically driven historical analysis, see Van der Pijl (2004). He examines the rise of, and tensions within what he calls the 'new transnational managerial cadre'.

15 For analysis of the racialised basis of the nation-state and interstate system, see for example Goldberg 2002; Nicholson 2001; Persaud and Walker 2001) For analysis of the gendered basis of the nation-state and interstate system, see for example, Enloe 2001; MacKinnon 1991; Tickner 2001).

or affirming an inextricable association of certain occupations with certain profiles of migrants.[16] Thus, state regulation is bifurcated with an obvious bias in favour of largely unrestricted capital flows on the one hand, and uneven immigration regulations governing different categories of foreign workers on the other hand. A key outcome is that some transnational migrants (signified by, and signifying their class-based, racialized/ethnicized and gendered identities) are deemed more worthy than others.

There exists, in the present time, relatively nascent knowledge of labour migration and the seafaring workforce especially on cruise ships (see ILO-SIRC 2003; Wood 2000; Wu 2005; Zhao 2001). The 2002 report, *Industry as a partner of sustainable development: Tourism* (collaboratively produced by the World Travel and Tourism Council, the International Hotel & Restaurant Association, International Federation of Tour Operators, International Council of Cruise Lines and the United Nations Environment Programme) commends the cruise industry for employing seafarers who come from contexts in which 'employment is often limited and difficult in terms of either opportunity or stability'. Aside from asserting that cruise line employment provides women 'across the globe' with opportunities 'to achieve increased economic, social and cultural equality', the report also claims that 'employees from developing countries' eventually will gain new skills that can be transferred back to their originating countries:

> Another aspect of the benefits gained through cruise ship employment lies in the value of the skills acquired in the course of work aboard a ship. Training in new technologies, cross-cultural awareness, certification in management practices and hands-on experience brings added benefits to the employee. There are comprehensive education and training programmes in place for crew members …When they return to their country of origin the employees utilise their experiences, training and resources for the benefit of the local economy and fellow nationals (2002, 48).

---

16 For example in Southeast Asia, sectoral demands for low wage labour are met not just by the entry of transnational migrant workers per se, but that women and men from specific labour-sending countries are given permission to enter and subsequently placed in a range of 3D (dirty, dangerous and degrading) jobs. With time, there has emerged an inextricable association of specific 3D jobs with women and men who come from different countries and who may also have different racial-ethnic and/or religious backgrounds. Employers in Taiwan express greater preference for Thai and Indonesian men factory workers as opposed to those from the Philippines because the latter are considered 'lazy and shiftless, quicker to demand rights than work and have a tendency to run away' (Devraj 2001). In Thailand, migrant Burmese men have the reputation of being strong labourers who can haul rice bags weighing approximately 150 kg. They also dominate the fishing industries in which they are assigned the tasks of catching fish, while migrant Burmese women have the responsibility for sorting the catch at central depots (Tang 2001). Thus, neoliberal economic restructuring processes coupled with immigration regulations and policies have produced stratified regional and global pools of low wage transnational migrant workers. For the most part, migrant workers are unable to command the same level of wages and/or the shrinking rights and benefits of citizen-workers in labour-receiving countries particularly given their immigration status that, in turn, is mediated by nationality, gender, class and racial-ethnic origins.

Noble as the objectives of gender equality and knowledge transfer may be, it is not clear at all that they can be achieved within the context of capital's demands for flexibilized seafaring labour in and from, different nationalities, genders, classes and racial/ethnic groups.

Most evidently, cruise lines registered in juridical tax havens of FOC states are able to socially reconstruct with ease the seafaring workforce into one with different temporal and spatial characteristics: most seafarers on cruise ships are temporary contract workers from around the globe. Of significance is that seafarers are not subject to restrictive immigration rules such as those confronted by transnational migrant workers on land.

Although FOC states are responsible for enforcing domestic and international regulations regarding work at sea, they make no attempt to manipulate seafarer identities via the enforcement of land-based immigration regulations to cruise ship employment. There are no real or perceived reasons for FOC states to do so especially since foreign seafarers need never set foot for work on their sovereign soil: they are not considered a potentially destabilizing socioeconomic force to landed communities. Thus, can distinct identities associating specific shipboard occupations with specific seafarers emerge in the absence of immigration rules designating some as more worthy than others, and if so, how?

Given open registries' relationship to the international maritime regulatory structure, seafarers are not transnational migrant workers as much as they may be considered 'stateless' or even 'de-nationalized' workers, many of whom sign labour contracts with crewing agencies in their home countries to work for a cruise line in which the parent company is incorporated in one country, while the cruise line is headquartered in another country and its ships are flagged by a third country (e.g., CCL's cruise line HAL is headquartered in Seattle, WA with its ships mainly flagged by the Netherlands via its autonomous region, Curacao in the Netherlands Antilles). At the same time however, the 'mini-UN' moniker celebrating cruise ship crew diversity, aurally and visually re-inscribes nationality onto seafarers while simultaneously conflating it with racial/ethnic origins, gender, culture and even the status of national economic development.

Chapter Five examines cruise lines' recruitment, placement and related manipulation of seafarer identities on cruise ships. Our analysis reveals that cruise lines are not motivated solely by the utility of low wage labour per se but that seafarers are placed in specific positions that affirm and display/express perceived traits amenable to the core business of producing pleasure at sea. In this way, persistent stereotypes and expectations of national cultural, racial/ethnic and/or gender identities are conveyed from land to sea.

With the exception of specialized seafarer education, training and certification that are required for those who work in the marine division of cruise ships, others with extensive or minimal experience in hospitality work may be able to secure employment in the hotel division of cruise ships. Cruise lines employ low wage contract seafarers especially in their hotel divisions to help keep down operating costs while providing passengers with unprecedented levels of service fit for 'dream' vacations. The discussion in Chapter Five ascertains the ways in which labour flexibilization processes at sea are mediated by identity modalities. Cruise lines place low wage seafarers from specific countries in specific positions to achieve stated and un-stated objectives, and accompanying these positions are uneven length of contracts, terms of work, compensation and benefits. North Americans, Western and Southern Europeans who are considered 'white' seafarers tend to have higher-level positions, wages and shorter contracts (i.e., three to four months 'tour of duty' followed by paid vacations) with more privileges (e.g., better cabin accommodations, shorter work days, officer and public dining spaces) than non-white seafarers from countries of the Global South (e.g., six to 12 month terminal contracts, four to six seafarers to a cabin, anywhere from 12-16 hour work days, mess hall dining). It is said that there is 'significant racial discrimination in the length of crew contracts' (ICONS 2000, 58).

Of equal importance is that the social construction and use of commercialized oceanic space remains distinctly masculinized despite changes in seafarer nationality and race/ethnicity. The overwhelming majority of seafarers in the global shipping sector in general, and cruise tourism in particular, continue to be men. Recruitment of women for shipboard work began in the 1980s when cruise lines experienced difficulties in hiring men seafarers. Even so, the ratio of women to men seafarers today remains at a paltry one to four or five. Similar to their land-based counterparts in service industries, women seafarers are concentrated in the hotel division of cruise ships mostly responsible for taking care of passengers (e.g., entertaining, baby-sitting, cleaning cabins and so forth).

Gender then is as important as that of nationality conflated with race-ethnicity in the recruitment and employment of seafarers for work on cruise ships. Women seafarers from the Global North who signify the physical features of being 'white' tend to be placed mostly in front-line or 'front stage' work, e.g., entertainment, spa-health and concierge services. Women from the Global South, on the whole, are placed in the back stage cleaning cabins and waiting tables on the ship.[17] An inescapable outcome is the construction of shipboard hierarchies reminiscent of those that characterized colonial societies in which white European men were situated at the apex, followed by a descending order of Others. Then as now, women's racial-ethnic origins also determine their insertion in the hierarchy.

Some men and women seafarers from the Global South, despite and because of their position on the lower rungs of the shipboard hierarchy, are considered exemplary at serving customers. This most evidently applies to Southeast Asian seafarers who are seen to come from 'service cultures' and are expected to fulfil stereotypical expectations of the always happy and smiling worker keen to please passengers. Not only does the stereotype have an effect of 'feminizing' Southeast Asian men in a shipboard work environment in which men outnumber women, it also comes with minimal base pay leaving seafarers dependent on passenger tips and gratuities to make up the difference.

---

17 The concepts of 'front' and 'back' stage were introduced by the sociologist, Irving Goffman in his analysis of social interactions. Using a dramaturgical framework, he asserted that the conduct of social life was much like the performance of a play, with the front and back stage 'self' (1959).

Chapter Five concludes by identifying the manner and consequences in which cruise lines shift a large part of select temporary contract seafarers' responsibility for earning the bulk of their monthly income primarily to gratuities or service charges paid by cruise passengers. Seafarers who clean cabins and wait tables are compensated this way on mass market cruise lines. Therefore, within the cruise ship workplace at sea, seafarers consistently must practice self-surveillance vis-à-vis their job performance. At the end of an itinerary, passengers are asked to complete 'comment cards' evaluating their experience and 'gifting' specific seafarers with cruise line suggested tips (or, increasing or decreasing 'service charges' added to their final bill). Positive evaluations from passengers do not guarantee continued employment beyond the end of short term contracts, although they can and do help seafarers to obtain future temporary contracts with the cruise line.

By flagging-out their ships to open and second registries, cruise lines can engage legitimately in the practice of 'recycling' seafarers (Petitpas 2005): in effect, they employ full-time workers on short-term renewable contracts that do not come with long-term benefits or job protection. From the perspective of free market transactions, seafarers indeed exchange their labour for wages. Yet, they have little control over labour recruitment and employment conditions.

Cast in this manner, the pursuit of profits, pleasure and work at sea in a global free market context can and will create its corresponding underside of loss, pain and servility. The underside's resilience is fuelled further by oft-invoked explanations that it is an unfortunate side effect that will dissipate with continued economic growth, and/or that it results from mistakes or miscalculations by individuals, firms and so forth. Such explanations fail to consider the ways in which repeated actions over time create and sustain social structures that in turn delimit the range and nature of present perceptions and actions. One major consequence is a missed opportunity to better understand the conditions in which different actors come to participate in free market transactions, and that their continued participation helps naturalize the free market imperative in and for the twenty-first century. Concurrent to this is a delimitation of what can be considered relevant or appropriate questions to ask and answer in efforts to address the underside of loss, pain and servility.

Taken collectively, on-going policies of economic privatization, liberalization and deregulation all over the world cannot but assign a privileged ontological status to the free market. Radiating from this ontological status is a sense of inevitability, i.e., free markets are the only route to reducing and eliminating inequities and inequalities. Applied to mass market cruise tourism, progress made toward addressing inequities and inequalities may be calculated in the form of total revenue from tonnage taxes, annual tourism receipts, berth occupancy rates, number of return cruisers, shipboard job creation, cruise line-passenger-seafarer expenditures on land, and so forth. These are quantifiable criteria that capture financial-economic impact. Manifestly absent are discussions of less quantifiable criteria for evaluating conduct per se in free markets. Why is it even important to pose such a question?

The answer begins from a simple fact that free markets neither have arisen from, nor operate in a vacuum (see especially Polanyi 1944). Free markets are constituted and reinforced by the actions of individuals (and, to be sure, collectivities made up of individuals) embedded in larger social contexts. Conduct in the marketplace, and indeed, is one of the many important acts of sociality that characterizes human beings as social actors par excellence. Since every society has standards for determining what are and should be good or right conduct, then it follows that free market practices also should be subject to, and not immune from questions of morality. Hence, what can be said of the relationship between morality and free market practices in general, and those that underpin the profit-pleasure-work at sea connection in particular? It is to this question that we turn in the final chapter of the study.

I emphasize here that the goal of Chapter Six is not to profess the 'immorality' of the profits-pleasure-work at sea connection. Rather, it is to foreground moral challenges generated from, and hidden by unconditional belief in the free market and its operations. Our discussion centres on the eighteenth century Scottish scholar Adam Smith. His well-known text *An Inquiry into the Nature and Causes of the Wealth of Nations* (1981, originally published in 1776, hereafter referred as WN) and especially its metaphor, 'the invisible hand' often are invoked to justify privatization, liberalization and deregulation policies in the construction and integration of free markets. Put simply, free markets are the panacea to what ail the national and global human condition (see, for example Wight 2002). By providing the free market its teleological nature, the invisible hand appears to make irrelevant explicit questions on morality. Conventional wisdom today has it that free markets ultimately benefit society (i.e., the 'invisible hand' at work) despite the fact that actors in the marketplace are motivated by self-interest unrelated to the highest good of others.

However there are two major issues associated with this kind of reasoning. First, Smith's arguments that were based on analysis of the rise of commercial society during his time (circa late eighteenth century) are given universal reach today i.e., the free market imperative applies across the board to all societies regardless of their contextual particularities resulting from long and complicated histories of inter-group contact. Related to this is the second issue. To transform what is a proposition into an axiomatic statement (i.e., free markets benefit society) is to insist on calibrating morality according to an exclusive economic dimension (with trickle down and side-way positive effects), and made applicable only to the outcome (the end) and not the processes (the means). All forms of conduct in the marketplace thus are shielded effectively from evaluations of what can or should be moral, i.e., good or right conduct.

Chapter Six specifically brings back in morality to the discourse on free markets by invoking Smith's other classic text, *The Theory of Moral Sentiments* (TMS) that offers a detailed examination of morality in society (1982b, originally published in 1759). An ostensible argument against this move is that WN and TMS are incommensurable since they encompass Smith's different authorial intents with their respective focus on economic and moral life. Smith, indeed, also wrote separately on other subjects such as law, rhetoric and so forth. It does not mean, however, that the respective works of Adam Smith—the political economist, the moral philosopher, the jurist, and the rhetorician—had no bearing on each other, or that his understanding of social life (as evinced from treatises on separate subjects) was segmented as opposed to holistic (see, for example Evensky 1987; Hirschmann 1977; Lamb 1974; Raphael and Macfie 1982). Perpetuating a separatist perspective facilitates mostly the argument for privileging the pursuit of self-interest that has a moral ending despite making no initial moral claims. This also silences Smith on what he observed to be the moral challenge of a free market-based society.[18] Thus, so long as Adam Smith continues to be invoked in policy, academic and lay discourse to defend the construction and integration of free markets on a global scale, there exists an obligation to examine his understanding of morality and its contemporary implications.

Smith asserted in TMS that human beings are driven not only by self-interest but also by the need for 'approbation'. The latter arises from individuals' capacity to imagine themselves in the position of others, i.e., to experience 'fellow feeling'. Even though the self cannot fully know an other, it is this drive to do so and in ways that affirm one's existence as a human being that builds and sustains viable communities and societies:

> And hence it is, that to feel much for others and little for ourselves, that to restrain our selfish, and to indulge our affections, constitutes the perfection of human nature; and can alone produce among mankind that harmony of sentiments and passions in which consists their whole grace and propriety (Smith 1982b I.i.5.5).

Crucially, individuals not only seek approbation but they seek what *ought* to be approved or disapproved in the course of social interactions (Smith 1982b III.ii.7). Smith, however, acknowledged that judgements made of the other by the self can be partial or biased. He then identified the 'impartial spectator' existing within the self that works to counteract such biases as it evaluates interactions from the standpoint of moral approbation: 'It is he, who, whenever we are about to act so as to affect the happiness of others, calls to us…that we are but one of the multitude, in no respect better than any other in it…' (Smith 1982b III.iii.5). The impartial spectator therefore is at work in every social situation, and not just that which occurs beyond the marketplace.

Of interest is that toward the end of his life and as recorded in the final edition of TMS that was published in 1790 long after WN, Smith observed the corruption of the impartial spectator. In the course of the rise of commercial society, material wealth and social status constituted the key criteria for dispensing moral approbation. Smith admitted that even though the exercise of self-interest in free markets benefited society by bringing about economic growth to sustain a growing population, it did little to encourage a deeper understanding of the moral self in relation to others.

---

18 Otteson asserts that there is no disjuncture between TMS and WN. He demonstrates that individuals' desire for mutual sympathy led to unintended moral rules in TMS, whereas individuals' desire for better living conditions led to unintended rules in WN. Otteson finds that there is an overarching framework in Smith's writings on morality, market and language, i.e., when left to their own devices, individuals' actions give rise to rules that, over time, become institutionalized. In this sense, 'the market explains the development of all human social customs and institutions' (2002, 7). His argument nevertheless evokes an essentialist stance on the ordering of social life, and in particular, the trajectory of which evolves according to a free market-based model. An inadvertent implication here is that majority of non-Western cultures somehow 'missed the boat,' so to speak, in their organization and legitimation of social life.

Before his death in the same year, he lamented the triumph of 'the rich and the great' over the 'wise and the virtuous' (1982b I.iii.3.2).

If, as Smith asserted, judgments of self and other are based on empirical observations over time in which general rules of morality emerge and are institutionalised (1982b III.4.8), then there is an unavoidable implication for our present time. When left unexamined, the utility of self-interest in free market transactions can and will help reshape criteria of, and for, what can be considered good or right conduct. Non-reflexive promotion and practice of exchange relations in the free market context may well desensitize people to persistent forms of inequities and inequalities that find new modes of expressions as we observe from the rise of FOC states, tourism as a national development strategy, competition between mass market cruise lines, consumer expectations and experiences, and seafarer recruitment and employment.

Applied to the profits-pleasure-work at sea connection, bringing back in the moral dimension can appear to be an incredibly lofty and virtuous goal. Such as effort also promises to elicit discussions fraught with the kind of controversy that can degenerate into what in different context Said called 'the politics of blame' (1993), e.g., 'It is the fault of greedy corporations', 'I'/We are not powerful enough to make changes', 'People wouldn't leave their families for work overseas if their political leaders were not corrupt', 'She was assaulted because she drank too much', 'FOC states are only interested in money', and so forth. Bringing back in the moral dimension does not mean at all that cruise lines should be barred from seeking profits, passengers criticized for wanting to have pleasurable leisure travel experiences and/or workers kept from being employed at sea. On the contrary, it means a rejection of this 'either-or' schema that has only precluded the search for viable long-term solutions.

Researching a World Beyond Land

> A legacy of one-too-many jibes about fieldwork in exotic locations, or fears of being trivialized, have given a sometimes desperately earnest tone to tourist studies. Reading the literature it would be hard to get a real sense that perhaps a central feather of tourism is pleasure, fun and enjoyment. We lack a language that can speak to the enjoyment and pleasure of tourism…through to academic writing whose subjectless passive prose denudes life from experiences, we engage in the social reproduction of seriousness. We need to be able to say tourism matters because it is enjoyable, not in spite of it.
>
> Franklin and Crang (2001, 14)

Over the past century and despite innovations in air and land transportation, the oceans remain an important site-space through which goods are moved from one land mass to another, as food is sourced to feed people all over the world. The oceans also have come to serve as an important site-space for which pleasure is produced and consumed in contemporary leisure travel and tourism. The construction and use of oceanic space unavoidably contours the human condition from the grounded everyday individual level to that of the more abstract global level. Given the centrality with which restructuring of the material and symbolic dimensions of life has commanded intellectual interest, then how is it that we know relatively little of what is happening at sea in comparison to contemporary land-based governance, industries and labour?

Perhaps, as Langewiesche eloquently put it, '[s]ince we live on land, and are usually beyond sight of the sea, it is easy to forget that our world is an ocean world, and to ignore what in practice that means' (2004, 3). With the exception of consistent detailed research on the global shipping sector conducted by the Seafarer International Research Centre (SIRC), Cardiff School of Social Sciences at Cardiff University in the United Kingdom, not much has been published by scholars working in fields such as International Political Economy, International Relations and International-Intercultural Communication and Tourism studies who, on the other hand, continue to produce a wealth of vital knowledge of neoliberal economic restructuring policies on land.

It should be said that site and subject accessibility can and do affect research of ocean-based industries and labour, e.g., logistical challenges of interviewing seafarers at work on open seas, increasingly securitized ports of call and/or the nature of funding interests. Researchers of the cruise industry, indeed, have commented on the difficulties of conducting fieldwork (for example, Garin 2005; ICONS 2000). Even though other industries within the global shipping sector allow, if not welcome, the assistance of seafarers' missions and centres throughout the world (e.g., provision of spiritual comfort, clothing and telephone calling cards for seafarers), cruise lines mostly have responded otherwise. In conducting research for its report on seafarers, the International Commission on Shipping (ICONS) encountered little, if any cooperation from cruise line management based in the US:

> The Commission formed the view that sectors of the US cruise industry operate in a secretive and harsh fashion. All requests to the industry for the opportunity to discuss allegations about its interests in safety and treatment of crew members were either declined or ignored. In fact, the US based cruise operators were the only major segment of the shipping industry that refused to meet with or provide input to the Commission's work (2000, 60).

For the most part, academic researchers have had to rely on the method of participant observation to investigate cruise ship operations in general and labour in particular (see especially research by R. Klein 2002a; and Wood 2000, 2004a). As A. Weaver asserted in his research on cruise ship space, '[t]he cruise excursion enabled the author to experience containment directly. They also enabled him to observe the ways in which tourists and service employees experience containment on board cruise ships' (2005b, 167). Another method is to secure employment on a cruise ship. Tracy, in her study of emotional labour performed by cruise ship workers, was hired as an assistant cruise director in the cruise department (2000). Zhao's study on emotional labour is a rare exception in which the researcher obtained permission to interview seafarers during a transatlantic voyage (2002).

The method of participant observation used in research on cruise ship operations, nevertheless, may and can leave researchers open to allegations of 'vacationing' while 'out at the field' so to speak. Tourism studies, in general, run such a risk: '[s]ome even claim that the study of tourism is the researcher's own excuse for traveling, an academic disguise for a joy ride' (Azarya 2004, 950). Related to this point is the mostly unacknowledged but accepted belief that leisure travel is a 'soft' topic when compared to the 'harder', more pressing or serious topics of transnational terror networks, the deregulation of telecommunication sectors and so forth. It could be said also that research on mass market cruise tourism is better left to the realm of business management and/or policy studies especially since the academic field of tourism 'has been dominated by policy led and industry sponsored work so the analysis tends to internalize industry led priorities and perspectives' (Franklin and Crang 2001, 5).

Questions of the researcher's motivation or 'real' intent out in the field (e.g., underwritten by the private sector, and/or the personal desire for leisure travel) can have an effect of weakening tourism studies as a legitimate academic field of inquiry. One consequence of this attitude is inadvertent affirmation of the socially constructed divisions between and within academic disciplines/fields of study, and in a way that mitigates attempts to better grasp the complexities of interrelated contemporary phenomena. The production and consumption of deep ocean pleasure cruises are located within a larger context that not only brings together economy, governance, security and labour, but does so in ways that intersect culture and identity. To accept this point is to understand that global-national-local forces are deeply intertwined and implicated in the conduct of social life that is lived in a holistic (albeit at times contradictory), as opposed to an analytically segmented manner.

Material for this study on profits, pleasure and work at sea are derived from archival sources such as newsprint media, government documents, academic and trade publications, as well as e-discussion threads on Cruise Critic, a popular cruise tourism website. The latter was the main source for examining the emergence of a virtual community of cruisers and their posts on the topics previously identified. To protect further posters' privacy, their on-line user names have been replaced with sequentially ordered 'CruiseCriticPoster1', 'CruiseCriticPoster2', and so forth, and only the dates of initial e-discussion threads are identified in-text.

Archival sources were complemented by field-work involving interviews of seafarers' missions and union representatives along the East Coast of the US; seafarers at a port of call; participant observation during a West Coast cruise itinerary; interviews of former cruise ship crew members in the US; and interviews of former crewing agents in Malaysia that were conducted between 2004 and 2005. My interviews with representatives of seafarers' missions along the east coast of the US confirmed that they had little contact with cruise ship crew, with the exception of arranging for transportation to take seafarers to nearby shopping malls at some ports of call. Among the posited reasons are the rapid turnaround time (a few hours at each port of call) of cruise ships; shortage of seafarer mission personnel or volunteers; and cruise ship-port security policies (e.g., access granted only to registered passengers, crew and port authorities).

While participant observation allowed me to gain first hand experience of a cruise itinerary, in the long-run this method was financially too prohibitive on an academic's salary. More importantly, it is not especially conducive to interviewing seafarers because they are extremely busy performing their work at sea, and some are quite reluctant to be seen chatting with passengers. For example, as I strolled the entire length of the ship's starboard side early one morning, I stopped to speak with a deck hand. He said 'good morning' to me, looked away and then proceeded to continue with his job of painting the metal railing. Wanting to confirm my reading of his nonverbal cues, I waited in the cabin for the woman whose job was to clean it. Surprised to find me in the cabin (seafarers are expected to wait for passengers to leave their cabins before entering to clean them), but upon learning from me that I originally came from her neighbouring country, the Indonesian woman said that certain categories of seafarers were not expected to interact with passengers. Although I succeeded in interviewing several seafarers in the hotel division, I realized that I had to find a more accessible site to do so.

Interviews of active seafarers turned out to be very challenging: my access to them was delimited mostly to those with shore leave at ports of call. Even then, the interviews were shaped by a number of factors such as seafarers' sense of 'urgency' (given limited shore leave time) in making phone calls to family and friends overseas; the rush to board seafarer mission-arranged buses (at some ports of call, cruise lines provide this service to seafarers) that will take them to the nearest Costco, Kmart or Walmart to purchase personal supplies; and in some cases, the fear that being seen interacting with me could be misread as sharing information with a journalist or union representative. In order to protect their identities then, seafarers are given pseudonyms in this book.

Unstructured interviews were conducted so as to minimize disruptions to seafarers' shoreside and/or shipboard activities. The length and content of interviews thus were shaped by seafarers' job responsibilities and/or sense of what they had to accomplish during the limited duration of shore leave. Importantly, dimensions of nationality and language also affected the interviewer-interviewee relationship. I was able to speak at different lengths with seafarers from Eastern Europe, Asia, Latin America and Southern Africa. After asking if they had time to speak with me, many replied with the question 'where are you from?' These uniformed crew members who wore ship badges identifying their names and countries of origin were interested firstly in knowing my country of origin. While some were not familiar with Malaysia, those who hailed from beyond Southeast Asia nodded as if they then knew where and how to place me, e.g., 'Near Indonesia? We have crew from there'. Such a response indicated to me one way in which seafarers gain cross-cultural knowledge while at sea. Of note here is that it is easy for passengers and fellow crew members to identify seafarers' nationality because they wear badges with two lines of inscription, i.e., their name followed by country of origin. Badges not only collectively represent the 'mini-UN' crew of cruise ships but they importantly can and do precondition shipboard interactions and expectations. As discussed in Chapter Five, seafarers' cross-cultural knowledge is characterized by ascribed national cultural traits that often are conflated with racial/ethnic origins.

All of my interviews were conducted of lower level support staff in the hotel division as opposed to officers from the marine division of cruise ships. European men and women officers were not as comfortable speaking with me, especially after I informed them that I was conducting research for an academic project. Without opportunities to converse further, I can only posit some possible reasons for the nature of our interactions, e.g., they were uncomfortable being seen conversing with a researcher; they placed me in the same social-cultural-economic category as Indonesian or Asian seafarers who are employed mostly in low wage and status positions; and/or they only had a limited amount of time to telephone their loved ones overseas, thus did not wish to spend it speaking with me. I was not privy to officers' backstage interactions with hotel staff while they were at sea or on land.

Of all the nationalities, Indonesian and Filipino men and women seafarers were most comfortable in conversing with me. The gender divide, in my interactions with men seafarers, did not seem to have as much impact as the fact that I am originally from a Southeast Asian country. According to Hamid, an Indonesian male seafarer who worked as a dishwasher on the ship, he had a sense when he first saw me that I was from his part of the world. Within minutes of our conversation, he said that even though he was so far away from his family, he felt as if he was 'home' because we could converse in *Bahasa Indonesia*. He then rushed (*'tunggu sini, tunggu sini'* literally translated as 'wait here, wait here') back on to the ship to find his compatriots because he wanted his friends to meet me. Similarly, Filipino men seafarers kept asking me if I was originally from their country. Even when I replied in the negative in English, they continued to insist that I was, in the words of Benjamin, a Filipino seafarer, 'my sister', claiming me as belonging to his regional cultural world.

I represented 'home' and 'hope' to them, a familiar stranger encountered near a dock thousands of miles away from their land of birth and loved ones. Seafarers from Indonesia and the Philippines took great pride in telling their respective compatriots that, not only was I from their part of the world but that I was a university professor. Raymond, an older Indonesian who worked in the ship's restaurants, felt the need to touch my arm as he said that he was proud (*'bangga'*) of me. In their world of work at sea, there were few opportunities for their fellow 'mini-UN' crew members to really get to know and interact with, or for these seafarers to be able to 'prove' that those from their part of the world can be and are more than the shipboard positions and related identities to which they had been assigned. Some hoped that one day their children would be able to make it further in life than they have been able to do so. Cruise ship employment gave them an opportunity to realize this, and others the hope to be able to do so. Still, there were seafarers who spoke of long work hours, low pay and being at the mercy of temporary contracts, their supervisors as well as 'picky guests' who complained about the service, or who demanded complimentary items and extra service. These seafarers were unanimous in their reason for bearing with such long and labour intensive work conditions, i.e., they do so for the sake of their families back home.

What emerged from the analysis of primary and secondary research is a complex picture of profits, pleasure and work at sea in which issues of capital mobility and state regulation intersect cruise lines' production and passengers' consumption of pleasure, with the employment of seafarers from all over the world. The following chapters tell a detailed story of these interrelated processes. Admittedly, there is no conclusive ending to this story: it will be contingent on the choices that we, as individual producer-consumers, as citizens of states, and as a global community continue to affirm or challenge in the present day.

Chapter 2

Flags of Convenience: Sovereignty-for-Lease in the Maritime World

Hey, no, no, no, no: my meaning in saying he is a good Man is to have you understand me, that he is sufficiently credit-worthy, yet his money is all tied up: he has a large merchant ship going to Tripoli, another to the Indies; I understand, moreover, in the Marketplace, he has a third to Mexico, a fourth to England, and other third at Mexico, a fourth for England, and other ventures he hath, squandered abroad.

Shylock in William Shakespeare's *The Merchant of Venice* Act I, Sc 3

During the imperial era, different powers sought strategic control of oceanic passage through or more direct access to their colonies. Following contestations over sea lanes, the high seas were clarified as belonging to all and to no one.[1] Since ships sailed mostly on this global commons, they then were constituted as oceanic signifiers of deterritorialized possession or nationality-at-sea: 'Freedom is thus the guiding principle of the law of the sea, but it is a principle strongly mediated by nationality'. In 1905, the Permanent Court of Arbitration at The Hague affirmed that the flag of registry rather than source of ownership determined a ship's nationality: 'the ship's national state has exclusive dominion over the ship; and no other nation can exercise dominion over that ship' (Alderton and Winchester 2002, 36).

Between the late nineteenth and early twentieth centuries, ships flagged by national or primary registries of traditional maritime states were a main source of national pride as evinced from competitive races between the United States and several Western European countries to construct the fastest ship for transatlantic crossings. These commercial vessels would soon be requisitioned to transport soldiers, war materiel and refugee-immigrants during interwar years. The unification of ship construction, ownership, management, operation and labour under the umbrella of a primary or national registry continued into the early post-World War II era.

Toward the end of that century, however, this unified system would be weakened considerably as the international shipping sector confronted an oversupply of ships in the midst of economic downturn. Since then, many ship owners have reflagged

---

1 See, for example, E. Mancke (1999). In the seventeenth century, the Dutch East Indies company hired a jurist, Hugo Grotius, to challenge Spanish, Portuguese and later, British attempts to control the high seas. In what is now considered one of the most important classical treatises on maritime relations, Grotius' *Mare Liberum* introduced the principle of the 'free seas,' i.e., the oceans belonged to no one and to all (2004, originally published in 1609). This principle remains operative today as discerned in UNCLOS that, among other key issues, delimits the differences between coastal and high or open seas.

or flagged out their ships to international or open registries with less restrictive regulations. Ships still fly national flags, but no longer are many identified clearly or exclusively with the nationalities per se. Ships may be built in one country, flagged in another country, their owners based in a third country, daily operations managed in a fourth country, and seafarers sourced from all regions of the world. The international shipping sector, thus, has gone 'global' in its structure of ship construction, ownership, management, operations and crew. How did the transformation happen within a relatively short period of time?

This chapter examines the historical development of open registries, also commonly known as 'flags of convenience' (FOC), from a particularistic origin to gradual widespread adoption all over the world. US strategic and commercial interests in the early twentieth century helped establish the world's first open registry in Panama. Since then, there are at least 30 open registries that flag foreign ships. Requiring little to no economic restructuring effort, these registries are attractive especially in a global era of economic deregulation, liberalization and privatization. As the maritime world's variant of 'offshore tax havens', open registries exchange minimal state regulatory power in return for ship registration fees and tonnage taxes. By delinking maritime capital's primary association with ship owners' countries of domicile-business, open registries are able not only to underwrite the denationalization of maritime capital but also that of the seafaring workforce, leading to new modes of ship management-operations, crewing sources and employment conditions. By flagging-out their ships to FOC states, ship owners are able to mask the chain of financial-legal accountability and liability while accruing tax-free oceanic revenue and controlling labour costs at the same time.

Liberated by FOC states from national or primary registries' strict citizenship requirements and labour regulations, ship owners can source all over the world for low wage contract seafarers. Even so, what makes the contemporary global seafaring labour force's overall profile unique is its explicitly gendered and racialized/ethnicized characteristics. The vast majority of seafarers are men, and within this gender, those from the Global North most often are placed in senior officer positions whereas those from the Global South tend to be employed as ratings or support staff. Pursuit of profits on the open seas then is not free of persistent racial/ethnic and gendered ideological practices most commonly found in landed life.

Open registries reveal that FOC states, by creating underregulated tax-free space for maritime capital, legitimizes a growing trend of constituting sovereignty as a commodity for lease in the twenty-first century. FOC states' exchange of minimal regulatory power for ship registration fees and tonnage taxes affirms the practice of free market exchange, and subsequently poses further challenges to port states and the global community with regard to pressing issues such as environmental pollution, ship and crew safety and possibly the identification and surveillance of potential terrorist threats at sea.

A Convenient System

Unlike a primary registry that has strict regulations governing all aspects of owning and operating oceanic vessels, an open registry is designed to offer 'ship owners internationally competitive terms, often as a means of earning revenue for the flag state' (Stopford 1988, 160). One account asserts that the gradual move to flag-out or reflag ships from a national registry to that of an open registry was initiated during the early decades of the twentieth century when ship owners in the US, in order to avoid Prohibition laws on the sale and consumption of alcohol, transferred their ships' registration to Panama. There also were some instances of European ship owners who had reflagged their ships elsewhere in the world (see especially Alderton and Winchester 2002). The practice of flagging-out ships to open registries, however, only became widespread toward the latter half of the century.

There was another reason behind initial practices of reflagging ships beyond owners' home countries. The US endorsed flagging-out of privately-owned ships in the early years of World War II as it sought to supply war materiel to the United Kingdom despite a declared stance of neutrality. By allowing ships to flag-out to Panama, the US could maintain neutrality—at least, until it was ready to formally enter the war—while aiding the UK (Boczek 1962; Garin 2005). Since then, the US continues to permit the flagging-out of ships as a way to facilitate its merchant marine's global competitiveness while maintaining a reserve fleet to be requisitioned in times of national emergency. As Susan Strange argued, the practice of flagging-out ships 'would never have been possible without the implicit consent of the world's leading economic and trading power—the United States' (1976, 360). Thus, it was the combination of US strategic and commercial interests that initiated and legitimized this practice.

The Spanish-American war served as an historical turning point for the maritime world: US experience of insufficient number of ships to carry war materiel prompted an aftermath build up of its merchant marine. So successful was the build up that by the end of World War I, the US Shipping Board began selling repossessed and/or confiscated enemy ships. Ship owners, however, soon complained that they could not compete on the international market because of strict US labour laws (e.g., La Follett Seamen's Act of 1915) that delimited citizenship and even dietary requirements of seafarers. The Shipping Board responded by allowing owners to flag-out their ships to Panama so long as these Panamanian-flagged ships did not compete on the same itineraries as their US flagged counterparts, and that during times of national emergency, the ships could be requisitioned for military service.

Ship owners were favourable toward Panama because of its weak regulations. As one shipping executive stated:

> The chief advantage of Panamanian registry is that the owner is relieved of the continual but irregular boiler and hull inspections and the regulations as to crew's quarters and subsistence. We are under absolutely no restrictions, so long as we pay the $1 net ton registry fee and 10 cents yearly a net ton tax (Carlisle 1981, 10).

Even though the Honduran registry already was in existence (established in the early 1920s by United Fruit Company to ensure consistent, reliable transport of produce back to the US), it was not deemed competitive because of the more restrictive ownership and crewing requirements.

Panama became the preferred country of ship registration for key reasons such as its geographic proximity coupled with the nature of its historical relationship with the US which, among other important outcomes, led to 'dollarization' of the Panamanian economy (i.e., adoption of US currency as legal tender) alongside pegging of the *balboa* or Panamanian currency to the US dollar at an exchange rate of one to one. Subsequently, the Hay-Bunau-Varilla treaty signed in 1903 between Panama and the US authorized the latter to construct the Panama Canal as well as to guarantee military protection for the former and its ships in the event of conflict. By World War II, the War Shipping Administration in Washington, DC even managed the Panamanian registry (Carlisle 1981, 99), and US consuls were expected to register Panamanian ships if there were no available Panamanian consuls to do so. Hence, the Panamanian registry's inception was linked intimately to intersecting US strategic and commercial interests in the region: 'Panamanian ship registration became an adjunct of American officialdom' (Carlisle 1981, 32).

In permitting ships to flag-out to the Panamanian registry, the US could protect its privately-owned ships flying Panamanian flags and ensure a vibrant merchant marine ready to be requisitioned by the military if needed *while* retaining the legal code and practice of labour rights for US seafarers on US flagged ships. It was a 'convenient' arrangement for both states and ship owners despite vehement objections from European states and labour organizations that, respectively, were concerned with the inability of European ship owners to compete with the US, and the registry's watered-down labour regulations.[2] In time, however, the Panamanian registry's popularity began to wane because of corrupt consuls who would charge for 'every service rendered' (even though they were legitimately given a percentage of fees collected), in addition to Panamanian student riots over the presence of US military bases, and opposition from US labour organizations (Carlisle 1981, 114).[3]

Shortly after World War II, US shipping firms operating tankers began to look toward Liberia. Former Secretary of State, Edward R. Stettinius Jr. established a corporation in 1947 to help develop the country (that had been settled and claimed by emancipated slaves as well as descendents of slaves approximately one hundred

---

2 Traditional maritime states in Europe initially resisted the flagging-out practice because it undermined the competitiveness of their ships. They took their case to the International Court of Justice arguing that there was not a 'genuine link' between flag and ship. They did not succeed in making their case. For more detailed discussion, please see Boczek 1962.

3 From the 1930s to 1960s, a series of legislative measures had a further cumulative effect of encouraging US ship owners to continue flagging-out their vessels. Although the Fair Labor Standards Act of 1938 exempted seafarers from minimum wage standards and over-time wages, labour unions eventually succeeded in securing pay raises for seafarers during the 1950s that only emboldened other ship owners to flag-out their vessels. In 1961, the US Congress extended minimum wages to cover seafarers but exempted those on foreign ships (thus encouraging the employment of non-national seafarers on foreign flagged ships), and in 1963, the US Supreme Court ruled that labour laws could not be applied to foreign ships in US territorial waters even if US citizens owned them (Nielsen 2000).

years earlier).[4] One year later, the Liberian Maritime Code was drafted and signed into law:

> Had it been known that those experts [in admiralty law] were members of the ship-owning company in the Stettinius organization and the ship management at ESSO, all involved in highly profitable tanker operations under Panama's flag, doubt might have been cast on their objectivity and independence (Carlisle 1981, 124).

Both of these open registries were drafted with the assistance, and catered to the needs, of corporate interests in the US. It was a 'win-win' arrangement for US commercial and strategic concerns. Ship owners were accorded unprecedented opportunities to pursue profits without the burden of paying income taxes or complying with strict regulations governing ship operations.[5] The US encouraged flagging-out of privately-owned ships to Panamanian, Liberian, and other open registries because these registries were considered 'under effective US control' (EUSC): ships flagged by these countries could be requisitioned during a national emergency.

The policy that places US-owned foreign-flagged ships under EUSC continues to this day. At the time of this writing, EUSC ships are those flagged by Panama, Liberia, Bahamas, Honduras and the Marshall Islands. Of significance is that this policy has never really been put in practice. As it exists, the policy is fraught with problems, not least of which are that (a) it is not legally binding, (b) the ships must be considered 'militarily useful', and (c) the potential challenge of meeting US citizenship requirements for crew on requisitioned ships. As W. Schubert, Maritime Administrator in the Department of Transportation testified in 2002 before the US House of Representatives' Armed Services Committee:

> The core of the EUSC concept is the assumption that the concerned nations will not interpose any objective to the exercise by the United States of its power of requisition over ships on their registries. There are no agreements, formal or otherwise, underlying the EUSC concept, which originated in the Department of Defense as a way to avoid the Neutrality Act prior to World War II, before our entry into that conflict, when we wished to supply Great Britain…Not all EUSC ships are militarily useful and the requisition power does not cover the crewing of any ship requisitioned (2002).

According to the US Joint Chiefs of Staff's 2005 report, there were over 60 ships in the EUSC fleet consisting mostly of tankers and dry bulk carriers, and they were crewed by non-US seafarers (2005, V-10). In January 2006 however, the US Department of Navy's Military Sealift Command listed only 32 tankers under EUSC.

---

4 For more detailed analysis on the origins and nature of nineteenth century settlements in Liberia, see Clegg 2004; and Shick 1980.

5 Based on the principle of reciprocity, US corporate tax regulations exempt foreign-owned corporations' revenues from the operations of commercial aircraft and oceanic vessels. Airlines, nonetheless, are incorporated in their home states and subject to home state income taxes on their global revenue. In the maritime sector, since 'beneficial owners' are based in one country while 'registered owners' are based in the FOC country, often times it is very difficult to determine the chain of accountability and responsibility.

In either case, no cruise ships are part of the EUSC, 'military sealift command', 'ready reserve force', or have 'readiness agreements' with the US military (2006).

That which began as a response to US strategic-commercial interests gradually would be adopted worldwide as open registries constitute a system of convenience for states and ship owners in search of profits. For flag states, open registries are a variant of the off-shore centre or tax-free haven in which underregulated space is created within sovereign territory for revenue generation that does not elicit the kinds of domestic opposition and unrest characteristic of economic restructuring policies. Especially since the latter half of the twentieth century, open registries allow ship owners an ability to select, if not demand, what are considered appropriate regulatory conditions for pursuing profits in the maritime world: the ease with which ships can be flagged by one FOC state means that they also can be reflagged to another. Still, what specifically prompted the eventual widespread practice of flagging out ships to FOC states?

The boom decades of ship building came especially after World War II, with the establishment of the Bretton Woods system overseeing the international economic order and the place of newly independent countries in it. The international shipping sector consequently grew in accordance with expanding international trade. Traditional sources of financing ships (i.e., from assets and profits) no longer were sufficient. New sources included state subsidies and institutional lenders. With expectations of high freight rates and expanding bulk trades, banks liberally approved loans to build ships. As the cost of constructing bigger and more technologically sophisticated ships increased, 'syndicated loans' were adopted to offset risks, i.e., banks sold to, or shared loan portfolios with other types of institutional lenders such as annuity and insurance firms (ILO 2001, 7).

A conjuncture of events beginning in the 1970s soon led to the sector's sharp economic downturn. Newly completed ships were delivered at a time of rising fuel prices and severely weakened commodity prices worldwide. International trade declined dramatically as the sector struggled with overtonnage or excess capacity in the market. Ship owners began defaulting on their loans. Institutional lenders responded by re-possessing ships and selling them at substantially lower prices to recover their costs. This had the effect of increasing competition in the sector as owners who purchased repossessed ships were able to offer cheaper freight rates while other ship owners grappled with the challenge of financing their new ships in the face of higher operating costs and lower freight rates.

With the Panamanian and Liberian registries serving as model open registries, other states especially those of the Caribbean and Pacific islands entered the business of exchanging minimal regulation for ship registration fees and tonnage taxes. For these FOC states, the business of flagging ships is an important mode of generating revenue, especially given the changing political economy. For ship owners, the flagging-out of their vessels to open registries allows them to remain competitive since they pay low ship registration fees and tonnage taxes, they are not taxed on revenue and profits from ocean-based activities, and they are allowed to employ foreign seafarers whose shipboard work conditions are governed by lenient regulations.

The International Transport Workers' Federation (ITF) defines open registries belonging to Panama and other countries as 'flags of convenience' because 'where beneficial, ownership and control of a vessel is found to lie elsewhere than in the country of the flag the vessel is flying'.[6] For example, the 'registered owner' is an individual or firm registered with the FOC state; the 'beneficial owner' most times is an individual or firm that actually owns the ship; and the 'operator or manager' is an individual or firm in charge of everyday ship operations. The operator or manager, in some cases, also may be the 'beneficial owner' who seeks to retain operational control without the legal responsibility assigned to the registered owner (Petitpas 2005). In this way, open registries complicate chains of financial-legal accountability by obfuscating the identities and responsibilities of beneficial ship owners.

Over 50 per cent of today's world fleet fly flags of convenience and the world's top three FOC states are Panama, Liberia and Bahamas (ITF 2005a).[7] Open registries' growing popularity easily can be discerned from fierce competition between these top three FOC states that has mitigated substantial increases in registration fees and tonnage taxes. Depending on the registry as well as the type and volume of ship tonnage, ship owners pay anywhere from USD0.10 to approximately USD0.50 per ton, excluding initial registration and annual fees of several thousands dollars. Ship owners also may receive discounted rates for registering more than one ship in their fleet (see, for example, websites of the Bahamas Maritime Authority; Liberian International Ship & Corporate Registry; Consulate of Panama in New York). The business of flagging ships is so competitive that the Liberian registry even waived its fees for new registrations (Liberian International Ship & Corporate Registry or LISCR), and Panamanian maritime consuls are rewarded financially when they generate revenue for the registry:

> A consul who generates between $100,000 and $150,000 for the Panamanian treasury, for example, is rewarded with $12,000, 30% of which goes to the office staff at the consul's discretion. "I made it more lucrative to work harder and longer," Sofer said. His aim is to attract the heavier, newer, more prestigious vessels, such as those operated by Carnival Cruise Lines of Miami. Six of Carnival's 10 cruise ships are registered in Panama, and a seventh -- the 101,000-ton Destiny, the world's biggest passenger vessel -- will fly the flag when it begins service at year's end (Morris 1996).

Ship owners need not be present physically in any of these countries to register their ships. The top three FOC states maintain offices in various capital cities throughout the world to facilitate ship registration, e.g., the Liberian registry has an office in the

---

6 The ITF is one of the largest and most powerful union federations in the world. It comprises of approximately 470 transport-based unions in 120 countries that collectively represent roughly 4.6 million workers. For more detailed information about ITF activities, please see the ITF website.

7 Even the People's Republic of China (PRC) flagged out ships from 1949 to the 1970s in response to its political economic isolation: ships had to be re-flagged in order for PRC to conduct international trade. Since then, the flagging out of PRC ships has continued because of economic competition, in addition to the ability of its ships to sail politically sensitive waters such as the Taiwan Straits (Wu 2004).

US state of Virginia, while the Bahamian and Panamanian registries have offices in New York. Indeed, open registries are what Palan calls 'fictional juridical locales', but they are not all the same (2003, 162). Liberia, in particular, 'franchised' its open registry to a private firm, i.e., first to the International Registries Inc., and then to the LISCR, both of which are based in the US. The Liberian state hence collects franchise or royalty fees from the privatization of its ship registry operations.[8]

FOC states, on the whole, rely on 'classification societies' generally chosen and paid for by ship owners and/or managers to certify that their ships are seaworthy, and that they comply with internationally accepted standards as delineated by IMO conventions. Discernibly at its worst, this kind of conflict of interest allows substandard ships to ply the oceans that, in well documented cases, have culminated in environmental disasters and/or abandoned crew at foreign ports (see especially ICONS 2000; Langewiesche 2004).

The allure of generating revenue from fictional juridical locales continues unopposed today. FOC states are

> [the] providers, solely, of a commercial service of ship registration. For these states such registration carries only minimal notions of any regulatory burden, whilst for the unscrupulous owner it represents an escape from any such [regulatory] burdens (Alderton and Winchester 2002, 39).

In 2005, the ITF specifically identified the following as FOC: Antigua & Barbuda, Bahamas, Barbados, Belize, Bermuda (UK), Bolivia, Cambodia, Cayman Islands, Comoros, Cyprus, Equatorial Guinea, Germany (German International Ship Register), Gibraltar (UK), Honduras, Jamaica, Lebanon, Liberia, Malta, Marshall Islands, Mauritius, Myanmar, Mongolia, Netherlands Antilles, Panama, Sri Lanka, Sao Tome & Principe, St. Vincent & the Grenadines, Tonga and Vanuatu. Note that even the land-locked state of Bolivia operates an open ship registry. At the time of this writing, the ITF has included three new FOC states: France (French International Ship Register), Georgia and North Korea (ITF, 'FOC Countries').[9]

Confronted by competition from FOC states, traditional maritime countries in Europe have created their versions of 'international' registries (pioneered by the Norwegian International Ship Register in 1987) existing alongside primary registries as a key way to minimize significant loss of revenue to other flag states.

---

8 Liberia's very public dispute with the International Registries Inc. (IRI) led to the transfer of its ship registry operations to the LISCR: 'LISCR was established and is owned by the lawyers who are acting for Liberia in their legal case against IRI. IRI has in turn lodged a US$ 400 million lawsuit against LISCR. There has also been a public dispute between the two companies over which of them has been authorised to issue certificates of registry and other statutory certificates on behalf of the government of Equatorial Guinea' (ITF's 'FOC Campaign Report 2000' that was quoted in Hekimoglu 2001, 2).

9 Under certain circumstances however, some open registries can surpass primary registries in their technical, safety and crewing requirements. In Eastern Europe, for example, the pursuit of economic privatization and deregulation policies has meant that national registries are filled with older, poorly maintained ships while newer ships are flagged out to open registries in order to earn more revenue (see ILO 2001).

More appropriately called 'second' registries, they may be considered 'hybrids' or 'half-way house[s]' (Klikauer and Morris 2002, 13) because the registries relax certain requirements, especially labour, to help maintain their citizen shipowners' competitiveness without having to flag-out to open registries. In the effort to prevent the haemorrhage of nationally flagged ships to open registries, such states have only hastened the deregulation of their seafaring workforce: depending on the second registry, ship owners are permitted to employ predetermined numbers of foreign seafarers for various shipboard positions. Italy's second registry for example restricts the percentage of foreign seafarers on a ship's total workforce but this may be waived with permission from the state.[10] Germany's second registry that did not have labour quotas, encouraged exponential growth in the employment of foreign seafarers. Klikauer and Morris found in their study on the German International Ship Register (GIS) that one year after the introduction of GIS, 'the percentage of foreign seafarers on board German ships increased from 6.6 percent to 34.4 percent' (2002, 20). Another year later:

> approximately 2,200 blue-collar seafarers worked on 450 GIS ships, and 80 percent of those came from the Philippines…[while] [t]he white-collar groups in the ship board labour force was less affected…The numbers of non-Germans in employment at officer level has not increased substantially' (2002, 21-22).

Meanwhile, the Netherlands has a second registry based in its overseas autonomous region of the Netherlands Antilles. Ships registered in the Netherlands Antilles (Curacao) fly the red-white-blue flag of the Netherlands while enjoying many benefits of an open registry (Britt 2003). An illustrative case is that of ships belonging to the cruise line, Holland America Line (HAL). HAL ships are registered in the Netherlands Antilles that permit the employment of non-national seafarers, and that complicate the chain of financial-legal accountability. Carnival Corporation & plc (HAL's parent corporation) in its Form 10-K Annual Report for 2005 identified the subsidiary HAL Antillen N.V. that owns, and charters some ships to HAL (CCL 2006b).[11]

It can be said then that the key difference between various types of ship registries is one of 'gradation', i.e., the degree to which a ship registry is able to accommodate the demands of capital. Whether flagged by open or second registries, oceanic vessels such as tankers, bulk carriers and cruise ships no longer are subject to restrictive regulations of primary registries.

Initial US support of the Panamanian open registry in the early twentieth century has come full circle as some of the major traditional maritime states devise creative ways of diluting national regulations so as to retain their primary registries while facilitating economic competitiveness. The overall consequence is direct and

---

10 International Marketing Strategies' *Official Guide to Ship Registries* provides detailed requirements of ship registries throughout the world (2005).

11 HAL's cruise contract with passengers also discloses that HAL charters cruise ships owned by different companies incorporated in the Netherlands Antilles (see HAL's website).

tacit state support for a minimal regulatory structure governing ship construction, ownership, management, operations and labour force in the maritime world today.[12]

State sovereignty is not eliminated so much as it is in the process of being commercialized by open registries: '[w]hile companies and tax haven states appear to undermine sovereignty by commodifying it, at the same time by paying for the right of abode, they are reaffirming sovereignty' (Palan 2003, 61). Premised on the leasing or renting-out of sovereignty, open registries represent one of the least political economic disruptive measures that states can pursue to generate much needed revenue in an era of economic privatization, liberalization and deregulation policies.

An important outgrowth of open registries is the phenomenon of third party ship management firms designed to rationalize the process of owning and operating ships for profits.

Third Party Ship Management Firms

Encouraged and legitimized by the minimal regulations of open registries, ship owners in the 1980s began to transfer management of daily ship operations to third party ship managers. Third party ship managers are those firms hired by ship owners to manage some or all aspects from finance (e.g., accounts, mortgage, insurance), operations and maintenance (e.g., specialized ships such as chemical and gas tankers), to the sourcing and placement of seafarers. They either are newly established firms or expansions of shipping lines into logistics in order to 'utilize spare management' capacity (ILO 2001, 13. See also Mitroussi 2003).

In the past, ship managers were located basically in 'old' metropoles of traditional maritime states. Today, they are joined by 'new' metropoles such as those in Hong Kong, Switzerland, Singapore and Malaysia. An example is UNIVAN, a third party ship management firm in Hong Kong. The firm manages over 70 ships whose owners are based in the U.S., Europe, and Asia. Their ships are flagged in various open registries and crewed by seafarers from countries such as India and the Philippines (ILO 2001, 14). Other ship managers such as Barber International have specific subsidiaries, and in this case, Barber Marine Team that specializes in sourcing and placing seafarers. The Marine Team is headquartered in Kuala Lumpur, Malaysia with crewing agencies in European and Asian countries. The centralization of computerized operations in Malaysia means that it 'will be able to deliver a product from any country the client would like' (International Cruise & Ferry Review 2002).

---

12 In the US, debates on repealing/strengthening cabotage laws (designed to protect domestic intercoastal trade by restricting coastal lanes to US-built, owned and crewed vessels) continue as some insist that protectionist cabotage laws have stifled domestic shipping industries while others call for strengthening potential US sealift operations and/or greater labour protection for domestic and foreign crew (The Merchant Marine Act of 1920, also commonly referred as the Jones Act, stipulates that ships for domestic intercoastal trade have to be built in the US, owned and crewed by US citizens and subject to domestic labour laws. The Act was amended several times to exempt certain routes and industries. See Jones 1995 for more detailed discussion and the potential ramifications of repealing the Jones Act).

Ship owners draw tremendous benefits from third party ship management firms' expertise in a range of services, together with their well established business networks in a variety of countries. For agreed upon fees, owners then shift the responsibility of compliance, book keeping, maintenance and/or seafarer recruitment to these managers. As such, shore side and shipboard operations can be made more efficient and cost-effective for the owners.[13]

> Professional ship management companies having developed expertise in operating efficiently with low cost labour while drawing on western technology and capital contribute to the development of new, more efficient factor markets to such a degree that they are instrumental in creating a new form of organization of shipping, its globalization (Mitroussi 2003, 78).

To reiterate, the blurring of this distinction between registered owner, beneficial owner and manager is one of the key advantages offered and protected by open registries.

Late twentieth century growth of third party ship management firms was shaped not only by ship owners' efforts at cutting costs via the rationalization of operations per se, but also a consequence of financial speculation in maritime commerce. By the 1980s and early 1990s, implementation of financial liberalization policies in various regions opened new markets of long and short term investments for denationalized-deterritorialized capital. Within the global shipping sector, this encouraged 'asset speculators' who may or may not have had any experience owning and operating ships but who saw opportunities in making profits from the quick purchase and re-sale of ships. In effect, the land-based phenomenon of 'flipping' real estate found its maritime equivalent in the 'flipping' of ships. These asset speculators turned to third party ship managers who, for a fee, would manage all aspects of ship operations on their behalf (Mitroussi 2003, 79).

The conjuncture of states' and capital's interests encapsulated in the exchange of fees for minimal regulation has meant that even though the search for profits encourages more efficient modes of ship management, it does so by affirming 'absentee or hidden ownership in plain sight' as complex webs of intra- and inter-corporate relations diffuses the chain of responsibility, accountability and liability. A similar process and outcome has occurred in the recruitment and employment conditions of seafarers.

---

13 It is not explicitly clear, however, as to the distinction between ship owners whose operations now include managing other owners' ships, and that of independent ship management firms with no ownership interests per se: '[M]any ship owning companies avoid connection with ownership, in order to avoid heavier taxation, legal responsibilities and claims and, thus, choose to appear as management companies. In this way, the secretive nature of the industry creates confusion about the real identity of the firms, that is which ship management companies appearing in directories constitute true third party ship management enterprises and which are in-house or manning firms' (Mitroussi 2003, 80).

A Global Seafaring Labour Force

The recruitment, size of shipboard work force, nationality and employment conditions of seafarers have been transformed by ship owners' adoption of new technologies coupled with open registries' more lenient labour regulations. Applications of technological innovations to oceanic vessels enhanced owners' cost-cutting measures, in part by reductions in crew size and consolidation of shipboard tasks. Especially on vessels that transport goods, the redesign of galleys and the automation of the engine and deck departments led to significant reductions in the number of seafarers of the officer and ratings levels. By the late 1990s, radio operators were gradually replaced with computerized communication systems such as the Global Maritime Distress and Safety System (ILO 2001, 16) and 'electricians merged with radio officers' as 'decks officers merged with engine room officers to create a 'nautical-technical officer'. Hence, that which accompany the implementation of new communication and information technologies are reductions in the total number of crew members on a ship while increasing seafarers' job responsibilities, e.g., the average number of crew onboard German ships declined from 35-50 in the 1960s, to 25 in the 1970s. By the 1990s, the number fell approximately to 15 crew members (Morris and Klikauer 2001, 187-88). On shore, the phenomenon of 'containerization' together with adoption of computerized systems linked and stream-lined daily global ship operations involving areas such as arrival and delivery of goods to staff payroll (Jensen 2004).[14]

In traditional maritime states, the flagging-out of ships initiated declining standards for seafarer education and training vis-à-vis technical competence, health and safety and so forth. A vicious cycle ensued as would-be seafarers looked to other professions while enrolments declined further in seafarer education and training institutions (Donn 2002). Even though senior and junior officers continue to hail from countries of the Global North, ratings/support staff and to a certain extent junior officers, now mostly come from countries of the Global South.

OECD countries provided the bulk of ratings prior to the 1970s. They soon were replaced by South Asians. Within a decade, South Asians in turn were replaced by Filipinos. Since the 1990s, competition to ensure a constant and reliable supply of low wage labour has encompassed nearly the entire globe: Filipinos, Eastern Europeans, and Chinese ratings are joined by junior and senior officers from countries such as the United Kingdom, Greece, Norway, Denmark and India. According to a representative of the International Ship Managers' Association, 'You go to a place, you harvest, then you abandon that place and go to the next one.' The net effect is that 'the hunt [for

---

14 'Containerization,' or the use of standardized containers to hold certain types of cargo, facilitates ease of loading on to ships, and off-loading directly on to rail cars or trucks for overland transport. Intermodal transport of this kind has helped decrease delivery time and the overall number of dock workers as on-off loading processes are taken over by computerized machinery (ILO 2001; Stratton 2000). Similar to the adoption of other forms of new technologies, the initial investment is high but over time, it can and does lower operating costs. Container shipping has become one of two industries (the other is cruise tourism) in the global shipping sector that continues to grow rapidly: within the last decade, the percentage of goods shipped via containers more than doubled, with prospects for continued growth.

low wage labour] is a tale of human arbitrage in an industry driven by globalization' (M. Cohen 2004, 47). Here, the nexus of denationalized-deterritorialized capital and flexibilized labour is made painfully evident as capital searches the world for the highest return on its investment in the seafaring labour force. The average monthly salary for contract workers at the ratings level is between USD400-500. Even if shipping lines comply with the ILO's minimum wage of USD435 per month based on 14 hour workdays, or 77 work hours per week, the incommensurability of wage to workload and conditions can only further repel potential seafarers from OECD countries (Donn 2002; ILO 2001).

Of note is that the phenomenon of manipulating seafarer identity is an integral dimension in labour deregulation processes. The presence of binational or multinational crews on ships today reveals that 'mixing seafarers of different origins to compose crews to attain objectives of cost and efficiency requires specialist knowledge' (ILO 2001, 34). Specialist knowledge dictates that wage levels are not the only defining characteristic: nationality, language proficiency, historical ties, cultural practices (including food preferences) also are central to the selection of seafarers. An ILO study on global seafarers has found that Russians and Koreans tend to be hired in groups because of their poor command of the English language while Filipinos and Poles, for example, can be integrated relatively easily with other nationalities. Crew mixing also may be and are informed by interregional preferences stemming from historical relationships, e.g., Indonesian crew on Dutch ships, and Koreans on Japanese ships, as well as intraregional linkages e.g., the 'Baltic connection' of Poles on German and Norwegian ships (ILO 2001, 40).

Deliberate efforts to mix crew on ships come with their own challenges, key amongst which are language proficiency and cultural preferences (Horck 2004; Sampson and Zhao 2003; Zhao 2001). While some seafarers want to work with their compatriots because of the comfort derived from shared linguistic and cultural backgrounds, others prefer working with seafarers from all over the world because they find that multinational crew have higher levels of respect and tolerance for difference, and that seafarers tend not to reproduce status hierarchies from their own societies (Sampson and Zhao 2003). As discussed further in Chapter 5, another important factor in recruiting seafarers of different nationalities is the need to mitigate their ability to organize collectively for their rights.

Ship owner-managers tend to rely on crewing agencies to recruit non-officer level seafarers. It is well known that many breach the ILO Convention No. 179 prohibiting crewing agencies from charging seafarers placement fees. Seafarers who seek union help to address wage or work related issues run the risk of being blacklisted by captains, ship owners and especially crewing agencies. In the Philippines, for instance, crewing agencies maintain a list of seafarers who have sought help from the ITF. Seafarers are 'blacklisted by fax' among agencies, e.g., a seafarer's picture and data can be sent via fax from one agency to another and at the bottom of the page, there could be a sentence 'offense---ITF involvement' indicating the perceived dangers of placing that particular seafarer. The International Commission on Shipping (ICONS) committee, in the course of its research on seafarers, came into possession of a fax with the sentence 'The above seafarer should be considered undesirable as he may destroy the integrity of your company and the manning industry as a whole'

(2000, 50). Seafarers' mission representatives along the east coast of the US confirm that crewing agencies' illegal practices are among the most frequent complaints of seafarers in general.

At the beginning of the twenty-first century, over 80 per cent of the world's seafarers come from Asian and Eastern European countries (ICONS 2000, 42). The Republic of the Philippines is considered the 'crewing capital' of the world, dominating labour supply for ratings and junior officers (Leggate 2004; Leyco 2004). In the early 1980s, there were roughly 50,000 Philippine nationals working as seafarers outside the country. The numbers increased exponentially in the midst of severe economic downturn during the late 1980s and early 1990s. By the early twenty-first century, over 200,000 seafarers left their countries annually for work on board ships (POEA 2003). This exponential increase came at a time in which the Philippine state officially entered the global migrant labour market by incorporating the 'export' of Philippine labour as a key strategy of development to mitigate the pressures of unemployment and underemployment exacerbated further by economic restructuring policies under the tutelage of the IMF and the World Bank (Ball 1997; Chin 1998).

So important are seafarer remittances to the country's economy that the state requires foreign employers to remit 80 per cent of seafarers' monthly salaries or 'allotments' directly to Philippine crewing agencies that then are responsible for disbursing the remittances to seafarer families even though some crewing agencies are known to delay disbursements of allotments to seafarer families in order to take advantage of fluctuations in the currency exchange rates (ICONS 2000, 44). The Philippine state established the Seafarer One Stop Processing Center to facilitate the processing of passports, seamen's booklets (record of ship job sites and performance), exit permits and so forth (Leyco 2004).

The state run Philippine Overseas Employment Administration (POEA) is responsible for implementing policies covering overseas contract workers: key amongst its tasks is to negotiate standardized work contracts for landed and ocean-based workers. Significantly, the President of the International Seafarers Action Center in the Philippines argues that the state considers its seafaring nationals 'as a commodity whose entitlements need to be diminished so they can be marketable' (Pabico 2003). In the past few years, revisions to the POEA standardized employment contract for seafarers reveal the privileging of seafarers' successful placement and completion of their work over seafarers' rights per se (Stevenson 'POEA' n.d.). Seafarers are expected to comply with 'company policy' that may not have been vetted by POEA or labour unions. They can be dismissed for 'creating trouble outside the vessel's premises' or for 'any activity which tends to destroy the harmonious relationship of the company' (Stevenson 'Illegal Contracts' n.d.).[15] POEA's standard contract also prohibits seafarers from negotiating higher wages with employers once they have agreed to the conditions of the contract by signing it (see also Ignacio 2005).

---

15 For more detailed information on the employment contract, please see the POEA's website.

POEA facilitates the global shipping sector's attempts to reduce coverage for sick or injured crew members' medical and living expenses by restricting compensation to direct 'work-related' incidences. This move undermines seafarers' long established right commonly known as 'maintenance and cure', in that ship owners are expected to pay for seafarers' medical care and living expenses until they have fully recovered or reached 'maximum cure' (Stevenson 2005). Exceptions to this occur when seafarers knowingly conceal pre-existing conditions prior to employment, and if seafarer injury occurred from 'willful misconduct'. Moreover, acceptance of any payment for injury/death automatically invokes the 'quitclaim' clause that prevents the seafarer or designated beneficiary from pursuing further monetary compensation in the Philippines or any other country. Even so, 'watered-down' POEA contracts signed in the Philippines are often substituted with a different contract (a practice called 'double bookkeeping') that seafarers are asked to sign upon embarking their assigned vessels overseas (ICONS 2000; ITF 2005b; Munro 2004).

Labour flexibilization processes have affected state-seafarer relations in the People's Republic of China (PRC) as well. Prior to the 1970s, seafarers worked for the state and shipboard relations were organized horizontally (i.e., collectivistically oriented), unlike the norm of traditional maritime shipboard hierarchies. Since the onset of economic reforms, however, Chinese seafarers have the option of working on state-owned or privately-owned ships, and those who elect the latter must learn to work within institutionalized shipboard hierarchies and relationships (Wu 2004; Zhao 2001). Fierce competition to place citizen seafarers overseas has led the PRC even to sanction Chinese seafarers for lodging complaints against their foreign employers (Zhao 2001).

Many observers and analysts anticipate that economic reforms in the PRC eventually will result in Chinese seafarers supplanting those from other nationalities in the global seafaring labour force. The Philippine state anticipated this threat by delaying the adoption of ILO mandated increases in the minimum monthly wage for its seafarers (Li and Wonham 1999; Philippine Seafarers Assistance Programme 1999). Yet, Chinese seafarers may not be competitive for other reasons, i.e., they are not as proficient in the English language as expected; they are perceived to be 'too clannish, refusing to eat Western food and generally failing to assimilate with other crew members'; and they are known to sign one-time contracts for work on foreign ships only to return to domestic assignments at the end of the contract (M. Cohen 2004, 47). Noteworthy here is the perception that Chinese seafarers are not 'interested' in working on foreign ships (e.g., their failure to 'assimilate') even though the standard practice is to offer temporary contracts without job security or long term benefits. A presumption is that low wage contract seafarers ought to want to have their contracts renewed.

It should be emphasized that the majority of seafarers are men, hence continued popular usage of the term 'manning' as opposed to 'crewing' agencies. With the exception of rare cases in the nineteenth century, there were no women officers on board merchant ships (Coons and Varias 2003; de Pauw 1982; ILO-SIRC 2003). At the turn of the twentieth century, women were recruited to work on passenger ships but in distinctly gendered positions and corresponding responsibilities. Women seafarers worked primarily as caretakers of women and children passengers.

By the mid-twentieth century, Scandinavian and Soviet women were employed as ship officers, and the number of women officers gradually increased worldwide as ship owners experienced difficulty in recruiting men counterparts. The PRC, however, has the sole distinction of an all-women officer ship, the *Fengtao*, that operated from the 1960s-1970s. The overall number of women officers declined during the 1980s when men were recruited from Asia (Central, South and Southeast) and Eastern Europe. Since then, women senior officers largely are absent on cargo ships while junior officers and ratings on passenger ships have increased because 'women clearly sell more products abroad' and 'women are welcome and increasingly preferred by our newly structured market' (Zhao 2001, 24). Today, the ratio of women to men seafarers in the maritime world is approximately one to 50-100 (i.e., one to two per cent of an estimated 1.2 million seafarers), and women are placed mostly in ratings or support staff positions (ILO-SIRC 2003, 9).

Thus, the social construction and use of oceanic space remains distinctly masculinized despite changes in seafarer nationality and racial-ethnic origins: it was not *fortuna* so much as the necessity of addressing labour shortages that helped women's entry into the world of work at sea. Still, gendered attitudes and expectations persist in dictating the terms and conditions of women's labour on ships in general, and deck and galley departments in particular. An ILO-SIRC survey of employers revealed disturbing kinds of gendered assumptions and practices with regards to the paucity of women seafarers. Managers either professed gender-blind policies that did not consider the particular needs of women (e.g., pregnancy, maternity leave, provision of sanitary napkins), or that they relied on stereotypes about the perceived bio-psychological nature of women that rendered them unsuitable for working with electronic and mechanical equipment, or for managing crew members from various parts of the world (2003, 29-32). Chapter Five will discuss the reasons for why there is a distinctly higher ratio of women to men seafarers (i.e., one to four or five) on board cruise ships.

Ostensibly, there are two general tiers of seafarers today: an 'upper tier' with higher status, wages and benefits, and a 'lower tier' with its corresponding status, lower wages and benefits (Donn 2002). Seafarers of the officer grade are mostly 'company men' with concomitant rights, privileges and benefits while seafarers of the ratings grade are temporary contract workers (ILO 2001, 67). The length of contract, as ascertained by the ILO, depends on seafarer nationalities as well as employers, i.e., the shorter the contract, the higher the crew member's status.

Western European officers are given contract lengths of three to four months, whereas Western European ratings have contract lengths of six months. Filipino officers and ratings are found to have nine-month contracts while Sierra Leonian ratings have 12-month contracts (ILO 2001, 65-67). Longer temporary contracts then denote lower positions and status, and in the words of an ITF inspector, exemplify the practice of 'recycling' seafarers who work for the specified length of contract, return home without vacation pay or benefits, and if lucky, will be rehired to work for the shipping firm or for another (Petitpas 2005). While officers have their own dining and entertainment rooms and even access to satellite phones and computer communications systems, ratings are restricted to mess halls and some may not even be provided with books, magazines, music and/or videocassettes for entertainment purposes. They mostly are able to communicate with family and friends via the phone or internet when they are given shore leave. Shipboard 'sensory deprivation' is addressed by a global network of seafarers' missions that offer ground transportation, telephones and calling cards, internet access, clothing and so forth.

Regardless of rank, Western and (to a lesser extent) Eastern European seafarers have shorter contracts and are paid higher wages than those from countries of the Global South. That which is troubling here is the nexus of nationality, race-ethnicity and gender in which non-white men seafarers are ranked and paid lower than their white counterparts.[16] Inherent in the maritime world's pursuit of profits at sea is an affirmation of hierarchical relations and concomitantly related compensation practices based on specific intersections of nationality-racial/ethnic-gender identities embedded within the shipboard workplace. Given that FOC states already have lenient labour regulations of which they may or may not demand strict compliance from ship owners, then what recourse do seafarers have in the event of disputes over terms of employment?

'Smoke and Mirrors'

Growing competition between FOC states to register and flag ships as an important source of national revenue has had a deleterious effect on flag state implementation of international conventions:

> Open registry nations over the course of the last fifty years have bid against one another to offer shipowners the most attractive possible labor, taxation and—tacitly—enforcement regimens until they've reached the point where such traditional functions of government become little more than empty formalities. When there is nothing to prevent a shipowner from transferring his investments back and forth among national registries, no questions asked, meaningful enforcement of international norms is all but impossible; it takes only a few rogue registries to undermine the entire system (Garin 2005, 185).

Open registries' 'sovereignty-for-lease' raises an important issue regarding maritime regulation in general. Primary oversight of ship maintenance and crew safety remains the responsibility of flag states. Once they have ratified the relevant international conventions, flag states are expected to comply with international regulations in addition to enforcing their respective domestic regulations on ship operations and labour.

There are important IMO conventions governing key aspects of life at sea, e.g., the International Convention for the Safety of Life at Sea or SOLAS (1974) covers ship and crew safety; the International Convention for the Prevention of Pollution from Ships or MARPOL (1973/1978) regulates pollution at sea; and the International Convention on Standards of Training, Certification and Watchkeeping for Seafarers

---

16 In an interview with Ed Munro, chaplain of the Baltimore International Seafarers' Center, he stated that he was aware of very few cases of shipboard racism in otherwise generally amenable work relations among seafarers from all over the world. He did note, however, that the national-racial hierarchy is very clear, e.g., 'Norwegians and Swedes [tend to be] officers and Filipinos are crew' (2004).

or STCW (1978) covers crew qualifications. The ILO, similarly, has a body of over 50 conventions and recommendations (collectively known as the 'International Seafarer Code') that set forth minimum standards governing all aspects of merchant seafarers, from recruitment to health and repatriation issues. Yet, given the IMO's and ILO's lack of enforcement powers, then flag states may and do ignore the substantial body of conventions even if they have ratified them:

> Both the ILO and the IMO, the regulatory agencies responsible for safety of life at sea, marine environmental protection and labour conditions for seafarers, are not empowered to ensure that its member States comply with mandatory standards that they themselves have approved. Both Organizations must rely on member States to voluntarily implement their convention obligations, although various political and moral pressures may be brought upon them (ICONS 2000, 94).

As early as the 1950s, there were international attempts to define more clearly what was meant by the phrase 'genuine link', i.e., there had to be a genuine link between a ship and its flag state. This phrase first was introduced in Article 5 of the Geneva Convention on the High Seas 1958, and later incorporated as Article 91 of the United Nation's Convention on the Law of the Seas (UNCLOS) despite opposition from Panama, Liberia and the US (United Nations n.d.). Despite the phrase's existence within UNCLOS, there is no agreement to date on its definition that could have clarified terms of ownership, employment of citizen-seafarers and so forth.[17]

FOC state privileging of revenue over seafarer rights, then shifts responsibility for protecting seafarers to seafarers' missions throughout the world. Seafarers' missions continue to perform similar kinds of service delivery as did their predecessors over one hundred years ago. Presently, some also engage in advocacy with regard to helping seafarers obtain lost wages or to mediate work-related disputes: seafarers' missions and union representatives are the workers' key advocates in disputes with their captain, ship owner and/or crewing agency. Apart from administering to the religious-spiritual needs of Christian (and in some cases, even non-Christian) seafarers, these missions help disseminate pertinent information to, and educate seafarers on their rights. ITF inspectors are called in, if and when missions require their assistance in resolving seafarer-captain/owner/manager disputes over contract and workplace issues.

For example, E. Munro who was the chaplain at the Baltimore International Seafarers' Center said that during a shipboard visit in 2004, the group of Filipino crew members requested that he contact the ITF on their behalf because they had not been paid in months and that they wanted to go home. By the time he returned to the dock, the seafarers had already debarked with their belongings. He advised them to return to the ship because that was the only way to conduct a legal strike. The ship owner immediately contacted the US Bureau of Immigration, Customs and Enforcement which meant that seafarers had the option either of voluntarily leaving the country or be subject to immediate deportation. The seafarers refused to leave the dock insisting that they would not have any legal recourse in the Philippines. After

---

17 For opposing perspectives on this issue, please see Churchill 2000; and Oude Elferink 1999.

lengthy negotiations, they left voluntarily but stamped on their respective seafarer's booklets was the phrase 'refusal to work' (Munro 2004). The failure to maintain an incident-free booklet will affect their future employment opportunities. Marking seafarers' booklets is a key way to manage their behaviour: the booklet becomes a disciplinary tool with which owners, captains and crewing agencies indirectly command compliance from seafarers.

The exercise of such power, however, can be and has been moderated to some extent by cooperation among non-governmental organizations and even port state authorities all over the world. Rev. J. Von Dreele, director of the Seamen's Church Institute in Philadelphia, related a case involving a Greek owned ship with Greek officers and Filipino crew members (2004). The Filipino seafarers had signed their POEA contracts with a crewing agency in their home country stipulating lower monthly wages than what had been agreed upon when the ship owner acceded to the ITF's terms for seafarer contracts. The Filipino crew informed Von Dreele that they had received only 40 per cent of their wages and had not been paid for many months thereafter. The total underpayment amounted to approximately tens of thousands of dollars. Von Dreele met with the ship captain who denied the existence of the ITF contract. With the assistance of the ITF, Von Dreele obtained a copy of the contract and threatened to involve an ITF lawyer (potentially to arrest the ship at port) in resolving the dispute. The captain, who took one full day communicating with the ship owner in Greece, finally admitted to the contract's existence and agreed to pay back wages including one month's bonus to prevent the crew from leaving for the Philippines (which would have halted the ship's operations, hence ability to generate revenue). Instead of closing the case, Von Dreele alerted other US and foreign ports on the ship's itinerary so that corresponding seafarers' missions and ITF representatives could monitor the ship owner's compliance.

This particular case illustrates a key challenge and response to protecting seafarer rights today. First, there exists an informal transnational network of seafarer advocates comprising non-state and state actors, i.e., seafarers' missions, ITF representatives (inspectors and lawyers), port authorities (e.g., Coast Guard), and the judicial system that can be called on to ensure ship owners' and captains' compliance with existing regulations. Secondly, the network's surveillance capability is facilitated by new communications and information technologies such as the Internet and satellite phones. In the context of an 'outlaw sea', this loosely formed transnational network's presence helps buffer seafarers from some ship owners' ability to exploit and abuse without much recrimination (Langewiesche 2004).

Given a largely unregulated work environment, Von Dreele emphasized that when necessary, the 'sheer raw naked power' of key actors in the informal network could be used to bring about ship owners' compliance. This power often takes the form of a basic threat to 'arrest a ship' at port. It is mainly the issuance of such a threat or what Petitpas calls 'smoke and mirrors' that, in many cases, has allowed some seafarers' missions and the ITF to resolve breach of contract cases (Petitpas 2005). The formal process of arresting a ship would involve port authorities and lawyers. The ship owner thus loses control of the vessel and future revenue. Ships can be arrested at port for a variety of reasons, e.g., failure to service mortgage, failure to pay wages, and/or safety and health-related issues.

A potential setback occurs if and when an arrested ship is found to be of substandard quality and the cost of repairs supersedes the ship's value. There continue to be cases in which ship owners have refused to make the necessary repairs and in effect, abandoned their ships for auction at a later date. As a result, seafarers may be left stranded at foreign ports. Given the US Coast Guard's aggressive inspections of ships today, the number of arrested substandard ships in US ports gradually has declined. This is not because the ships are better maintained per se, but that some ship owners have responded to stricter US enforcement by redirecting substandard ships to non-US ports, potentially leaving the latter to deal with abandoned ships, stranded foreign seafarers and/or coastal pollution (see especially Langewiesche 2004).

The continued absence of a globally-integrated regulatory framework with enforcement powers to sanction ship owners and/or flag states means that efforts to monitor and secure seafarers' global rights rest partly on non-governmental organizations, e.g., domestic labour unions, the ITF, and seafarers' missions throughout the world. This latter group of actors collectively temper the degree and nature of exploitation made possible in a maritime world that increasingly is enclosed by free market practices especially in ship regulation and labour employment.

In light of FOC states' inability and/or unwillingness to enforce existing international conventions governing ship safety and labour, the formal responsibility increasingly falls on port states to do so, e.g., the ILO's Merchant Shipping (Minimum Standards) Convention No.147 (in effect 1981) that gives port states the right to apply minimum labour standards to foreign-flagged ships even if the flag state has not ratified the convention.[18] The IMO has helped spearhead discussions and consequent agreements on 'port state control' (PSC) that allows for port state inspections of foreign flagged ships to ensure compliance with international regulations. To date, there are signed regional Memorandum of Understanding (MOU) that cover every ocean in the world (IMO 2002).

Standardized PSC, however, remains elusive. Bloor et al's cross-national study of PSC in UK, Russia and India, revealed divergent (political economic and/or cultural) inspection practices.[19] Inconsistencies in regulatory practices among port

---

18 Even though ILO Convention No. 147 gives port states the right to apply the minimum labour standards to ships whether or not the corresponding flag states have ratified it, many port states tend not to pursue wage related issues alone but will do so in conjunction with other violations e.g., safety, technical and environmental issues. In this way, port states try to adhere to the 'comity of nations' principle. This is the case with the US that does not want its citizen seafarers to be subject to the regulations of other port states (Stevenson 2005).

19 For example, 'The level of attention accorded by UK inspectors to hygiene and seafarers' living and working conditions was very much greater than that accorded by their Indian and Russian counterparts. Although both Russian and Indian inspectors were observed on occasion to inspect the galley, galley stores, accommodation and ship's hospital, they did not do so routinely, unlike their UK counterparts. Further, Indian inspectors on occasion did not regularly check medical certificates and hours of work and rest, unlike their Russian and UK counterparts...Even in the UK – despite some well-publicised detentions of ships for carrying insufficient food or insufficient bedding – instances were observed where inspectors, faced with multiple deficiencies in ship standards, would simply omit examination of health and labour standards altogether' (Bloor et al. 2004, 2).

states, thus, constitute a major challenge to effective port state enforcement of international conventions.[20]

Since 9/11, key focus in the maritime world gradually has shifted to the protection of ports and ships from terrorist attacks. The US Maritime Transportation Security Act of 2002 stipulates various requirements such as a 96-hour notification prior to ship arrival at US ports, submission of ship manifest within 24 hours, and the demand for individual seafarer visas as opposed to entire crew visas. The US-led Proliferation Security Initiative of 2003 calls for increased interdiction of ships at sea, while the Container Security Initiative of 2002 identifies and targets any containers considered potential terrorist targets in the top 20 megaports of the world. The IMO's International Ship and Port Facility Security Code (ISPS Code) introduced in December 2002, and that came into effect July 2004, stipulates conditions for shipboard and port security. An ISPS Code Certification is issued to ports and ships that have complied with the requirements (Hesse 2003; Shie 2004). Although these are important measures to strengthen maritime security, that which is left visibly unaddressed are existing recruitment and employment conditions for seafarers on FOC ships, together with (uneven) implementation of seafarer rights as delineated by ILO conventions. Heightened emphasis on maritime security can have an effect of constituting seafarers as potential terrorists instead of important maritime intelligence sources for global efforts to stem terrorist acts.

Borne from early twentieth century US strategic and commercial interests, the widespread practice of flagging-out ships to open (and, in other cases, that of second) registries have contributed to the transformation of a maritime regulatory structure designed primarily to facilitate the free flow of capital. At the same time however, this structure elicits and sustains contradictions that are experienced directly by port communities, the oceans and seafarers. Overall responsibility for monitoring seafarer rights, port communities' security, and oceanic health in effect shifts from flag states to international organizations, NGOs and port states. Open registries, at their best, may be read as an innovative way for those states to affirm their sovereignty in a neoliberal era while accruing much needed revenue from leasing it to capital. At their worst, open registries threaten to naturalize a way of thought, conduct and life that affirms and privileges free market transactions above all else.

Given on-going efforts to ensure the free flow of capital all over the world, open registries exemplify a unique response to capital's demand for unobstructed flows in a world apportioned according to geopolitically-based governing entities called states: 'where the nation state is the bulwark of international regulation, sovereignty is for sale in the context of ship registration and the state enjoys the privilege' (Alderton

---

20 For example, 'In contrast to UK inspection practice, it was not *normal* Indian practice to check medical certificates, rest hours log books, galley, accommodation or the ship's hospital – although all these were observed by the researcher to be checked on at least one occasion during the Indian fieldwork and, in a few cases, deficiencies were recorded. Moreover, not all the inspectors were intellectually convinced of the rectitude of enforcing global standards of living and working conditions: one assiduous inspector expressed a concern that the advocacy of global labour standards was a developed world strategy to inhibit competition in the shipping industry from the developing world' (Bloor et al. 2004, 16).

and Winchester 2002, 30). The commercialization of sovereignty in this manner redefines the state's identity and legitimacy as the highest legally empowered moral agent within geopolitical borders, not in terms of relinquishing moral education to the free market per se but 'modelling' the kind of conduct commensurate with, and supportive of, free market exchanges.[21] States with open (and increasingly, second) registries help extend, validate and reinforce the inexorability of free market practices. Thus, evaluations of marketplace conduct are delimited for example to whether or not an exchange occurred between 'willing' buyers and sellers, as opposed to structural conditions that shaped the need to participate in, and/or the direct and indirect ramifications of that exchange.

Late twentieth century deep ocean pleasure cruising emerged from, and continues to grow within this minimal state-based regulatory structure in the maritime world. It should be noted here that the major mass market cruise lines do not operate substandard ships, and their terminal and ship security plans for protection against terrorist threats are considered to be some of the best in the maritime world. Underwritten mostly by FOC states, however, cruise lines' pursuit of profits at sea does affect oceanic health, port community development, passenger safety and seafarer rights. The next chapter analyzes the emergence of mass market cruise lines, their major business strategies for pursuing profits and contradictions emanating from these processes.

---

21 See Antonio Gramsci, *Prison Notebooks* for a lengthier discussion on the manner in which states work to build 'new national civilizations' via consensual strategies within civil society (1971). See also Axtmann 2004; and Chin and Mittleman 2000.

Chapter 3

Floating Resorts: Political Economy of Pleasure Production

> The great virtue of capitalism—the quality that always confounded socialist critics and defeated rival economic systems—is its ability to yield more from less.
>
> William Grieder (1997, 45)

Deep ocean pleasure cruising became a mass phenomenon only during the latter half of the twentieth century, commensurate with the widespread practice of flagging-out ships to open and second registries. Its origins, however, can be traced to the nineteenth century when 'packet ships' carried cargo and passengers to and from distant lands (especially overseas colonies) separated by vast oceans (Cartwright and Baird 1999; Coons and Varias 2003; Mancini 2000; Maxtone-Graham 1985). Steam engines later would increase the speed and comfort of oceanic passenger transport. Ship building at that point was a matter of national pride encompassed by competition between Europeans and Americans for 'The Blue Riband' award given to the fastest and biggest ship (e.g., those belonging to Cunard Line, White Line, Peninsular & Oriental Steam Navigation Company) in transatlantic crossings. These ships were considered a primary mode of transportation rather than the site of, and for, pleasure per se even though elite passengers travelled in first class accommodations that segregated them from poor immigrants: 'while pleasure cruising was already evident by the 1880s and 1890s, for the masses of people traveling on ships, necessity was the main impulse' (Coons and Varias 2003, xvi).

The shift from oceanic 'crossing' to 'cruising' began in the 1920s when some ship owners responded to two key pieces of US legislation (National Prohibition Act of 1919, and the Immigration Act of 1924) by refitting, reflagging and redeploying their vessels for regional itineraries (Maxtone-Graham 1985, 66). Oceanic crossings for passengers declined at the onset of World War II particularly when vessels were requisitioned for military transport. The early post-World War II period could have reinvigorated transoceanic voyages except for Pan American Airways' first transatlantic jet service in 1958. Mass passenger air transport that dramatically shortened travel time across the Atlantic left ocean liners' manifests filled mostly by those considered the 'newly wed and the nearly dead' (Mancini 2000, 6). While some shipping lines folded, others reconceptualized their business strategies and soon refitted, reflagged and redeployed their ships exclusively for pleasure cruising.

During the late 1960s, cruise lines began marketing the Caribbean and Mediterranean respectively to North American and Western European passengers as regional sites for pleasure cruising especially during the winter months (WTO

2003). For example, the founder of Carnival Cruise Lines (Ted Arison) refitted and marketed old vessels as 'fun ships' in which families could take affordable all-inclusive vacations throughout the Caribbean basin.[1] In the United Kingdom, pleasure cruising was stimulated by a specific piece of legislation designed to stem currency haemorrhage, i.e., tourists were prohibited from taking more than £50 (approximately USD80) in foreign currency out of the country. Cruise ships thus offered an attractive alternative mode of mass tourism because tourists only needed to use foreign currencies during short stays at ports of call (Cartwright and Baird 1999, 28).

Today, cruise lines have expanded beyond the Caribbean and Mediterranean routes to encompass other regions of the world. The business of cruise tourism, situated at the intersection of the shipping and tourism sectors, averages an enviable annual growth rate between 8-9 per cent per annum (CLIA 2006b; WTO 2003; Ahmed et al. 2002). Since the late twentieth century, roughly 100 million passengers have taken deep ocean pleasure cruises of two or more days. Nearly 40 per cent of this number did so in recent years. Forty new ships were introduced in the 1980s and the number doubled to 80 new ships within one decade.[2] Over 20 new ships are expected to join existing fleets by the end of this decade (CLIA 2006b, 36). Further, new destination ports are being added in Asia, Middle East, Europe and South America, e.g., in the near future, Costa Crociere that specializes in the European cruise market is expected to take delivery of a 3,800 passenger ship and Cunard Line (Cunard) will take delivery of a new 2,000 passenger transatlantic ocean liner, while Star Cruises (Star) has signed letters of intent for two new 1,500 passenger ships (*SuperStar, Sagittarius II* and *Capricorn II*) for its Asia-Pacific routes.

Despite expanding global coverage, deep ocean pleasure cruising remains overwhelmingly regionalized and weighted toward the US which is the 'dominant source of cruise passengers' worldwide: it is home to the world's top embarkation ports for the top destination ports, and it serves as the top deployment site for new ships (WTTC 2002, 44). Cruise ships carried approximately 11.5 million passengers globally in 2005, of which 9 million passengers resided in the US (CLIA 2006b, 4). A majority of the world's top embarkation ports are located in the US, especially the state of Florida (e.g., Miami, Port Canaveral and Fort Lauderdale) while some of the top destinations ports are located nearby in the Caribbean basin (including Bermuda), Alaska and Mexico. According to Cruise Lines International Association (CLIA), the Caribbean 'represents the number one destination [for its member lines] with almost 49 per cent capacity development. The Mediterranean, Europe, Alaska,

---

1 For a detailed discussion of Ted Arison's relationship to the founding of Carnival Cruise Lines in the US, please see Dickinson and Vladimir 1997; Garin 2005; and Klein 2005. For a detailed discussion of British cruise companies such as P & O, and Fred Olsen, please see Cartwright and Baird 1999. Garin discusses the personalities, business relationships and ensuing power struggles between major players such as Ted Arison, Knut Kloster (co-founder of Norwegian Cruise Lines), and the Norwegian shipping companies of Anders Wilhelmsen, I.M. Skaugen, and Gotaas-Larsen (of Royal Caribbean).

2 By 2002 for example, the 12.3 per cent increase in the industry's net capacity was met with 15.3 per cent increase in passengers. One year later, an eight per cent increase in capacity was met with 10.1 per cent increase in passengers (Conroy 2004, 13).

and Mexico follow the Caribbean in popularity' (2006b, 3).[3] Large, technologically advanced cruise ships tend to be deployed for itineraries originating from US ports as older ships are sent elsewhere in the world.

This chapter analyzes the manner in which cruise lines pursue profits, and the contradictions experienced by port communities. We begin by examining horizontal and vertical business integration strategies characterizing the emergence of the 'Big Three' cruise corporations and their related cruise line holdings. This is followed respectively with the development of niche market segments in mass market cruises, and the deployment of large and mega cruise ships. By rationalizing the production of pleasure at sea and on land, cruise lines simultaneously shape and affirm the larger context from which passengers come to expect and consume pleasure in mass market cruise tourism. The last section discusses how cruise lines and their ships can and do resist proposed legislation by Caribbean and Alaskan port authorities that are designed to address contradictions emerging from the operations of mass market cruise ships.

Mass-ification of Pleasure Cruising

In 1909, Cunard's *Mauretania* that was built, owned, flagged and crewed by the British had recaptured the Blue Riband award from the Germans for the fastest transatlantic crossing. Approximately nine decades later, the *Mauretania* and other oceanic trophies of national pride have been replaced with large ships such as those belonging to the cruise line Royal Caribbean International (Royal Caribbean) that is headquartered in Miami, Florida, e.g., Royal Caribbean's *Voyager of the Seas* was built in a Finnish shipyard, flagged in the Bahamas, and crewed by over 60 nationalities of seafarers:

> What these companies [cruise lines] have achieved, they have won through a profound mastery of the emerging global economy…Entirely within the bounds of the law, or nearly so, cruise lines like Carnival and Royal Caribbean have managed to create a global enterprise of unparalleled flexibility and freedom (Garin 2005, 9).

To be sure, the 'juridical residences' of open ship registries created by FOC (flag of convenience) states make possible global parcelling-out of the construction, ownership, registration, management and crew of cruise ships to various countries in the world. Other states such as the Netherlands and Italy have responded to growing competition from open registries by establishing second registries with more lenient regulations.

The open registries of Panama and the Bahamas that flag many mass market cruise ships help constitute and legitimize a minimal maritime regulatory structure. These registries underwrite cruise line pursuit of profits at sea such as charging low ship registration fees and tonnage taxes in lieu of taxes on revenue generated from

---

3 Majority of mass market cruise lines have membership in CLIA. The last section in this chapter will discuss briefly CLIA's activities. For more information, please see CLIA's website.

ocean-based activities. Open registries also have no restrictions on the employment of foreign seafarers.

On the open seas, cruise ships are under the legal oversight mainly of their respective flag states. Importantly, it is not in FOC states' interest to strengthen weak regulations since their registries are premised on the convenience accorded ship owners in registering, and operating their vessels. Thus, this regulatory structure ensures unparalleled flexibility and freedom for cruise lines to pursue profits at sea. Dickinson and Vladimir, two leading cruise line executives confirm some of the advantages in this way:

> When a ship carrying an international crew is registered in Liberia or Panama, it is not subject to union and other restrictive crewing policies. ..This means that owners are in a better position to negotiate fair and equitable compensation packages in a global, free-market environment. Of course, ships registered in these flag-of-convenience nations pay lower wages and are taxed on an aggregate basis than those registered in the United States (or Norway or Italy for that matter). But that makes it possible for them to offer cruises at a much lower cost than if their ships were registered in countries with restrictive hiring policies (1997, 66-7).

In his explanation for reflagging ships from Norway to the Bahamas, the Chief Executive Officer of Royal Caribbean said that: '[T]he competitive nature of the cruise industry is intense, and we must ensure our competitiveness throughout the business' (DuPont 2004b).

Open registries facilitate a very important and unique process, i.e., to liberate maritime capital from restrictive national regulations only to be reinvested in, and re-presented as superficially national yet fundamentally mobile in its physicality. Unlike land-based industries with their fixed assets, primary assets in the shipping sector in general and the cruise industry in particular are what Wood calls 'physically mobile' and 'massive chunks' of capital. Ships can be reflagged with relative ease to other registries; they also can be positioned and repositioned to ports in different parts of the world without being subject to a host of differentially restrictive national regulations regarding investments, taxations, profits, and employment (2000, 352).

The mobility of this form of capital clearly was evident in the early twenty-first century when cruise lines responded to the spread of Severe Acute Respiratory Syndrome (SARS) in Asia by repositioning ships to North America and Europe as a key way of offsetting declining sales of Asian cruise vacations. Following security challenges emanating from terrorist attacks on the US, cruise lines also began redeploying their ships to sail from new and old 'homeland' ports in the US, as opposed to foreign ports. Marketed variously as 'homeland cruising' or 'drive-to' cruising, this has reduced total costs of cruise vacations by eliminating air travel to foreign embarkation ports while significantly increasing economic activities in newly designated US home ports such as Seattle, Houston and Norfolk (Figueroa 2002; Sottili 2004). A few years later, Carnival responded to consecutive hurricanes that affected states along the Gulf coast of the US as well as the Caribbean basin by rerouting its ships: 'Maneuverability [physical and operational] is one of Carnival's greatest assets' (Palmeri 2004). Unlike some of the key problems that continue to confront the airline industry, cruise lines are able to respond relatively quickly and effectively to political, economic and/or environmental crises especially given that the unique maritime regulatory structure is no longer dominated by primary registries. The mid to late twentieth century ascent of open registries has legitimized parcelling-out of ship construction, ownership, management, operations and crewing sources to different countries, and in the process ensures ship owners' right to reflag and reposition oceanic vessels anywhere in the world for uninterrupted generation of revenue and profits.

Horizontal Integration

Consolidation within the cruise industry accelerated during the late 1980s as smaller cruise lines based in the US confronted mounting debt in the midst of heightened competition for passengers. By 1995, Regency Cruises' bankruptcy announcement was followed by Dolphin Cruises. Premier Cruise Line that eventually bought several of Dolphin's ships later would declare bankruptcy in 2000, as did Commodore Holdings that controlled the Commodore, and Crown Cruise Line. Renaissance Cruises, the fifth largest cruise line in the world covering the Asia-Pacific, European, Mediterranean and Caribbean routes eventually collapsed in the midst of post-9/11 weak sales and burgeoning debt. Renaissance's bankruptcy declaration would be joined later by American Classic Voyages and Royal Olympic. Their assets either were laid-up or sold to shipping interests in the US and/or Europe (Cordle 2001; DuPont 2004c). These and other smaller cruise lines were not able to compete against the expansion of mass market lines and their new ships with large carrying capacities that offered more amenities at highly competitive prices:

> Along the way of course, the bottom feeder lines like Regency, Premier and Commodore went out of business—despite the price advantage derived from operating older, fully depreciated ships—because the new, larger ships' economies of scale allowed the mass market lines to close the price gap. This drove the bottom feeders into bankruptcy (Dickinson and Vladimir 2004, 276).

In the past two decades then, cruise lines' 'growth by acquisition' or horizontal integration strategies fuelled by the collapse and/or buy-out of competitor lines, have culminated in three distinct cruise corporations with coverage of the world's oceans and dominating approximately 80 per cent of the global cruise industry (R. Klein 2005, 22).[4] The 'Big Three' are Carnival Corporation & plc (CCL), Royal Caribbean Cruises Ltd (RCL), and Star Cruises Ltd. (SCL). Other well-known cruise lines such as Disney Cruise Line, Crystal Cruises and Regent Seven Seas Cruises (renamed from Radisson Seven Seas Cruises in 2006) remain as respective subsidiaries of the entertainment conglomerate, the Walt Disney Company; the global shipping line, Nippon Yusen Kaisha Group; and the privately-held corporation specializing in travel and hospitality, Carlson Companies Inc.

---

4 For more information on conceptualizing and implementing horizontal integration and vertical integration strategies in other industries, see for example, Ensign 1998; Fan and Goyal 2006; Goshal and Patton 2002.

CCL is the largest cruise corporation in the world. Carnival Corporation is incorporated in Panama, whereas Carnival plc is incorporated in the UK. Carnival Corporation and Carnival plc respectively are listed on the New York Stock Exchange and the London Stock Exchange. Even though Carnival Corporation was publicly listed first in 1987, both began operating under the structure of a 'dual-listed company' in 2003. Headquartered in Miami, CCL owns and/or has controlling interest in 12 cruise lines, including Carnival (founded in 1972), Holland America Line (HAL) and its subsidiary Windstar (acquired in 1989), Princess Cruises (acquired in 2003), Costa Crociere (Costa, acquired wholly in 2000), Seabourn (acquired part ownership in 1993), and Cunard (acquired in 1998). By 2005, CCL and its cruise lines had 79 ships plying the oceans, of which Carnival dominated with its 22 ships (flagged by Panama and Bahamas), followed by Princess's 14 ships (flagged by Bermuda and Gibraltar) and HAL's 12 ships (flagged by Netherlands, i.e., Netherlands Antilles). Meanwhile, other cruise ships such as those belonging to Cunard are flagged by the UK, while Costa's ships are flagged by Italy.[5]

In that year, CCL had assets totalling approximately USD28 billion, with USD11 billion in revenue, USD10 billion of debt and USD2.2 billion in net income. It paid USD73 million in income taxes, an increase from USD47 million that were paid in 2004 (CCL 2006a, F-1). One half of the increase or USD18 million was due to taxes on a US government contract (CCL 2006a, F-21). Carnival was awarded a contract by the Military Sealift Command in September 2005 to provide temporary housing for Hurricane Katrina evacuees and relief workers on three of its cruise ships (Wiseman 2005).

When taxes related to the US government contract are deducted from the total income taxes paid in 2005, there is an increase of only USD8 million from taxes paid in the prior year. This in part is due to the Internal Revenue Service's (IRS) final regulations interpreting Section 883 of the Internal Revenue Code that no longer allowed across-the-board tax-free exemption of income considered 'non-incidental' to the international operations of foreign-flagged cruise ships. As CCL explained:

> For fiscal 2004 and 2003, we believe that substantially all of our income, with the exception of our U.S. source income principally from the transportation, hotel and tour businesses of Holland America Tours and Princess Tours, is derived from, or incidental to, the international operation of ships, and is therefore exempt from U.S. federal income taxes. For fiscal 2005, regulations under Section 883 of the Internal Revenue Code limiting the types of income considered to be derived from the international operation of a ship first became effective. Section 883 is the primary provision upon which we rely to exempt certain of our international ship operation earnings from U.S. income taxes. Accordingly, the 2005 provision for U.S. federal income taxes includes taxes on a portion of our ship operating income that is in addition to the U.S. source transportation, hotel and tour income on which U.S. taxes have historically been provided (CCL 2006a, F-21).

---

5 Information on cruise lines and corresponding registries for different ships are available from CCL's Form 10-K (CCL 2006a and 2006b), as well as the website of CLIA that provides detailed ship information (e.g., registry, initial year of service, tonnage and so forth) for all member cruise lines.

The second largest cruise corporation in the world is RCL. RCL is incorporated in Liberia, listed on the New York Stock Exchange (initial listing in 1993) as well as the Oslo Stock Exchange, and headquartered in Miami, Florida. RCL owns and controls Royal Caribbean (founded in 1967) and Celebrity Cruises (Celebrity, acquired in 1998), RCL had a total of 28 cruise ships in 2005: 19 in Royal Caribbean's fleet (flagged by Bahamas and Norway), and 9 in Celebrity's fleet (flagged by Bahamas and Ecuador). In that year, RCL's assets totalled approximately USD11 billion, with USD5 billion in revenue, USD 4 billion of debt, and USD700 million in net income: 'We and the majority of our subsidiaries are currently exempt from the US corporate tax income from the international operation of ships' (2006a, F-16).

Similar to CCL, RCL claimed exemption under Section 883 of the International Revenue Code because

> We and our subsidiary, Celebrity Cruises Inc., the operator of Celebrity Cruises, are foreign corporations engaged in a trade or business in the United States, and our ship-owning subsidiaries are foreign corporations that, in many cases, depending upon the itineraries of their ships, receive income from sources within the United States. Under Section 883 of the Internal Revenue Code, certain foreign corporations are not subject to United States income or branch profits tax on United States source income derived from or incidental to the international operation of a ship or ships, including income from the leasing of such ships (RCL 2006, 12).

However in light of the IRS' final regulations that 'narrowed the scope of activities... to be incidental to the international operations of ships,' RCL acknowledged that, '[t]he application of these new regulations reduced our net income for the year ended December 31, 2005 by approximately USD14 million' (RCL 2006a, F-17).

SCL, the third largest cruise corporation in the world, is incorporated in Bermuda, headquartered and listed on the Stock Exchange of Hong Kong (initial listing in 2000) and the Singapore Exchange.[6] In 2005, SCL owned 18 ships operating in Star (founded in 1993), Norwegian Cruise Line (NCL), NCL America, Orient Lines and Cruise Ferries. NCL dominated with its 9 ships (flagged by Bahamas), followed by Star's six ships (flagged by Panama and Bahamas) and NCL America's two ships (flagged by the US). SCL acquired NCL in 2002 to access non-Asian routes, particularly those in the US, Canada, the Caribbean and Mexico (Ng 2002). As discussed at greater length with regard to US seafarers in Chapter Five, NCL took over the bankrupt American Classic Voyages and gained exclusive rights via NCL America to cruise the Hawai'ian islands. NCL America ships are the only mass market cruise ships flagged by, and subject to US regulations governing ship construction, ownership, management, operations and labour.

In 2005, SCL assets were calculated at approximately USD5 billion, with USD2 billion in revenue, USD3 billion of debt, and USD18 million in net income. It paid USD2.6 million in income taxes. The total amount paid in taxes increased from the previous year's amount of USD1 million because of 'the provision of U.S. federal

---

6 SCL is a member of the Genting Group that was founded by a Malaysian Chinese business tycoon (Tan Sri Lim Goh Tong. For more information on the Group's activities, please see its website.

income tax for the tour operation in U.S. and corporation tax for Indian operations' (SCL 2005, 19). In the same vein as its competitors CCL and RCL, SCL encompasses very complex relationships between ship ownership, registry, management and operations. For example, the parent corporation SCL, two of its subsidiaries NCL Corporation Ltd and Star Cruises Asia Holding Ltd are incorporated in Bermuda, whereas Star Cruise Management Limited is incorporated in the Isle of Man. Companies owning different NCL ships are incorporated either in Bermuda (e.g., *Norwegian Spirit*) or the Isle of Man (e.g., *Norwegian Star*) but all ships are flagged by the Bahamas (SCL 2005, 107-8).[7]

It is in this way that open registries' exercise of their minimal regulatory power collectively facilitate and legitimize new modes and sites of maritime capital accumulation in which chains of liability and accountability effectively are obscured in the process.

Strategies of horizontal integration have allowed every one of the Big Three either to access, or increase market share in different regions of the world (e.g., DuPont 2003a). At the same time, the cruise corporations can achieve unprecedented economies of scale for ship operations and management especially in those cruise lines with large numbers of ships. For example, Carnival minimizes food costs by serving identical meals in all of its ships plying the Caribbean: 'In the restaurant business good costs should run between 25 and 30 percent of the selling price, while a mass market cruise line has costs of around $10 a day' (Berger 2004, 6). Carnival's reputation for offering 'cheap cruises' (at times, less than USD500 for a one week cruise) in the Caribbean reportedly has led even some Norwegian captains of Royal Caribbean cruise ships to draw their passengers' attention to Carnival ships passing nearby with the moniker, 'K-Mart of the Caribbean' (Garin 2005, 164). While this moniker pokes fun at Carnival's business philosophy of squeezing the most out of every dollar while offering affordable cruise vacations for individuals and families, it also connotes a degree of veiled condescension based on an almost nostalgic preference especially for the golden days of elite voyages operated by Europeans.

Vertical Integration

After roughly a decade or so of implementing horizontal integration strategies, cruise lines belonging to the Big Three now are focused on competing with land-based interests as opposed to one another exclusively. Competing against landed hospitality firms entails strategies of vertical integration involving the establishment and/or acquisition of companies offering shore excursions, and pre- and post-cruise packages, e.g., Royal Caribbean's *Royal Celebrity Tours* in Alaska offers landed tour packages.[8] The case of CCL is even more illustrative. CCL controls over 60 per cent

---

7 For more information on CCL and RCL subsidiaries, please refer respectively to Exhibit 21 "Significant Subsidiaries of Carnival Corporation and Carnival plc" (CCL 2006b), and Exhibit 21.1 "List of Subsidiaries" (RCL 2006b).

8 In the UK, well-known tour operators such as Fred Olsen, Thomson and Saga own and manage travel agencies, chartered cruises and flights, hotels, and tour coaches, also to control quality and costs (WTO 2003, 94-5).

of the cruise market in Alaska (via Carnival, Princess and HAL cruise lines), together with '13 hotels, 5 wilderness lodges, 18 luxury railcars and 440 motorcoaches and vans.' From this perspective, CCL owns and operates upstream and downstream landed operations. Vertical integration of this kind helps the corporation to control quality and costs. At the very same time, CCL's contracts with externally-owned tour operators provide additional revenue as it receives a percentage share (as much as 40 per cent in some cases) of profits for advertising select tour operators to passengers on various cruise lines (Kroll 2004, 96). Encouragement of passengers to choose cruise line-owned or vetted land operators include the ship's promise to wait for those who are delayed by their shore-side excursions. No such promise is given to passengers who contract with other land operators: the ship may and can sail without them (Pattullo 1996, 168).

Unique to Caribbean itineraries is the addition of leased or purchased 'private islands' such as NCL's *Great Stirrup Cay*, Royal Caribbean's and Celebrity's *Coco Cay*, Princess's *Princess Cay*, and HAL's *Half Moon Cay* (Showalter 1994; Turner 2004 and Turner 2004b).[9] The offer of private-exclusive recreational activities to cruise passengers on these islands means that cruise lines can ensure greater security for passengers, control labour costs (on some islands, seafarers debark first to set up for food and fun) and charge for extra services without having to share profits with externally-owned shore excursion operators.

As vertical integration strategies facilitate cruise corporations' control of nearly every aspect of mass market cruise tourism from pre- to post-cruise landed activities, horizontal integration strategies maintain or increase market share in and for different geographic regions (Ahmed et al. 2002; Miller and Grazer 2002). Cruise corporations' pursuit of profits, however, requires more than the acquisition of cruise lines and landed firms. Especially since profits inextricably are connected to potential passengers' willingness and ability to purchase pleasure, then cruise line production of pleasure must account also for different kinds of consumers. Key to this are the development of niche market segments, and the deployment of new cruise ships.

Niche Markets

Late twentieth century transition from Fordist to post-Fordist modes of production has transformed not only the manufacturing sector but also the tourism sector as mass production of goods and services for mass consumption gives way to niche production of goods and services for niche consumption (Ioannides and Debbage 1997; Meethan 2001; Poon 1993, 1990; Urry 2002, 1990). Within the tourism sector, this can be discerned readily in the shift from standardized production techniques and services characteristic of the mass holiday market (e.g., large resorts and packaged tours), to that of specialized production techniques and services designed

---

9 According to Showalter, NCL pioneered this concept by docking at Great Stirrup Cay in the Bahamas. The success of this port of call led to NCL's purchase of the Cay. In the case of Royal Caribbean, it first called on an island belonging to the Dominican Republic but 'hustlers and petty thieves' soon prompted the move to Labadee, a gated port on the Northern tip of Haiti (1994, 109-110).

for 'discerning' consumers of various income levels, tastes and preferences, among which may be and are demands for 'authentic' experiences. Examples of niche tourism are that of eco-tourism, ethnic tourism, cultural tourism and so forth.

At the outset, it appears that this movement of disaggregating the mass market into niche segments similarly is reflected in the business of deep ocean pleasure cruising. Closer analysis, however, will reveal otherwise. When the Big Three cruise corporations acquired cruise lines, they respectively elected to maintain independent identities for each line. Until recently and depending on the typology used (e.g., income level, ship ambience and size), cruise lines could be distinguished according to categories such as 'contemporary' (e.g., Carnival and NCL), 'Premium' (e.g., HAL and Princess), 'Luxury' (e.g., Cunard and Regent Seven Seas Cruises) and 'Ultra-Luxury' (e.g., Windstar and Seabourn). The last category of cruise lines are those with significantly smaller capacity (e.g., a few hundred as opposed to a few thousand passengers) that offer high-end cruise vacations for the wealthy. The rest are geared toward a range of middle class consumers.

Making the apparent shift from mass market to niche market consumption even more obvious are the changing profiles and interests of cruise passengers. During the first half of the twentieth century, the general profile of cruise passengers in the US was that of the elderly who had the financial means and leisure time to cross the Atlantic ocean. Cruise passengers today include what the industry calls 'condo commandos' or 'condo dragons' (Dickinson and Vladimir 1997, 127), i.e., retirees who live in Florida or who regularly travel south to board cruise ships for their silver or golden anniversaries; 'DINKYS' or 'double income no kids yet' (Cartwright and Baird 1999, 16) in search of fun and festivities at sea that appeal to their hobbies or lifestyle interests; and families interested in all-inclusive vacations complete with respective activities for parents and children.

The average annual income and age of cruise passengers have dropped considerably since the early twentieth century (WTO 2003). As Table 3.1 demonstrates, US cruise passengers (the dominant nationality in cruise tourism) i.e., those considered frequent 'cruisers' predominantly are white (at 91 per cent, with 4 per cent 'Black' and 5 per cent 'Other'), with an average age in the late 40s and average household incomes of approximately USD104,000. More than half of cruisers are college-educated and approximately 80 per cent are married. The general profile of cruise passengers from the world's top embarkation ports today thus may be said to be 'usually middle class and white,' and they constitute the 'mass market' (Mather 2002, 5).

Notably however, members of the middle classes beyond the US also are being drawn to pleasure cruising. In 1992, consumers from the US, Canada and Western European countries constituted 96 per cent of all passengers, but declined to 83 per cent in 2000 (WTO 2003, 5). The decline is paralleled by an increase in the number of wealthy and middle class Asians who opt for pleasure cruising as an alternative leisure activity. Southeast Asian cruises have become the third largest market for cruise tourism after that of North America and Europe. The new middle classes in Southeast Asia constitute 85 per cent of the cruise passenger market there with the rest coming from East Asia, Australia and New Zealand (Singh 2000, 139-144). Significantly, data collected on general passenger profiles ascertained that 60 per cent of the market was dominated by those who were 39 years old and younger

Table 3.1   2006 Profile of US Cruise Passengers

	Rep. Sample 2002	Rep. Sample 2004	Rep. Sample 2006	Cruisers	Non-Cruiser Vacationers
Age					
25-29	6%	6%	7%	6%	9%
30-39	22	23	24	24	25
40-49	26	28	30	26	33
50-59	19	24	21	22	20
60-74	19	17	15	18	12
75+	8	2	3	4	1
Total	100%	100%	100%	100%	100%
Average	50	48	47	49	45
Median	46	44	43	49	42
Income (Different Categories 2002)					
USD40,000 to less than USD50,000	14%	10%	15%	11%	16%
USD50,000 to less than USD60,000	13	15	14	11	15
USD60,000 to less than USD75,000	19	21	18	17	18
USD75,000 to less than USD100,000	11	23	21	22	22
USD100,000 to less than USD200,000	8	27	27	31	24
USD200,000 to less than USD300,000	1	3	3	4	3
USD300,000+	1	1	2	4	2
No Answer	5				
Total	90%	100%	100%	100%	100%
Average	USD64	USD90	USD94	USD104	USD90
Median (in 1,000s)	USD50	USD71	USD75	USD84	USD73
Gender					
Male	49%	49%	46%	49%	49%
Female	51	51	54	51	51
Marital Status					
Married	74%	82%	80%	83%	79%
Single/Divorced/Separated	26	13	20	17	21
Employment Status					
Full-time	56%	63%	56%	57%	56%
Retired	23	13	13	16	11
Educational Attainment					
College Grad or Higher	49%	58%	52%	57%	50%
Postgraduate	18	18	20	23	20
Race					
White	92%	93%	90%	91%	88%
Black	3	3	5	4	5
Other	5	4	5	5	7

Source: Reproduced with slight modifications from 'Figure 8 Demographics Summary' CLIA 2006b, 12.

(WTO 2003, 44). The rise of the new middle classes and changing consumption patterns during the early 1990s encouraged the growth of Star that now controls approximately 70 per cent of market share in Asia. Expected expansion of cruise itineraries in Asia has led to orders for even bigger cruise ships (Chung 2001).

With tropical-like weather and geography, the islands of Southeast Asia are marketed as a geographically closer alternative to the Caribbean, or what Wood has identified as the 'Caribbean of the East' (Wood 2004a). Star has three different categories of ships respectively offering two to three day cruises for those who are interested primarily in 'cruises to nowhere' (so that some may gamble legally in international waters), week-long large ship cruises for middle class families, and small private charters for the wealthy. As a result of cruise tourism's growing popularity in Southeast Asia, several states are in the process of upgrading, or will build new port facilities to accommodate large cruise ships.[10] Hence, it has been claimed that cruise tourism is 'democratic' given the wide variety of global cruise products appealing to an equally wide variety of consumers within the middle classes as well as the wealthy (Conroy 2004, 13).

Cruise lines' ability to cater to shifts in consumer profiles and demands does not necessarily indicate a transition from mass to niche production-consumption in cruise tourism per se. Rather, it reveals the adoption and offer of specialized or customized services within a mass market context. On land, cruise passengers can customize their shore-side excursions. At sea, they can elect to travel on cruise ships with specific itineraries that accentuate their lifestyle preferences and identities, select from a range of cabins, i.e., from the least expensive inside cabins to luxurious ones complete with personal butler and concierge service, and so forth (see, for example, McDougall 2004).

Major cruise lines also offer 'themed cruises' appealing to specific segments within the mass market. Tour operators block book a number of cabins on certain ships for those interested, for instance, in a celebration of rock-and-roll music or even for motorcycle enthusiasts. On Cunard ships, there are themed cruises ranging from faculty lectures on the history of art, Shakespeare and other topics, to gourmet cooking classes by world-renowned chefs. Cruise lines then can generate additional revenue by sub-contracting a certain percentage of cabins and related activities to third parties: 'Travel agents or promoters purchase cabin space and work with cruise lines to make sure additional meeting rooms are also provided. Rather than dedicate an entire cruise to a theme, most leave room for several hundred passengers to mix among those who are just along for the ride' (M. Martinez 2004). By marketing

---

10 The PRC awarded Star the right to wholly own and operate a tour agency in Shanghai ('Star Cruises gets China Approval,' *Business Times* (Malaysia), August 14, 2004. See also Star's website. State authorities in Malaysia, Singapore, Thailand, Vietnam, Indonesia and the Philippines are investing in port facility upgrades to attract more cruise passengers. Singapore now has a Cruise Division within the state-controlled Tourist Board (*United Press International* 2004). This kind of state involvement in infrastructural improvement attests to a belief in, and an expectation of the industry's continued growth well into the twenty-first century.

Teen, Gay/Lesbian, Family, Adventure, Romance and other themed cruises, cruise lines strive to affirm brand identification and strengthen consumer loyalty.

Specialized production of services accommodating diverse consumer tastes and lifestyles neither represent niche production per se, nor a transitional stage between mass and niche modes of cruise tourism. Rather, the embeddedness of niche segments and services within the mass market is a necessary condition characterizing cruise lines' pursuit of profits at sea in the contemporary era: 'segmentation therefore relies on the generation, or recognition of difference, and its purpose is to achieve 'greater efficiency in the supply of products to meet identified demand' (Meethan 2001, 73). This generation or recognition of difference is commensurate with changing demographics of those who purchase cruise vacations. With the exception of ultra-luxury cruise lines such as Windstar operating significantly smaller ships with more exclusive, intimate experiences geared for elite consumption, the others are considered mass market cruise lines that produce pleasure for middle class consumers:

> The new ships began to blur the distribution between mass-market and premium lines. The premium lines countered by building larger and larger ships themselves, making it far more challenging for premium lines to offer the type of intimate service on which they had built their reputations. Moreover, as premium lines added capacity, they found themselves marketing to broader (mass market) segments of the population (Dickinson and Vladimir 2004, 275).

Ships with large and even larger carrying capacities facilitate what can be called the 'nesting' of niche market segments within mass market cruise tourism.

Larger/Mega Cruise Ships

The design of deep ocean vessels for passenger transport has changed dramatically in the past century. Transoceanic liners that carried cargo and passengers on fixed schedules and routes were organized spatially along vertical hull segments, i.e., first class cabins and public spaces in the front, second class in the middle, and steerage class in the back or aft of the ship (Maxtone-Graham 1985, 54-57). In the early twentieth century, immigrants to the US travelled in steerage class that vertically segregated their living and dining spaces from 'first class' and 'second class' passengers.

However, when the US implemented its Immigration Act of 1924 that severely curtailed immigration from Asia and South-Eastern Europe, passenger lines had to identify other kinds of passengers to fill empty berths. One example is the Netherlands-American Steamship Company that later became HAL.[11] Steerage class soon was replaced with 'tourist third class' cabins for students, writers and young women who wanted to visit foreign locales but who did not have the means for first or second class travel (Coons and Varias 2003, xvi). A few years earlier other passenger lines already had responded to US implementation of its National Prohibition Act of 1919

---

11 For detailed information on HAL's earlier history, please see Maxtone-Graham 1985; and the website of HAL.

by refitting ships for pleasure cruising, and their subsequent flagging-out to Panama that then permitted shipboard consumption of alcohol.

An important related outcome of these two key pieces of US legislation was the reorganization of cabin and public space from vertical hull segments to horizontal deck arrangements, i.e., first class cabins on upper decks that spanned the entire length of the ship, while second and tourist third class cabins were resituated on lower decks (Maxtone-Graham 1985, 66). By the end of the twentieth century, mass market cruise ships have multiple decks (as many as fourteen to fifteen) that hold a variety of cabin sizes on each deck. Further, cruise ships no longer are considered exclusively a mode of transportation from one port of call to another. They also have become deterritorialized vacation sites in mass market cruising especially on North American-Caribbean itineraries. In some cases, mass market cruise ships are considered *the* main destination that is followed by port calls. This begs the question, 'From where do cruise lines draw the inspiration for their production of deterritorialized pleasure in, and for deterritorialized vacation sites?'

The blueprint for this kind of vacation-at-sea comes from all-inclusive landed resorts. Since the US middle classes dominate cruise tourism, shipboard activities and amenities then reflect and/or appeal to their consumption preferences and expectations. This is evident from the construction and deployment of large and even larger ships with the space for activities and amenities such as those found in popular resort destinations of Las Vegas, Florida and the Caribbean (see especially Ritzer and Stillman 2001). The dimensions of culture and economics intersect as mass market cruise tourism shapes and is shaped by middle class US cruise passengers' interests and preferences. Of importance also is that an ever growing list of activities and amenities offered by these ships simultaneously facilitates cruise lines' profit maximization efforts.

According to the logic of capital accumulation in mass market cruise tourism, the larger the cruise ship, the greater the amenities and economies of scale, hence more profits for cruise lines (Mathisen 2004a). Cruise ships averaging 80,000 GRT were considered large in 1980 (1 GRT is equivalent to 100 cubic feet of enclosed space that generates revenue on a ship). By the early twenty-first century, there already exists the deployment of cruise ships over 100,000 GRT. These mega-ships with a larger carrying capacity of several thousand passengers and seafarers allow for more efficient distribution and use of resources.

Princess took delivery of *Grand Princess*, the world's largest ship at 109,000 GRT in 1998 but was soon superseded by Royal Caribbean's *Voyager of the Seas* at 138,000 GRT and with a carrying capacity of over 3,000 passengers. Carnival, Royal Caribbean, Costa and Princess are some of the major cruise lines that have ordered ships exceeding 100,000 GRT. In 2006, Royal Caribbean launched its 160,000 GRT *Freedom of the Seas* that carries 3,600 passengers. Royal Caribbean also intends to build an even bigger behemoth: 'Project Genesis' will develop a 220,000 GRT ship with the carrying capacity of 5,400 passengers (Cruise Critic News 2006). These post-Panamax ships (i.e., too large to cross the Panama Canal) are designed with different hulls and taller superstructures better suited for calmer seas.[12] Fuel costs will not increase substantially since, unlike the era of the Blue Riband, speed is not a deciding factor in pleasure cruising. Thus, cruise lines' deployment of larger or mega ships allows them to achieve optimal economies of scale as capacity is increased while operating costs remain relatively the same (Walsh 2000).

Aside from increasing the number of cabins, mega ships can hold a variety of new activity sites such as miniature golf courses, bowling alleys, basketball courts, ice skating rinks, shopping plazas, and rock-climbing structures. By designing space and activities in this way, cruise lines are able to compete directly with landed resorts:

> It is not enough to win business from rival cruise lines; that is just rearranging the market. What is needed is a concentrated attack on other parts of the leisure industry, such as land-based resorts and hotels. But to attract people from land-based holidays, the cruise industry needs a product that offers a comparable level of activity and diversion (Mott 2004, 94).

With collective coverage of the world's oceans, the three cruise corporations and their respective holdings of cruise lines now are positioned to compete with land-based resorts. Yet, the 'war' metaphor that encapsulates and drives this strategy of taking away market share from landed resorts, is experienced mostly in pleasurable ways by cruise passengers.

Mass market cruise ships in the present era may be considered oceanic variants of Ritzer's land-based 'cathedrals of consumption' into which consumers venture for temporary escape from the rigours of everyday life:

> The new means of consumption can be seen as 'cathedrals of consumption'—that is, they are structured, often successfully, to have an enchanted, sometimes even sacred, religious character. To attract ever-larger numbers of consumers, such cathedrals of consumption need to offer, or at least appear to offer, increasingly magical, fantastic, and enchanted settings in which to consume (Ritzer 2005, 7).

A major contradiction, nonetheless, emerges from transforming cruise ships into the main production sites of and for passengers' dream vacations (most readily ascertained from cruise lines' television and print advertisements promoting dream vacations). Large and even larger ship settings and operations can elicit disenchantment because of longer queues at check-in, embarkation/debarkation, meal services, show-times and shore excursions. Cruise lines make the effort to mitigate potential disenchantment of the cruise experience in significant ways such as offering additional and varied outlets of alternative restaurants, in-cabin dining service, shopping alleys, multiple recreation sites, and health and fitness programs that have a cumulative effect of dissipating passengers' sense of being on a ship with thousands of other people.[13]

---

12 For an excellent and accessible discussion of historical shifts in ship design, please see Maxtone-Graham 1985.

13 This degree of 'dedifferentiation' on the ship in which retail shops, eateries, sports and entertainment venues are contained in a very large space, may lead some to argue that cruise

Significantly, the four principles of efficiency (the most value for money), predictability (no unpleasant surprises), calculability (ability to control costs) and controllability (scripted or mapped activities and movements) inform cruise lines' production of pleasure in these floating cathedrals of consumption (Ritzer and Liska 1997). Put in another way, even though cruise passengers can and will choose from a variety of cabin categories, decide where and when to eat their meals, select among different entertainment outlets, shore excursions and so forth, these decisions are made within an institutionalized context informed by the familiar principles on which landed life increasingly is being reordered. Phrased succinctly, structured diversity informs the production and consumption of pleasure in mass market cruise tourism (Chapter Four discusses the nature and extent to which consumers challenge or not the institutionalization of pleasure at sea).[14]

Ship décor and round-the-clock programming offer passengers that which is expected of all-inclusive landed resorts. The experience of deep ocean pleasure cruising projects a sense of drifting in time or timelessness on what may be called 'dream ships': 'The overarching effect of moving around the new means of consumption is the loss of a sense of time and a dream-like state in which the passage of time seems not to be occurring or does not matter' (Ritzer and Stillman 2001, 94). In practice, the dream context encourages passengers to pay for additional goods and services despite their purchase of all-inclusive vacations, e.g., charges for soft drinks and themed-night specialty drinks, tuxedo rentals, photographs taken at the point of embarkation and formal dinners, and fees for dining in specialty restaurants. For some passengers, the dream experience concludes abruptly when detailed bills are slipped under their cabin doors on the last night of a voyage. One passenger noted in an e-discussion thread that, '[o]n my first cruise I had a great deal of fun overhearing people talk about the bill they got at the end of the cruise and watching their eyes bug out!' (CruiseCriticPoster1, 17 December 2006).

Mass market cruise lines' production of pleasure may and does deliberately conflate the ship with the destination, i.e., the ship becomes a deterritorialized 'touristic place,' a floating resort designed and operated to offer many of the amenities

---

vacations signify the post-modern life that no longer draws distinctions between separate spheres of social activity. While this may apply particularly to applications of new information and communication technologies in everyday life, in the case of mass market cruise tourism, I would say that it is not a post-modern condition so much as the manner in which cruise lines can maximize shipboard profits. MacCannell puts it in this way, 'I am not prepared to argue that the accumulation of materials called 'postmodern' constitute the end of history, or even a distinct historical epoch, nor can I say that I believe they touch humanity in its tenderest parts. They are more a repression and denial necessary to the dirty work of modernity so that it can continue to elaborate its forms while seeming to have passed out of existence or to have changed into something 'new' and 'different'' (1989, vi).

14 Bauman writes, 'The market might already have selected them as consumers and so taken away their freedom to ignore its blandishments; but on every successive visit to a market-place consumers have every reason to feel that it is they – perhaps even they alone – who are in command. They are the judges, the critics and the choosers. They can, after all, refuse their allegiance to any one of the infinite choices on display. Except the choice of choosing between them, that is – but that choice does not appear to be a choice' (1998, 84).

of its landed counterparts.[15] As a mode of transportation and a site of pleasure, the cruise ship exemplifies Sheller and Urry's twin concepts of a 'place in play' and a 'place to play' (2004). Indeed, Cartwright and Baird's study found that:

> for many cruisers, it was the cruise itself, i.e., the shipboard experience that was the major motivator, although all of the sample agreed to some extent…that they wanted authenticity in the place they visited but perhaps not too much, especially if it involved confronting poverty (1999, 96).

Different kinds of cruise itineraries such as those that do not call at ports, and those with relatively brief stays at numerous ports of call with officially vetted shore excursions and/or visits to exclusive 'private islands', encompass the changing nature of mass market cruise tourism particularly in the Caribbean basin that is home to many of the world's top cruise destination sites. While private islands have 'decided advantages for the company as they are in control of spending and thus do not have to share any income with shore-based traders,' passengers still can claim that they have visited the Caribbean, albeit without having to confront contradictions generated by many Caribbean economies' dependence on tourism as the major strategy of development (Cartwright and Baird 1999, 146. See also Courtman 2004; Duval 2004; Pattullo 2005). The inclusion of 'private islands' in cruise itineraries highlights and promotes further the 'extraordinariness' of cruising on dream ships by helping to keep at bay 'criminal' elements that potentially can 'pollute' passengers' pleasurable experiences.[16]

Integral to the idea and practice of the cruise ship as a 'touristic place' is its function also as a 'gated community' at sea and at port in the twenty-first century. Cast in this way, mass market cruising redirects Urry's notion of the 'tourist gaze' in the sense that the ship and shipboard activities may share in, or even supersede shore-side excursions in passengers' search for extraordinary sights and experiences.

Cruise itineraries in the Caribbean basin today appear to be a far cry from what was intended during the 1970s, especially by NCL. One of its co-founders, Knut Kloster (the other was Ted Arison who founded Carnival), envisioned cruises in the Caribbean as a way to redress the area's colonial legacies by encouraging 'passengers to interact on a deeper, more challenging level with the people and places they were visiting' (Garin 2005, 48). Thus, Kloster and his Vice-President for Public Relations developed the 'New Experiences' program in 1971 in which middle class US passengers could visit with Jamaican families and/or their professional counterparts. The program ultimately failed because they neither anticipated nor

---

15 Since, the touristic culture 'is more than the physical travel; it is the preparation of people to see other places as objects of tourism, and the preparation of those places to be seen', the mass market cruise ship can then be considered a major touristic place at sea (Franklin and Crang 2001, 10).

16 Urry calls it 'social pollution', i.e., 'individuals or social groups in a particular location whose beliefs or actions are seen as "polluting." Some examples are alcoholics, the homeless, prostitutes, drug users, pickpockets, dangerous drivers, teenage gangs, and even other tourists.' (1992, 182).

expected resentment from Jamaicans who perceived it as a postcolonial variant of servitude, in addition to the resilience of racist attitudes in NCL's main office.[17]

For cruise passengers who choose to debark at ports of call, they often are encapsulated by what Jaakson calls 'tourist bubbles' of informal spatial boundaries circumscribing their movements and activities (2004). Tourist bubbles delimit what already may be a mere one-half day experience at a foreign port:

> Overall, cruise passengers' whole experience is highly controlled, well organized and to some degree even contrived. Cruise line surveys, however, consistently show this to be the highest and most satisfactory shore feature on most cruises when it is offered (Showalter 1994, 111).

Some ports of call in the Caribbean basin even have created tourist zones such as duty-free San Miguel in Cozumel, and the Tourism Village in Belize City. The latter was designed specifically for cruise passengers (E. Brown 2002). These tourist enclaves offer passengers opportunities to experience/purchase previously vetted goods (many of which may be provided by transnational duty-free retailers) and services without having to venture into 'unknown' spaces inhabited by the locals.[18] Hence, tourist bubbles help preconfigure the shore-side tourist gaze for many cruise passengers.

Cruise line production and marketing of pleasure on large and mega cruise ships conjure the allure-promise of 'dream vacations' on 'dream ships' wherein passengers or 'guests' can live—albeit temporary—fantasy lives of having their 'staterooms' cleaned twice a day, all their meals served in elegant restaurants and/or cabins, and a selection of entertainment venues ranging from Broadway-like shows/revues to casinos. The size of mass market cruise ships and related interior décor illustrate Sampson's notion of cruise ships as 'hyperspaces' characterized by 'monotonous and universal features. They are in many senses culturally indeterminate, reflecting neither one culture nor another' (Sampson 2003, 256). Restating this from a Ritzerian perspective, cruise ships and shipboard activities signify the globalization of 'nothing' or 'a social form that is generally centrally conceived, controlled and comparatively devoid of distinctive substantive content' (Ritzer 2003, 195).[19]

---

17 Garin writes: 'Outright contempt among some in the Miami offices didn't help things. The *New York Times* may have praised the program, but Florida was still the Deep South, and Kloster's efforts were unfolding in the middle of the most racially charged period in American history. "Not all our people in Miami appreciated what we did" he remembers. "One of the most influential people in our organization referred to this program as the "Take a Nigger to Lunch Program"' (2005, 53).

18 Much controversy erupted in Belize when respective contracts on the construction of new tourism villages that were signed between the Government of Belize with Carnival, and Royal Caribbean were seen overwhelmingly to favour the cruise lines (e.g., docking fees, employment of local labour, infrastructural development) over that of the local communities (see, for example, *The San Pedro Sun,* 2004).

19 Ritzer argues that the concept of 'nothing' always exists in relation to something: the marketing of dream ships and cruise experiences can be contrasted to that of significantly smaller ships that may reflect more accurately local cultural and geographic environments of their itineraries (2003).

Perhaps with the exception of cruise ships on localized itineraries (e.g. NCL America ships with exclusive Hawaiian itineraries), the majority of mass market cruise ship decors are designed to facilitate ease of repositioning from one geo-cultural region to another. Mass market cruise ships may be said to possess 'non-spaces' with standardized décor; and some of them can sail to and around 'non-places' such as 'private islands' and 'cruises to nowhere'. Even when ships call at foreign ports, the generally short duration of port calls together with cruise line promotion of select shore excursions tend to capture constructed images and identities of local cultures and communities. Ships also may be said to be staffed by 'non-people' who, despite and because of their different geographic and cultural origins are expected to be demonstrative always of 'happy' personalities. Nonetheless as ascertained in Chapter Five seafarers are distinguished according to key intersections of identity modalities.

For some of the most popular cruise itineraries in the Western, Eastern and Southern Caribbean, large and mega cruise ships are the classic Barthesian 'sign' in which the relationship between the signifier (the ship) and the signified ('dream' or 'fantasy' experience/life) exposes, yet hides the Caribbean basin's painful historical experiences and legacies of racial-economic subordination (Barthes 1973; Momsen 2005; Pattullo 2005). The construction of ships as main destinations supplemented by calls to private islands and tourism villages in mass market cruise tourism has the intended effect of increasing revenue and profits while minimizing passenger confrontations with poverty and crime. This cannot but force the retreat of local Caribbean cultures and peoples into designated background space only to reemerge under sanitized conditions of providing shore-side goods and services.

Brochures advertising cruise ships and their Caribbean itineraries help manage consumer expectations. The 'brochure discourse' as represented by advertisement pictures and copy foregrounds different kinds of ships, their restaurants, amenities, and cabin types, in addition to the islands' natural landscapes and a variety of water sports and activities (A. Weaver 2005a). Largely and unproblematically rendered semi-invisible or invisible are the local peoples (Jansson 2002; Strachan 2002).[20]

Cruise ship names, moreover, invoke specific emotions relating to the production of pleasure in cruise tourism. Celebrity, RCL, NCL and Princess ship names for instance signify limitless earthly and heavenly horizons (e.g., *Celebrity Constellation* and *Celebrity Galaxy*; Royal Caribbean's *Vision of the Seas* and *Explorer of the* Seas; NCL's *Norwegian Sun* and *Norwegian Dawn*; Princess's *Regal Princess* and *Grand Princess*). HAL ship names are reminders of the Netherlands' long and glorious maritime past, e.g. *ms Maasdam* and *ms Zuiderdam*.

The naming of Carnival's cruise ships appear to shift in accordance with particular trends. Ships delivered in the mid to late 1980s, appear to have been named to symbolize Carnival's brand image, e.g. *Holiday* and *Celebration*. During the early

---

20 This quote from a travel guide on shopping in Caribbean ports captures a key point: 'I believe that there are two Caribbeans—the rich, isolated, hidden, private and personal Caribbean where royalty and rich folks tuck away from the winter winds; and the real world Caribbean, seen on the surface as offered up to cruise ship passengers, day-trippers and those who will not go off the beaten path' (Gershman 1997, 1).

1990s, however, ship names reflected a somewhat different ethos: collectively, ship names such as *Ecstasy* and *Sensation* help articulate--by sensualising--the promise of a Carnival cruise experience in the Caribbean basin. By the end of that decade, Carnival began prefacing all ship names with 'Carnival' that seem to replace the ethos of sensuality with domination and patriotism. One possible interpretation is that ship names such as *Carnival Triumph, Carnival Victory, Carnival Conquest and Carnival Liberty* reflect Carnival's position as the global leader in cruise tourism, and/or they attest to the triumph of the cruise line's founder and his dogged vision amidst all odds, to build a successful business. In the post-9/11 era, newer ship names also have the effect of instilling the foreign flagged cruise line's commitment to, and support of distinct values characterizing US national history and the conduct of its international relations. Paradoxically, given Carnival's dominant market position and itineraries in the Caribbean basin and the west coast of Mexico, certain ship names also may be interpreted as hinting at, or revivifying the conquest of the Americas, i.e., what were bloody and cruel historical experiences for the indigenous peoples and eventually African slaves, now are reworked as a modern celebration of victory, prowess and posterity at sea.

For this region, modern cruise ships indeed have replaced imperial galleons of the past. Buoyant, camera-touting ordinary folk have taken the place of stern-faced uniformed soldiers and officials commanded by kings and queens. Whereas sugar cane fields, bauxite mines and salt ponds may have symbolized exploitative development of a region past, the sound of ship horns calling at ports and subsequent debarkation of thousands of passengers symbolize the growth of a region present. For some port communities, however, contradictions seem to follow the arrival and departure of modern cruise ships.

Power of 'Leased Sovereignty'

Cruise ships flying foreign flags have been likened to 'sovereign islands' (see Frantz's 1999 special series in the *New York Times*) or, 'floating cities with their own zip codes' (Fraser 2003). These ships are visible exemplars of 'leased' sovereignty at sea especially since cruise lines exchange fees for lenient flag state oversight of their maritime operations. The minimal regulatory structure brought into existence by open and second registries has woven a complex web of legal-financial accountability and liability in the maritime world that facilitates cruise lines' direct and indirect ability to pursue profits at sea, inclusive of efforts to resist port communities' attempts at redressing different aspects of ship operations.

There is little doubt that cruise ships generate revenue and employment for US home ports and economy. In 2005, the total economic benefit of the cruise industry to the US economy exceeded USD30 billion. For example, direct spending by cruise lines, passengers and crew in the US economy reached upwards of USD16 billion as hundreds of thousands of jobs were created in addition to over USD13 billion paid in wages to US employees (ICCL 2005, 1).[21]

Nonetheless, cruise lines' deployment of large ships has had contradictory consequences particularly for ports of call. In Alaska, although small towns like Skagway and Juneau with respective resident populations of less than 1,000 persons derive over 50 per cent of their revenue from cruise line and passenger spending, the towns' infrastructural services (including sewage and waste management) often can be overwhelmed by the simultaneous arrival of ships during high season that collectively debark thousands of passengers. In 1991, the port community of Haines passed a four per cent tax on organized tours to help pay for services. Royal Caribbean responded by removing Haines from its Alaskan itineraries. The immediate drop in revenue soon led to rising unemployment rates, followed by the closure of shops and schools. Haines repealed the tax shortly thereafter (Kroll 2004).

Moreover, a large cruise ship carrying thousands of passengers and crew generates tremendous volumes of waste: on a weekly basis it can produce several hundred thousand gallons of sewage, over one million gallons of grey water (e.g., galley and bath water) and tens of thousand gallons of oily bilge in addition to toxic chemicals produced by photographic processing equipment (see, for example, Bluewater Network 2005). Technologically advanced cruise ships have not been used consistently to reduce environmental pollution at sea. Although some ships are equipped with marine sanitation devices to treat waste, it has been proven in various law suits that some of them continued to release untreated waste within and beyond the territorial limits of destination ports.[22]

Since the 1990s, major cruise lines have been fined variously for dumping raw sewage, grey water, or oily waste/bilge within the specified limits of territorial waters from Alaska and California, to Florida and the Caribbean islands (R. Klein 2003a and 2003b). In 1998, Royal Caribbean pled guilty to, and paid fines for polluting the ocean. One month later, one of its ships was discovered to have discharged oily waste, and that officers had falsified logs in the process. The cruise line argued that it was 'immune from criminal prosecution because its ships fly foreign flags'. Investigation into the incident revealed that Royal Caribbean had a policy of offering year-end bonuses to its officers for staying under budget, hence by disposing the oil at sea as opposed to separating oil from water via the use of expensive filter membranes, the officers could save USD50,000 annually (Frantz 1999k. See also Frantz 1999b; 1999h and 1999i; R. Klein 2003b and 2002a).

There exists an important international convention governing pollution at sea, i.e., the IMO's International Convention for the Prevention of Pollution from Ships (MARPOL). Enforcement of MARPOL, to be sure, depends on the willingness and capacity of flag states to do so. In 1992, the US Department of State referred 111

---

21 A similar case has been made for the economic contributions of Star to Asian economies (see Arshad 2003).

22 For examples of offences by different cruise lines, please see the website of Cruise Junkie Dot Com, as well as Arakawa 2005; Gardner 2003; Hanks 2002; Laidman 2004; Lebowitz 2003; and Oceans Blue Foundation 2002.

cases to flag states that, in turn, acknowledged only the receipt of 35 cases. Of that, only two cases were given small fines (Frantz 1999k).

Within the US, Alaska has had some success in limiting the number of ship dockings, and entry into environmentally sensitive waters such as Glacier Bay. This is due partly to community activism and lobbying efforts within the state, and partly to the unique site of Glacier Bay that is not found elsewhere in the world. The bay's centrality to a majority of Alaskan itineraries encourages cruise ship compliance. Some cruise lines nevertheless, could and did 'retaliate' against proposed port taxes by reducing the time their ships spent at port, and/or even by reducing donations given to local charities and civic organizations (Frantz 1999b; Kroll 2004).

In late 2004, California passed three Cruise Ship Pollution Bills that prohibited the dumping of sewage and grey water into state waters, as well as the burning of garbage in ship incinerators within three miles of the California coast (Bluewater Network 2004b). At the federal level, the bipartisan Cruise Ship Pollution Bill that prohibits dumping within 12 miles of the US coastline was introduced in early 2004 but has not yet received full Congressional support at this time of writing (Bluewater Network 2004a). While Alaska and California successfully pursued the legislative route in their dealings with cruise lines, other states such as Washington and Hawai'i elected to sign respective Memorandum of Understanding (MOU) that do not convey legal enforcement powers if and when cruise lines contravene the agreements (R. Klein 2003a). Such was the case with one of NCL America's ships that was found to have discharged 70 tons of treated effluent into Honolulu harbour. NCL America responded by stating that, '[i]t was clearly human error but we have put in place procedures to make sure that that doesn't happen' (Arakawa 2005).

In the Caribbean, however, attempts to address cruise ship-generated infrastructural stress and pollution have not met with much consistent success. The Organisation of Eastern Caribbean States (OECS) tried to increase the minimum passenger head tax in 1992 to finance much needed infrastructural improvements but ultimately failed in its attempts. One of Royal Caribbean's executives explained the cruise line's 'divide and conquer' strategy:

> Let's say that five islands form an alliance, and we have no way around the alliance. We decided that, instead of calling at three of them we're going to call at two—and we pick which ones. The other members of the alliance are going to get pissed at the other two; that's been the case before that, and that's, I think, what didn't allow the islands to go forward...They like to blame it on us, but the fact was that because of their own individual interests, they couldn't get it together---they couldn't make it (Garin 2005, 286).

One year later, the larger organization of the Caribbean Community (CARICOM) announced its proposal to levy a tax of USD10-15 per head. Tax revenue then would help address the strain on infrastructure as well as to ensure the viability of local businesses that could not compete with duty-free transnational retail franchises such as those that specialized in precious gems. The proposal also came at a time in which hoteliers complained that their businesses, already subject to a variety of taxes, also could not compete against that which cruise ships offered to their passengers (Pattullo 2005, 197-8). Cruise lines responded by threatening to remove ports of call from their itineraries.

The OECS again tried to implement a levy of USD1.50 per head in 1997 to subsidize construction of waste management systems that were needed to deal with massive amounts of cruise ship waste (Garin 2005; R. Klein 2002a and 2002b; Wood 2004b). When the World Bank confirmed that the OECS was 'required to ratify the MARPOL agreement for making the Caribbean into a special area', the majority of cruise lines acceded to the tax (Wood 2004b, 164). Carnival ultimately resisted: it boycotted Grenada by explaining that although the additional tax of '$1.50 a head—on top of the current $3 arrival tax, the lowest in the region—seems paltry… The reason that Carnival Corp. makes the kind of money we do is because we pay great, great attention to controlling our costs' (Fineman 1998). Earlier discussions to regulate work conditions were met with a similar threat: 'any attempt to legislate salary, safety or other employment practices would cause them [cruise lines] to flee the Caribbean' (Nevins 1989)

In 2003, the Secretary-General of the Caribbean Tourism Organization (CTO) proposed a Caribbean-wide tax of US $20 per cruise passenger, so that the revenue could be divided among member islands to deal with rising cruise passenger traffic and its effects on local communities and the environment. Carnival reacted by calling the proposal 'outrageous.' According to one report, the proposal was dropped soon thereafter because:

> these multi-billion dollar cruise ship operations were using strong-arm tactics to drive the 'fear of God' into Caribbean governments. He [Secretary-General] illustrated this by reference to the tactics of the Florida Caribbean Cruise Association (FCCA) that represents major cruise lines operating in the region, as 'unacceptable by reasonable men…and of making considerable profits while bearing a disproportionately small share of the burden of maintaining those resources which they rely on' (Fraser 2003).[23]

Cruise lines' threat tactic of dropping ports from ship itineraries is effective because of what cruise passenger expenditures as well as the possible conversion of cruise passengers to future landed hotel guests represent to Caribbean economies. In the decade between 1993 and 2003, cruise passenger arrivals in the region grew from approximately 10 million to over 17 million. In 2002, while the total number of tourists in the region declined by about 2.7 per cent, cruise passenger arrivals grew by 8.2 per cent (CTO 2004, Section II Tables 1 and 3, n.p.). However, changing cruise itineraries and ship size (whether or not existing ports can accommodate them) means that the total number of arrivals for different ports can and will fluctuate. St. Maarten, Jamaica, Belize and British Virgin Islands registered double digit growth in 2003, while decline was experienced by Curacao, Aruba, and St. Vincent and the Grenadines (WTTC 2004, 23).

Proposed by the World Bank and the IMF as a development strategy in the mid twentieth century to diversify Caribbean economies from reliance on demands for, and fluctuating prices of commodity exports, tourism today has become the main export industry for many islands. So long as the majority of Caribbean economies

---

23 FCCA was formed in 1972 to develop better relations between cruise lines and Caribbean authorities, i.e. to mitigate tensions arising from treating 'ports of call [as] merely additions to the ship.' (WTO 2003, 140).

are dependent mostly on tourist receipts in a global era that privileges unfettered economic competition, then they cannot but be at the mercy of cruise lines' individual and collective bargaining power vested most evidently in the ease with which ships can be repositioned, and ports of call can be removed from itineraries. Seen from this perspective, cruise lines can be said to have an ability to 'hijack' ports so to speak, by demanding lower port charges, more amenities and services. Many ports simply give in so as to retain the revenue generated by ship, passenger and crew spending. From a free market perspective nonetheless, port communities are seen voluntarily to exchange low port taxes for revenue from sale of tourism-related products and services.

Yet, cruise passenger traffic may not be as financially beneficially to local Caribbean economies as previously thought. Wilkinson's study identified three major factors for this: cruise passengers' shore-side spending decreased as shipboard revenues increased (duty-free shops, alternative restaurants, casinos and so forth); passenger profiles have changed from the days of elite cruisers; and the inclusion of private islands in itineraries together have 'shifted revenue from local governments and vendors to the cruise line' (Wilkinson 1999, 274). Bahamas is illustrative of these points. In 2003, it had the highest number of cruise ship calls in the region at 1,970 (CTO 2004, 61). Yet, cruise passengers spent an average of USD53 (CTO 2004, 63). The US Virgin Islands, known for duty-free shopping, hosted 888 cruise ships in the same year (CTO 2004, 61), but had the highest average cruise passenger expenditure at USD273 (CTO 2004, 63). Landed tourists (including same-day and non-cruise sea arrivals) spent considerably more than the above amounts, i.e., USD 1061 and USD1248 respectively in the Bahamas and US Virgin Islands (CTO 2004, 63) As asserted by the WTTC:

> Despite the fast growth of cruise passenger arrivals, their contribution to the region's economies is in many cases negligible, accounting for less than 10 per cent of total international tourism receipts. Moreover the cruise industry's growth is largely due to its tax-free status. When some governments have dared to consider imposing head taxes on cruise passengers the result has usually been a pull-out from that particular country by the cruise ship operator' (2004, 65).

Large and mega ships are double-edged swords for some destination ports. On the one hand, many of the islands seek to welcome them in the hope that passengers eventually will return as landed tourists even if the initial capital outlay (dredging for port construction/enhancement and other infrastructural costs to accommodate large ships) may divert already limited resources to this sector (Chase 2001; Wilkinson 1999). For some islands, the arrival of these ships has had a distinct negative effect, i.e., as cruise ship passenger traffic increased, the total occupancy of hotel rooms decreased. Put differently, hotel rooms cannot compete effectively with ship cabins since pricing of the former has to take into consideration occupancy and other taxes, worker benefits (especially if there are collective agreements) and so forth. Take for example the Bahamas and US Virgin Islands. In 2003, cruise passenger taxes respectively were USD15 and USD7.50 (CTO 2004, 8). Meanwhile, hotel room taxes respectively were six and eight per cent, excluding airport departure/exit taxes. The managing director of a hotel chain sharply worded the disparity in this way,

'You've got a land-based tourism industry that is being taxed to death competing with a sea-based tourism that is virtually tax-free' (Wise 1999, 44-5). One exception is Bermuda. In 2003, there were only 156 cruise ship calls (CTO 2004, 61). Yet, it had the second highest average cruise passenger expenditure at USD224 (CTO 2004, 63). This is due, in part, to some cruise itineraries that allow passengers to overnight on land.

Particularly for island states or territories with small domestic markets and population bases, their relationship to cruise tourism is symptomatic of a contradiction inherent in the path of export-oriented development within an increasingly integrated free market-based global economy. Tourism development entails the 'export' of services that are expected to generate employment while increasing foreign exchange earnings. Even more extraordinary is that some Caribbean island states/territories also operate open registries to flag foreign-owned ships (i.e., another mode of 'exporting' services). Approximately one-third of 'flags of convenience' identified by the ITF are located in the Eastern, Southern and Western Caribbean chain of islands: Antigua & Barbuda, Bahamas, Barbados, Bermuda, Cayman Islands, Jamaica, Netherlands Antilles, and St. Vincent & the Grenadines, with Bahamas holding the distinction of being one of the largest FOC states in the world. The co-existence of open registries as a form of offshore tax haven for maritime capital with that of landed tourism industries cannot but expose further key contradictions arising from state governance in a free market era. Even though an open registry is a 'fictional juridical residence' created to facilitate the flow of denationalized or deterritorialized maritime capital, it cannot be presumed that the conduct of business in space will not affect the conduct of business in place.

Phrased differently, while both open registries and tourism-related firms may be engaged respectively in the 'export' of regulatory and tourism services geared to generate revenue, the former operates on a premise of 'leasing out' sovereignty that, given cruise line practices in the past, may and does undermine attempts to bolster the latter (especially landed tourist firms and activities). This strongly suggests the need for future in-depth critical review of the relationship between open ship registry and the tourism sector if an intent is for the latter to remain a viable path to sustainable development in the Caribbean and/or elsewhere. Until then, the practice of flagging foreign-owned ships will give to, while taking away from, Caribbean economies. Meanwhile, major cruise lines continue to benefit from flying flags of convenience and calling at their choice of Caribbean ports and private islands.

Mass market cruise lines, however, neither take for granted the ways in which they are allowed to operate legally on the open seas, nor do they expect to be able to do so indefinitely and without opposition from environmental and labour groups, port communities and so forth. This is evident from the ways in which they are well organized to protect their interests, such as anticipating and deterring attempts at curbing their political ability and economic power to navigate the oceans.[24] Within the US, there are regional cruise line associations such as the FCCA and the North West Cruise Association (NWCA) that represent member lines with corresponding regional itineraries. At the national and international levels and until 2006, the Cruise Lines International Association (CLIA) and the International Council of Cruise Lines (ICCL) operated as separate entities. Among CLIA's primary responsibilities were the marketing of cruise tourism and training of travel industry personnel. The ICCL, on the other hand, dealt with advocacy and regulatory issues. The majority of ICCL's member lines also participated in the UK's Passenger Shipping Association, and a few of them were active as well in the European Cruise Council.

The ICCL represented its members in international organizations such as the IMO and ILO, and had committees on technical, legal and legislative activities.[25] Its objectives included advocating for perspectives and interests of member lines, as well as promoting the overall practice of self-regulation. ICCL was the collective public face and voice of member cruise lines as seen in responses to highly publicized and controversial allegations of shipboard crimes (e.g., sexual assault and theft), environmental pollution and seafarer exploitation. ICCL's responses included the introduction of the following policies on 'zero tolerance for [shipboard] crime,'[26] 'New Mandatory Environmental Standards for Cruise Ships' (ICCL 2001), and the 'Shipboard Workplace Code of Conduct'.[27] These ICCL initiatives are demonstratively sensitive and responsive to important issues of passenger safety,

---

24 Cruise lines based in the US can and do cultivate relationships with legislators representing states in which there are home ports. At the federal level, they also cultivate relationships with legislators serving on committees that oversee different dimensions of maritime commerce. R. Klein provides detailed analysis of the cruise line-US legislator relationship e.g., election campaign donations, financial and travel perks, and so forth (2005).

25 'One of its [ICCL] most important roles is representing the industry's best interests before key US and international organizations with the power to establish new international maritime laws that may affect its members. They include the IMO (international maritime organization) that sets the recognized safety standards known as SOLAS (Safety of Life at Sea) and the basic regulations for training crews, STCW (standards of training certification and watchkeeping) and the ISM Code (international safety management)' (WTO 2003, 57).

26 Augmenting this policy are efforts to interpret data by juxtaposing shipboard incidences against the total number of cruise passengers and/or landed rates to establish proportionality, and by citing continued cooperation with federal intelligence agencies and compliance with US and international maritime law. See the 2005 testimony of J. Michael Crye (then President of ICCL) at the joint hearing by the US House of Representatives' Committee on Government Reform; the Subcommittee on National Security, Emerging Threats and International Relations; and the Subcommittee on Criminal Justice, Drug Policy and Human Resources (US House of Representatives 2005).

27 Amongst key items covered by the code of conduct are that (a) 'All personnel, shipboard and shore side, have the basic right to be respected and treated in a fair and just manner at all times by superiors and fellow employees…and provide a workplace free of discrimination based on gender, race, religion, age, disability, nationality, sexual orientation, social or ethnic origin'; and (b) 'Hours of work and hours of rest will comply with flag state

the environment and labour. Nevertheless the emphasis on voluntary/self-regulation for an industry professedly in pursuit of ocean-based and now land-based profits portends largely a continuation of status quo practices.

The merger of CLIA and ICCL in 2006 furthers processes of rationalization within the industry (CLIA 2006a). Retaining CLIA's name, the new organization is expected to better coordinate and streamline the regulatory, marketing and training aspects of cruise tourism. This new organization, then, has the potential to be even more effective in promoting and protecting cruise lines' interests on the national, regional and global levels.

Straddling the oceanic transportation and tourism sectors, cruise corporations and their holdings of cruise lines are positioned uniquely to draw on, and affirm the efficacy of free market operations. As a mode of oceanic transportation, modern cruise ships have arisen from, and are sustained by a maritime regulatory structure in which open registries and their lenient regulations have prompted traditional maritime states to establish second registries (with somewhat relaxed regulations) co-existing alongside primary registries. Yet, cruise ships are more than just another mode of transport since the core business is that of producing pleasure for profits. After approximately two decades of intra-industry consolidation, the Big Three corporations now compete with landed interests for tourists via the deployment of even larger mass market cruise ships and new itineraries that, collectively, transform vessels into all-inclusive floating resorts filled with middle class consumers. Large and mega cruise ships, in effect, simultaneously transport people and pleasure in an under-regulated maritime world.

As ascertained, the production of pleasure for profit within this larger context can and does generate an underside of loss for some landed firms, port communities and the environment. However, given global emphasis on, and the privileging of free market operations, this underside of loss may be, and is explained away at best as an unintended side effect of growth in the industry, or at worst as an anticipated outcome of competition (e.g., to compete is to have 'winners' and 'losers'). Left in the wake is an ever shrinking space to question the criteria on which competitive conduct and transactions in the marketplace can be considered good or right since free market competition already is assigned an inherently positive attribute and value.

Our discussion on the production of pleasure elicits also the related dimension of pleasure consumption, e.g., to what extent are cruise passengers aware of contradictions emanating from the pursuit of profits, pleasure and work at sea? The following chapter offers an examination of the consumption of pleasure in cruise tourism.

---

regulations and/or applicable collective bargaining agreements' (ICCL 'Shipboard Workplace Code of Conduct', n.d.)

Chapter 4

Structured Hedonism: Consumption of Deep Ocean Pleasure Cruising

It is often said that the consumer market seduces its customers. But in order to do so it needs customers who want to be seduced.

Zgymunt Bauman (1998, 83)

The previous chapter examined how mass market cruise lines pursue profits via the production of pleasure at sea and increasingly, on land as well. Their strategies for doing so collectively help constitute cruise tourism's 'institutionalized leisure' context. One important strategy entails transformation of the large/mega cruise ship from a primary mode of transportation to a floating resort with brief port calls. Especially for the more popular itineraries in the Caribbean basin, cruise lines' production of pleasure in this manner cannot but involve the elision or erasure of some port communities' complex colonial histories and legacies. Erasure of this kind hardly may be considered a problem if one comes from the perspective that the business of deep ocean pleasure cruising first and foremost is concerned with producing pleasure as opposed to resurrecting pain for profits.

This last point brings up the requisite dimension of consumption. Since cruise lines produce pleasure to be consumed by passengers, then what are the latter's views of cruise line strategies and related consequences? Are consumers passive social actors who uncritically accept the context of institutionalized leisure, or do they actively evaluate the conditions and consequences in which pleasure is produced by cruise lines? What are the ramifications of either outcome?

We begin in this chapter with a brief discussion of conceptualizing tourist motivations as shaped by the human agency-social structure nexus. Following this is analysis of consumer postings on a popular website's e-discussion boards to better ascertain their perceptions and explanations of major aspects of cruise vacations. Our analysis of e-discussion threads on these boards reveal that consumers become 'producers' when they share knowledge of, or educate others on different aspects of cruise vacations. Another important finding is that consumers' tendency to privilege the human agency perspective frames their understandings of, and proposed solutions to contradictions arising from the larger structure shaping cruise lines' ability to produce, and consumers' experiences of, pleasure in cruise tourism. By minimizing or dismissing structural forces, the majority of posts echo cruise lines' official positions and in ways that affirm free market exchange. Information highly critical of cruise line practices, on the other hand, are found on alternative websites such as those established by former cruise passengers and/or their families that bring attention to the need for more effective state regulation and oversight of the industry.

'(In)Authentic' Experiences

Researchers of tourism studies continue to grapple with conceptualizing tourist motivations as the shift from Fordist (mass) to post-Fordist (niche) production is accompanied by a concomitant shift from Fordist to post-Fordist consumption. One key issue is whether or not tourists are driven by the search for 'authentic' experiences. While packaged holidays of the 1970s and 1980s were seen to be based on the production and consumption of inauthentic experiences (Azarya 2004; Britton 1991), on-going expansion of the new middle classes with concomitant new consumption patterns evince their search and demand for 'authentic' vacations ranging from the 'self-planned' trip inclusive of apartment/flat/villa rental to those offered by 'cultural' and 'eco-' tourism firms in the Global South.

Even though niche tourism may come to be equated with the search for authentic experiences, it should be emphasized that some degree of institutionalization is inherent given the participation of tourism ministries/departments, specialty travel agencies, transportation and lodging interests. MacCannell is more realistic when he writes that:

> Touristic consciousness is motivated by its desire for authentic experiences, and the tourist may believe that he is moving in this direction, but often it is very difficult to know for sure if the experience is in fact authentic. It is always possible that what is taken to be entry into a back region is really entry into a front region that has been totally set up in advance for touristic visitation (1989, 101).

MacCannell asserts that tourists will always search for authenticity even though the nature and degree of institutionalized leisure affects their ability to distinguish between real and 'staged' authenticity.

Urry agrees with the notion of institutionalized leisure but rejects the distinction between authentic and inauthentic experiences in his conceptualization of the 'tourist gaze'. In the past, the tourist gaze indeed was a manifestly institutionalized gaze (e.g., 'socially organised and systematised' [Urry 2002, 1]) particularly since tourist decisions concerning places to visit were 'sustained through a variety of non-tourist practices, such as film, TV, literature, magazines, records and videos, which construct and reinforce that gaze'. Even so, it was not a monolithic gaze because gazes shifted depending on the social positioning (e.g., gender, age, class, educational background and so forth) of tourists (Urry 2002, 3).

MacCannell, nonetheless, critiques Urry for failing to distinguish between the 'tourist gaze' particularly with reference to the search for extraordinary experiences, and the 'second gaze' in which the tourist is:

> always aware that something is being concealed from it...the second gaze knows that seeing is not believing. Some things will remain hidden from it...The second gaze turns back onto the gazing subject an ethical responsibility for the construction of its

own existence. It refuses to leave this construction to the corporation, the state, and the apparatus of touristic representation (MacCannell 2001, 36).

From Urry's perspective, however, MacCannell misses the point because tourists are not driven by the desire for authenticity as much as they are by 'extraordinary' experiences. Efforts to distinguish between authentic and inauthentic experiences are futile at best especially in an era of new information and communication technologies: travel and tourism take on new meanings as consumers are able to experience them in embodied and/or cyberspatial contexts. Ultimately, tourists search for extraordinary corporeal and/or hyperreal (simulated) experiences that contrast with their highly regulated everyday lives.[1] These 'post-tourists', especially those of the 'service' or new managerial middle classes, are not concerned with authenticity per se since the extraordinary can be experienced as real or staged (Urry 2002, 12). From post-tourists' perspective, tourism 'is a series of games with multiple texts and no single, authentic tourist experience' (Urry 2002, 91).

Taken to its logical conclusion, the conceptualization of tourists as players in a series of games (i.e., depending on their choice of game in which to participate, presumably they are aware and accepting of the ensuing contradictions in that particular institutionalized leisure context) can render them apolitical social actors who privilege pleasure above all else. Cast in this way, conceptualization of the post-tourist paradoxically may not be much different from the one of mass tourism.

Research on tourism's transition from mass production-consumption to niche production-consumption, tourist motivations, and the role of new information and communication technologies have yet to account in greater empirical detail for the ways in which tourists may critique and/or explain away contradictions and their related consequences. What we do know from cruise tourism is the continued if not expanding popularity of all-inclusive cruise vacations especially to the 'sun-sea-surf-shops' of the Caribbean islands.[2] If we are to retain the concept 'authenticity', then cruise passengers may, as Selwyn in another context points out, be interested in 'authentic social relations and sociability (which would certainly include an authentically 'good time') as well as some sort of knowledge about the nature and society of the chosen destination' (1996, 8). Hence, a major issue concerns the sources and content of consumer knowledge shaping affective and cognitive demands that can be used to affirm/challenge the relationship between production and consumption in cruise tourism.

Fordist and post-Fordist modes of production and consumption coexist in mass market cruise tourism. As discussed in Chapter Three, niche tourism need not necessarily have to supplant mass tourism: in fact, niche modes of production–consumption are nested within mass production-consumption. This point is taken up partly by Ritzer and Liska as they move away from a focus on human agency to revisit structural forces in their discussion of tourism. Contra to Urry's perspective, they argue that tourists 'want to experience much of what they experience in their day-to-

---

1 See also Urry's earlier response to his critics in 'The Tourist Gaze 'Revisited' 1992.

2 The 3S of mass tourism refers to sun, sea, and surf (E. Cohen 1998). Momsen adds a fourth 's', i.e., shopping or sex in the case of Caribbean tourism (2005, 209-221).

day lives. That is, they want their tourist experiences to be about as McDonaldized as their day-to-day lives' (1997, 99).

'McDisneyization' is the tourism sector's variant of 'McDonaldization' in society. Vacations that are highly predictable, highly efficient, highly calculable and highly controlled reflect and affirm the larger social context or world in which tourists have and continue to be socialized.[3] McDisneyized tourism exists because tourists seek vacation contexts that are extraordinary, yet offer familiarity and comfort because of the way in which they are structured:

> Those who rebel against McDonaldized tourism will unquestioningly force some tour operators and tourist sites to de-McDonaldize. Most importantly, there will continue to be a market for McDonaldized vacations. Raised in McDonaldized systems, accustomed to a daily life in those systems, most people not only accept, but embrace, those systems... many will gravitate toward them (Ritzer and Liska 1997, 100).

What needs to be emphasized here is that the 'extraordinary' view on which tourists gaze and the context in which they participate, is based on the four principles of efficiency, predictability, calculability and controllability that similarly frame their day to day lives. It does not mean that McDisneyized/McDonaldized tourism is a rigid structure that *dictates* preferences and activities. Flexibility in McDisneyized tourism comes in the form of different choices of activities, food outlets and trip/ show schedules and so forth: 'as society itself grows more and more McDonaldized, there is less and less need rigidly to standardize the package tour' (Ritzer and Liska 1997, 99). Ritzer and Liska cite landed resorts and cruise ships as prime examples of McDisneyized/McDonaldized tourism. They make a major point that is applicable to the production and consumption of pleasure in mass market cruise tourism since cruise ship designs, itineraries and overall operations are grounded in the four principles of efficiency, predictability, calculability and controllability.

The issue for us here is not that these four foundational principles applied to generate profits constitute a deterministic structure which, in turn, can only produce hedonistically-oriented social actors despite and because of flexibility that is built into institutionalized contexts. Rather, it is the manner in which tourists' views and activities are informed by, and inform what may be called 'structured hedonism'. Indeed, cruise lines draw from, and shape changing consumer demands and expectations. CLIA surveys, frequent cruiser/loyalty programs, passengers' comment cards (completed at the end of cruise itineraries), and travel agencies are main venues for gathering information that informs the production of pleasure at sea. Tourists, however, also become producers when they 'broadcast' their experiences to friends, families, and even strangers via letters, postcards, reviews, souvenirs, photographs, gifts and so forth. Tourists then participate in, or reenter the production process as they integrate or incorporate cruise vacation experiences into their everyday lives. Seen in this way, the relationship between tourism production and consumption can be a mutually constitutive 'circuit' (Ateljevic 2000; Meethan 2001).

---

3 Sheller and Urry write that 'We might thus say that Mickey Mouse has escaped from his special kingdom and now seems to occupy almost every place across the globe---there are an extraordinary number of global places for Mickey to play in' (2004, 5).

To a certain extent, Ritzer and Liska anticipate this circuit albeit in an *a priori* manner when they conceptualize human agency as determined by structural forces, i.e., when the mode of consumption arises from and reinforces the mode of production.[4] Urry, on the other hand, places emphasis on human agency as tourists participate in the games of tourism: structural forces recede into the background and seemingly remain unchanged. As opposite sides of the same coin, both require empirical elaboration on how dominant meanings and practices of tourist consumption are shaped by and shape tourism production.

Aside from traditional sources of information such as the 'brochure discourse' of cruise lines (of which travel agents play an important part as well), who and/or what other sources inform cruise tourists' expectations and experiences of pleasure? What can new sources of information tell us about the manner in which tourists affirm or not the deployment of big ships; dominant meanings assigned to, and derived from the 'Caribbean' and private islands; the role of making and sharing visual records; shipboard incidental charges in all-inclusive vacations; and to be sure, the topics of environmental pollution, shipboard labour and passenger safety?

Virtual Community of Cruisers

Contemporary applications of new communication and information technologies are in the process of 'mediatizing' tourism (Buhalis 1998; Jansson 2002; Prentice 2001). It appears that an era of post-tourism has come as a result of the internet's expansion with concomitant accessibility and visual representations of places that blur the distinction between real and simulated experiences: consumers now have the choice of travelling in place and/or cyberspace (see, for example, Dewailly 1999; Molz 2004; Urry 1995 and 2002; Wilson and Suraya 2004). Even Ritzer and Liska observed that for some, 'virtual touring' may be more attractive because of the degree of predictability and calculability even though cyberspatial travel does not offer the same kind of experience as corporeal travel (1997, 101). It may be an overreach, however, to assume that virtual touring can and will supplant physical travel especially given global growth in landed and sea-based tourism, in addition to published empirical research demonstrating internet use as a major source of travel planning (see especially Bei, Chen and Widdows 2004; Jansson 2002; WTTC 2004).

The internet, to be sure, encourages firms and consumers alike to collect and share information in cyberspace (Buhalis 1998).[5] Reviews and sales of cruise vacation packages are cogent examples of this, e.g., proliferation of on-line travel agencies offering or specializing in cruises, and the establishment of discussion

---

4 For example, in their examination of the rise of the service economy in Europe, Gershuny and Miles assert that changes in consumer lifestyles and interests are related directly to changing production structures and processes that offer innovative products for consumption (1983).

5 Particularly for the tourism sector, consumers increasingly rely on the internet for 'experience' products (i.e., the experiences of other consumers) as opposed to 'search' products (L. Klein 1998).

sections for consumers within these websites. Some websites of major cruise lines are designed similarly for consumers to ask questions and post comments. What these internet-based phenomena collectively signify are emerging virtual communities of 'cruisers'.

For those who define community as place-based in the traditional sociological sense, then the existence of list-servs, e-chat and e-boards (especially those located within e-commerce sites) does not constitute a community of social actors living and interacting in embodied lives within specific locales. Preece, however, argues that these e-groups should be considered virtual communities if they fulfil four functions respectively of exchanging information, providing support, facilitating socialization and creating space led by moderators for the discussion of ideas and issues (2000). As aptly summarized by Wang, Yu and Fesenmaier, 'a virtual community is place in manifestation, symbolic in nature, and virtual in form' (2002, 411; Smith and Kollock 1999). It follows then that alternative virtual communities can and will be established if moderators do not provide space for articulation of radically different and opposing perspectives.

The phenomenon of cruise-oriented virtual communities indicates that consumer knowledge no longer is restricted to that which is disseminated mostly by cruise lines and/or travel agents. Analysis of discussions within these virtual communities can be informative of what consumers consider important issues to share/discuss; how they do so; and the extent to which they are able to express their acceptance of or resistance to different dimensions and consequences of consuming pleasure on integrated sea-land vacations.

An example of a virtual community can be found on Cruise Critic, one of the most popular websites for those interested in such vacations. This website was established in 1995 by a New Jersey-based corporation, The Independent Traveler. Funded in part with advertisement revenues from major cruise lines, on-line travel agencies and other firms, Cruise Critic has garnered accolades from national newspapers and travel magazines for being one of the most comprehensive consumer-oriented sources for all aspects of cruise tourism. The website averages over 1.5 million visits and 20 million page views per month. Its primary audience are 'baby boomers with high incomes': approximately 60 per cent are between 36-55 years old; 57 per cent are college/post-college graduates, 60 per cent earn incomes of over USD75,000, 90 per cent have taken one or more cruise vacations, and women outnumber men readers by an approximate ratio of two to one (Cruise Critic, 'About Us' n.d.). The data published by Cruise Critic are not disaggregated according to nationality although a cursory review of posts on message boards reveals that US residents overwhelmingly outnumber non-US residents (identification of place of residence is voluntary, as are addresses and genders).

Cruise Critic contains e-sections ranging from 'Planning First Cruise, 'Cruising Styles' (e.g., Teens, Gay/lesbian, Golf, Gourmet and so forth) and 'Destinations', to Community', 'Cruise Lines,' 'Latest News' and 'Boards'. Readers can participate in limited virtual touring offered by Cruise Critic's 'virtual cruises' (located within the 'Cruise Lines' section). Given comprehensive information offered by the website, virtual touring of this kind can encourage physical travel as readers get to anticipate/ imagine day-to-day activities on a ship and at different ports of call. In the Community section, members of Cruise Critic can organize group cruises by selecting the ship, itinerary and month of cruise, after which the Community Manager will help with coordinating and promoting the group cruise (Cruise Critic, 'Group Cruises' n.d.). Members with similar lifestyle interests, thus, can organize to cruise together, after which they may post reviews of their cruise experiences on the site.

The 'Boards' section (open forum, registration required for posting rights) that facilitates communication among Cruise Critic members who are frequent cruisers and/or who are planning to cruise for the first time, offers an unprecedented opportunity to examine consumers' discussions of their expectations and experiences of pleasure at sea and on land (Cruise Critic, 'Boards' n.d.). According to statistics published in this section, there were nearly 200,000 registered members, over 300,000 threads and roughly 6 million posts in March 2006. The Boards contain nine categories, e.g., individual cruise lines, ports of call, 'roll call' (searching for members who will be on a specific cruise ship/itinerary), special interest cruising (e.g., singles, teens and so forth), reviews of Cruise Critic member-organized cruises and miscellaneous cruise discussion topics. Discussions on the 'Ask a Cruise Question' message board encompass a wide range of issues in pleasure cruising, e.g., from things to do in destination ports, watching sports on the ship's satellite television, appropriate travel documents and cabin choices, to ground transportation, advice on sleeping the night before a cruise and dealing with children on board the ship.

Cruise Critic members or 'posters' are expected to use their 'user names' in order to post on the boards (in some cases, members publish photographs of themselves next to their user names).[6] It is worth emphasizing here that they establish their legitimacy in e-discussions not only via the content of their posts/replies but importantly, the 'signature' following posts that list their cruise experiences according to (and not necessarily in this order) cruise ship name, date and/or itinerary. The more they have cruised, the more weight their posts may and can carry.

Cruise Critic posters must abide by 'Community Guidelines' covering issues such as on-line demeanour,[7] content (advertisements are barred from posts),[8] and language (Cruise Critic, 'Community' n.d.). Travel agents, cruise industry executives and so forth are encouraged to participate: they must identify themselves as 'experts' on a particular topic but they must post only their 'user names' instead of their 'business name', and they are not allowed to promote their businesses in the posts. The intent

---

6 To protect further the privacy of posters, all user names here are substituted with sequentially ordered 'CruiseCriticPoster1' 'CruiseCriticPoster2', 'CruiseCriticPoster3', and so forth. Only the dates and not the titles of initial e-discussion threads are identified.

7 'Treat the cruisers here the same way you'd treat anyone you'd met for the first time. This is important because anyone is welcome to participate in our community. You shouldn't make a cruise decision just because some stranger (or even an online friend) talks it up. Basically, you shouldn't treat cyberspace any differently than you would real life'.

8 'Our Cruise Boards are meant to be a cruiser's exchange of advice and tips where cruisers can talk about their travels -- not a marketplace for advertising and selling services. There are thousands of cruise professionals online and if we didn't insist on a non-solicitation policy the cruise boards would be very quickly overrun with nothing but ads'.

here is to draw on expert knowledge without commercializing the e-discussion boards.[9]

The Community Guidelines call for non-discriminatory treatment of all posters ('don't attack their race, heritage, or their sexual orientation, etc. If you disagree with someone, respond to the subject, not the person'), while legitimizing the English language as this virtual community's lingua franca:

> Our forums are accessible from around the world. We welcome the participation of everyone. All we ask is that if you POST in your native language, that you simulaneously [sic] post your questions/comments in English -- in the same post. ...each and every posting is read by a volunteer moderator. They must be able to understand your posting to allow it to remain. Additionally, you will receive a far greater response to your question if you consider that the majority of our cruise community do only converse in English.

Taken together, the guidelines shaping this virtual community reflect and are reflected by the general profile evinced from Cruise Critic's readership, as well as that of CLIA market surveys, i.e., predominantly middle-class, English-speaking North Americans.

Pleasure on/in Paradise

Given mass market cruise lines' continuing efforts to shift the tourist gaze and related activities from ports of call to the cruise ship, then to what extent do posters affirm this practice? CruiseCriticPoster2 initiated an informal poll on whether the ship or the port of call is more important to decisions on cruise vacations. Of the 152 members who voted, 33 per cent agreed with the sentence 'I book because of the ship I choose'; 47 per cent agreed with the sentence 'I book solely because of the intinarary [sic]' and 20 per cent agreed with the sentence 'It really does not matter to me' (Cruise Critic, 'Boards' 17 June 2006). Some posters explained further their respective positions:

> 'I book based on the itinerary first and foremost' (CruiseCriticPoster3)

> 'I vote on the ship, because what I'm buying is a 'Cruise Vacation!'...When I pay for a cruise, I want a ship, food, and service! Now THAT'S a Cruise Vacation!!' (CruiseCriticPoster4)

> 'All of the above! I did not care what ports, but do go for certain areas like Alaska. But I am happy anywhere that is not home and at work!' (CruiseCriticPoster5)

Other posters were quick to point out that their ship or port choices depended on the regional itinerary, i.e., the distinction between Caribbean itineraries and those elsewhere in the world:

---

9 Requiring travel professionals to remain anonymous, however, runs the risk of skewed responses that may be designed to achieve unstated objectives while masking the identities of contributors or 'posters'.

'The more I cruise, the less important the 'Caribbean' ports are. But when we did the Panama Canal, Hawaii, and Canadian cruises, it was ALL about the ports!' (CruiseCriticPoster6)

'I mean come on, do you really think people sail to Europe, Hawaii, Alaska, Tahiti, Australia and more for the ship and not the ports…By reading these posts it seems the ones that sail for the ship only sail the Caribbean and have been there many times. They need to venture out and see that there is more out there to explore'. (CruiseCriticPoster7)

'A few months ago, as we tried to decide Eastern vs. Western Caribbean, I realized that it's the journey rather than the destination that we care about when cruising to the Caribbean…However, there is no question that the itinerary is more important when we go to Europe or exotic places'. (CruiseCriticPoster8)

As far as these posters are concerned, the cruise ship is the main destination in mass market cruises to the Caribbean. For this specific region, the cruise ship and its amenities are placed in the foreground with the islands serving as a large backdrop. This perspective is ascertained once again from Cruise Critic members' responses to Royal Caribbean's 2006 launching of its new ship, *Freedom of the Seas*. Even though some posters complained of substandard service on the ship's inaugural voyages, the majority of them revelled in its size (158,000 GRT ship that has a carrying capacity of 3,600 passengers), beauty, new amenities and entertainment venues (Cruise Critic, 'Boards' 25 June 2006). The main attraction is the cruise ship as opposed to the Caribbean islands.

Many Cruise Critic members, however, were unabashedly critical of Royal Caribbean's announcement that it planned to build a 220,000 GRT ship with a proposed carrying capacity of 5,400 passengers. Cruise Critic reported that its poll titled 'How Big Is Too Big?' elicited a record 3,243 votes of which over 75 per cent agreed that the ship would be too big, and that approximately 65 per cent would refuse to sail on it. It quoted one member anticipating that the ship's size potentially would disenchant dream vacations because '[e]mbarkation and debarkation would be a nightmare, and even exiting at ports would be just too big a mess. Dining would be a nightmare as well', while another said that 'I foresee any number of nightmarish situations. Long lines for boarding, disembarkation at ports, getting through buffet lines, getting into the various venues at night' (Cruise Critic, 'Features' 'How Big is Too Big?'n.d.). Overwhelmingly negative responses to the planned behemoth ship, weakens the assertion that tourists understand and accept tourism as a series of games from which to cull pleasure regardless of the circumstances. Even though these posters may accept the fact that embarkation and debarkation times are lengthy on large and mega cruise ships, they reject the idea of a behemoth ship in which passenger queues will be even longer than that to which they have become accustomed. It remains to be seen whether or not new amenities can mitigate potential disenchantment of passengers.

Another member was concerned that such a ship could negatively affect smaller ports of call (e.g., 'What port can you dock at?'). Despite the fact that an overwhelming number of respondents criticized the idea of a behemoth ship for reasons of ambiance, safety ('a surefire terrorist target') and/or impact on the environment, a minority of 25 per cent polled affirmed Royal Caribbean's decision to gain even greater economies of scale in mass market cruising, e.g., 'More things to look at, more things to do, just more and more...of a good thing?' and 'It will be a fascinating floating hotel with all sorts of options'.

When Cruise Critic asked the question, 'Do you care about destinations at all on a ship like this?' it is notable that over two-thirds of respondents 'felt that the itinerary was irrelevant'. Briefly put, they understood that this behemoth ship is to be considered *the* destination at sea. Cruise Critic reported that 'of those potential cruisers who did care about where this behemoth would end up, the vast majority preferred a Caribbean itinerary to anything else'. What, then, is the significance of the Caribbean islands to consumers in mass market cruise tourism?

To be sure, brochure discourse 'performs' the Caribbean islands as what Sheller calls shore-side 'places to play' (2004a). Still, representations of the Caribbean islands as playgrounds in paradise are not the exclusive purview of cruise and advertising executives and/or travel professionals. Posters who have cruised the Caribbean and who share detailed information also may be considered experts in this virtual community. Their postings reinforce the Caribbean islands as landed sites of and for what are '3+1S' vacations (i.e., 'sun, sand, surf and duty-free shopping').

In response to a post seeking advice on Caribbean islands (Cruise Critic, 'Boards' 19 June 2005), one member replied by identifying specific Caribbean islands with water sports, quality of beaches, landscape and/or shopping:

> 'Jamaica - some great scenery and cultually [sic] interesting, snorkling [sic] is poor St. Thomas - nice scenery but a bit over-developed (shoppers love it). Snorkling is OK at Coki Beach. It is also a short ferry ride to St John were snorkeling is quite good...St. Martin: developed but with a nice European ambiance, some great beaches (Orient, Dawn), some scenic areas. Shoppers love Philipsburg but if you don't shop - get out of Philipsburg and head to the beaches. Some decent snorkeling at Dawn beach (depending on ocean conditions)' (CruiseCriticPoster9).

This was the case also on another e-discussion thread concerning the Caribbean (Cruise Critic, 'Boards' 13 September 2005):

> 'Put me in that group that doesn't tan, swim or drink, too. But that doesn't mean I can't enjoy the Caribbean. Exotic tropical islands. Cruising the fresh-aired open sea. Sightseeing. Shopping. Wearing ridiculously loud and large clothing (and not having anybody say anything about it' (CruiseCriticPoster10).

> 'You sound just like me. I also don't swim, don't tan and don't drink...I am a history buff, mobility challenged and love local cultures. He [husband] is a newly retired biology teacher and loves the flora and fauna. I also enjoy the shopping, both local markets and duty free ports' (CruiseCriticPoster11)

'CruiseCriticPoster10's' reply epitomizes the uninhibited tourist in the tropics whose search for the extraordinary manifests in new sights and activities as well as the suspension of rules governing apparel in everyday landed life.[10]

---

10 The dress code for island cruising contrasts sharply with the dress code for transatlantic crossing as encapsulated in a debate between posters (Cruise Critic, 'Boards' 12 January

'CruiseCriticPoster11', on the other hand, is attracted to the beauty of the physical environment, experiencing local cultures as well as shopping. Contravening the constructed boundaries of 'tourist bubbles' as part of the search for the extraordinary, 'CruiseCriticPoster12' explained that:

> 'We [she and her husband] love being entertained and enlightened by local performance groups. We love to have an authentic local meal in some off-the-beaten track restaurant. We love to find local art…We love the Caribbean because it is such a lifestyle change from our busy Chicago days'.

Overall, what the above posts collectively indicate is that cruise passenger-tourists seek and expect to be removed from the ordinary, mundane conduct and context of their everyday landed lives. They are motivated to experience pleasure in and from markedly different physical contexts (e.g., on board the ship, shore-side excursions, planned tourism villages, and so forth) most of which, paradoxically, have been constructed from the same foundational principles (predictability, calculability, efficiency and controllability) to which they have become accustomed.

Narratives focusing on the Caribbean islands' natural physical beauty and/or recreation sites support Britton's argument that institutionalized leisure strengthens instead of challenges the existing social order for accumulating capital (1991). Since its nineteenth century colonial construction as an 'earthly paradise,' the Caribbean's physical beauty has been re-presented and enhanced in this way:

> In touring 'through' the islands, moving from one to another, the ideas of ease, luxury and relaxation were crucial. The tourist immersed his or her body in a tropical experience of sights, scents, and tastes in which nature was understood to be more bountiful, more colorful, with more flowers, exotic fruits, and leafy greenery. In these Edenic places where others labour and living is easy, tourists are encouraged to believe that they can engage guiltlessly in sensuous abandon and bodily pleasures (Sheller 2004b, 177-8).

Aurally and visually marginalized by dominant discourse arising from, and characterizing the production and consumption of mass market cruise tourism in the Caribbean, are the local communities. Posters' differentiation of the Caribbean from Alaska, Europe, Hawai'i, Australia and Asia exposes a major effect of culturally sterilizing a region, one that has been stripped of its complex histories in favour of a near-exclusive focus on its paradise-like natural qualities:

> Meanwhile, those largely romantic 'desert island' images of the brochures and the magazines triumph over the real and painful complexities and paradoxes of Caribbean life and culture. The fantasies mock the history of the Caribbean: from the almost complete annihilation of the Amerindians, through slavery and the plantation system, to migration,

---

2006). 'CruiseCriticPoster 13' who initiated this discussion thread reported an incident on one of Cunard's cruise ships in which British cruisers complained of the 'vulgar, American dress codes' (especially jeans and polo shorts on formal nights). Some members agreed that Americans ought to dress appropriately when in Europe since they represented their country and culture, while others resisted the suggestion by arguing that dress code neither signifies nationality nor 'proper upbringing'.

the difficulties of nationhood and the forging of new identities and economic strategies (Pattullo 2005, 177).

Ports elsewhere in the world, on the other hand, are valued for their rich political-social-cultural histories in addition to their natural physical beauty. It is in this way that the production-consumption circuit in mass market cruise tourism reworks complex colonial histories of the Caribbean by folding its inhabitants into the physical landscape, hence perpetuating their absence in an unproblematic way (or conversely, 'naturalizing' their presence within the larger context of consumption, i.e., as providers of physical and emotional labour in tourism goods and services).

Contributing to the further marginalization of Caribbean histories and cultures is the concept of the 'private island'. Cruise lines' inclusion of private islands to their itineraries normalizes the Caribbean as the main source of and for shore-side recreational activities (in many instances, made possible by seafarers' shore-side labour of serving meals, facilitating water sports and so forth) while limiting (unpredictable) interactions between tourists and local peoples. So important are private islands to Caribbean itineraries that there is a discussion forum specifically dedicated to the topic.

In reply to one member's post concerning a missed opportunity to visit a particular cruise line's private island, 'CruiseCriticPoster14' wrote that:

'When we cruise the private island is our main destination. We won't book a cruise unless their [sic] is a private island. Getting off the ship and spending a relaxing day with no worries of excursions or getting lost or where to eat or getting back to the ship late and no extra charges for enjoying a nice lunch on the beach are just some of the highlights. IMHO [In My Humble Opinion] a day on private island in the Caribbean is an absolute must! This is what being on vacation in the caribbean is truly about' (Cruise Critic, 'Boards' 28 October 2004).

Some posters consider another cruise line's private island to be one of the more popular private islands because of its beaches and activities such as horseback riding and jet ski-ing. 'CruiseCriticPoster15' confessed that, 'I have never in my life seen such a perfect beach -- probably made even more perfect by the waiter in a tux who waded out to serve me drinks on my floating mat. AHHHHH... I took a second cruise on HAL just because of the island'. For cruise passengers, then, private islands offer an unprecedented degree of exclusivity that is not possible in ports of call 'belonging' to local inhabitants. E-discussion threads on private islands and their respective characteristics allow potential cruisers to select what they deem to be the most appropriate cruise ship and corresponding itinerary that maximizes their experience of pleasure: private islands simultaneously yield pleasure from the physical, and protection from the social (if any) environments. For cruise lines, private islands in the Caribbean are another important venue for the production of pleasure and the pursuit of profits.

Visual Records of Pleasure

Cruise Critic members share their experiences on the Boards not only via their narratives but also the medium of photography. Photographs taken while on vacation serve as visual records or evidence of their experiences at sea and on land. When shared with friends, families and strangers, photographs represent another way in which consumers participate in the production process. On the one hand, tourists' photographs of sites and activities are visual records of their experiences. On the other hand, some photographs may also be considered re-presentations of representations because tourists can and do take the kinds of photographs of sites and activities modelled from those published by different media outlets and/or other passengers: 'many of the images that we visually consume when we are traveling are, in effect, the memories of others which are then visually consumed by us' (Crawshaw and Urry 1997, 179).

In an e-discussion thread initiated by 'CruiseCriticPoster16' on photographs taken during a cruise vacation (Cruise Critic, 'Boards' 10 February 2006), posters discussed the pleasure derived from viewing such photographs. 'CruiseCriticPoster16', a self-identified 'cruise addict' wanted to know from fellow Cruise Critic members what they thought of his need to 'turn on the internet to look at other peoples [sic] cruise pictures...I see what a great time those strangers are having and then I want to be on a cruise'. Other posters endorsed this 'need' by replying that:

> 'It's terrible to have to view all those people having fun in all those places when I'm not with them or booked to go to those places...It just makes me have to plan another cruise' (CruiseCriticPoster17).

> 'We love to look at other peoples' cruise pictures. Sometimes it gives us ideas of what to bring along on board. Other times, it gives us ideas of things to do in port' (CruiseCriticPoster18).

> 'I am so new to this and am so disappointed I did not start cruising sooner BUT all that said, these boards have taught me so much about cruising NOT to mention how wonderful all the pictures have been while reading everything' (CruiseCriticPoster19).

> 'I love looking at pictures. I will be on my first cruise this summer in the Med. And it took me a long time to convince DH [Dear Hubby/Husband]. After showing him pictures of different ships and ports, he finally caved and I won...Any info helps me plan better compared to a couple of months ago, I feel like I'm on top of things. Really all the help and pics are truly appreciated' (CruiseCriticPoster20).

Contrary to that which inheres in the post-tourism or end-of-tourism perspective, tourists' consumption of photographs published on the internet has the effect of encouraging as opposed to discouraging the yearning for physical travel.

The above narratives tell us that photographs are more than records, or even representations of representations of the tourist gaze. They constitute a visual language of communication containing non-verbal 'grammatical' rules. Photographs taken by cruisers are viewed not just for pleasure or as records of experiences, but crucially for information on what to bring on board the ship, what to do, where to go and when to do so. Photography then is a social act: it is a 'particularly powerful signifying practice which reproduces a dominant set of visual images, at the very same time that it conceals its constructed character' (Crawshaw and Urry 1997, 183). The sharing and concomitant consumption of photographs helps establish rules or rituals that can be followed on a cruise vacation. Posters' photographs help affirm cruise lines' promise of pleasure and 'proven' ways to experience it.

To Cheat or Not to Cheat

Arguably, since the Cruise Critic website is operated by a commercial enterprise and its membership is filled with 'cruisers' or self-styled 'cruise addicts', then it should not be surprising that mostly positive discussions and reviews of cruise vacations are published there. This does not mean that Cruise Critic members are unaware of cruise lines' continued efforts to manage the institutionalized contexts for their experiences of pleasure. Of interest here is how e-discussion threads on shipboard incidental charges, gratuities given to seafarers, romantic/sexual relations, as well as the environmental impact of cruise ships, disclose posters' explanations of their viewpoints and in ways that support the centrality of consuming pleasure, while affirming key tenets of the free market.

E-discussion threads are replete with posters exchanging information to help limit or cut shipboard expenditures, for example, by monitoring usage of the identification-credit card issued to each passenger during shoreside check-in. Among the more controversial issues are smuggling alcohol for consumption on board ships and the sharing of 'soda cards'.[11] 'CruiseCriticPoster21' initiated an e-discussion thread by asking other members if they had been successful in bringing mini bottles of liquor on board cruise ships (Cruise Critic, 'Boards' 9 May 2006). Posters shared their experiences smuggling alcohol in different sized containers and/or by wrapping them in clothing. 'CruiseCriticPoster22' responded first with a cautionary note, i.e., some cruise lines monitor e-discussion boards so as to identify the novel ways in which passengers smuggle alcohol on board their ships:

> 'Be careful not to post your sailing date, cat or deck when planning to smuggle contraband on board. NCL monitors this site and has removed liquor from those passengers [sic] luggage. One poster thoughtfully posted his cabin # and NCL removed everything he has so carefully disguised in water bottles (Vodka). Yes people on a roll call [another message board section specifically for passengers scheduled to travel on specific cruise lines/ships/ dates] that had a CC [Cruise Critic] meeting planned and set up with the ship's staff (so [NCL] knew who they all were) plotted for months on their Roll Call exactly how they would get massive amounts of booze on board. No one was successful'.

While open forums such that of Cruise Critic message boards encourage consumers to gather and/or share information, they also facilitate cruise line surveillance

---

11 Policy on alcohol purchased shoreside varies according to cruise lines. For example, some lines do not allow passengers to bring on board alcohol purchased at home ports, and/or to consume duty-free alcohol purchased from foreign ports, while other lines have restrictions on the total permitted volume, or bottles.

of consumer practices that, in this case, can undermine shipboard policies and profitability.

'CruiseCriticPoster22' then questioned the ethics of smuggling liquor by drawing an analogy to dining in a restaurant: 'Given the cost of a cruise, is it that much of an imposition to pay for your on board beverages. Would you smuggle liquor into a restaurant?' Some posters argued that the practice is acceptable because it is an avenue through which passengers can lessen the impact of cruise lines' profit-generating efforts from their consumption of pleasure at sea, or somewhat to 'level the playing field' so to speak:

> 'The imposition is not being able to bring liquor into your cabin to enjoy a cocktail in your cabin (not a restaurant) while getting ready to go out. The cruise line will make its $$ on us the rest of the time' (CruiseCriticPoster23).

> 'I really don't like having a bar tab of $300 when my cruise only cost $600—seems a bit steep' (CruiseCriticPoster24).

A more heated discussion occurred in one e-discussion thread on shipboard beverage cards (Cruise Critic, 'Boards' 1 December 2005). 'CruiseCriticPoster25' thought it was prudent to share a cost-cutting practice with regard to soda consumption: 'I just realized on my last cruise that if I buy one drink [soda card], they [cruise ship management] don't check to see if it is yours or not. It worked GREAT the whole week for my whole family. Just wanted to share'. 'CruiseCriticPoster25' neither could anticipate the degree of disapproval from other members nor the manner in which they conveyed it. While many of the replies were laced with sarcasm, e.g., 'So I gather that means that your family can't all sit in a lounge and have soft drinks together and you have to have your drinks in shifts?' (CruiseCriticPoster26), and 'Are you familiar with the term: keel haul?' (CruiseCriticPoster27), other responses were vociferously critical. Two posters insisted that while smuggling alcohol could be considered acceptable conduct under certain circumstances, sharing a soda card was a reprehensible act:

> 'Bringing alcohol on board only takes away a sale from the cruise line, in fact many people that bring a bottle don't even use it, they end up buying drinks from the ship. Using a drink card for multiple people is actually taking away a product from the cruise line, it cost them money' (CruiseCriticPoster28).

> 'It's simply dishonest and cheating. Using this reasoning, one passenger should buy one card for soft drinks, then everyone on the ship drinks for free, why limit it to one family? I can't believe we're having this discussion...Sick' (CruiseCriticPoster29).

The operative logic here is that alcohol smuggling is an individual act, and that at the end of the day, the cruise line will recoup any potential monetary loss since passengers end up purchasing and consuming alcohol outside of their cabins anyway. The act of sharing soda cards, however, cannot but involve more than one person thus it takes away revenue from cruise lines. Notably, this act is not interpreted as resistance toward some cruise lines that charge passengers for soda even on all-inclusive packages, but that of unethical conduct on the part of the individual. Eventually, criticisms of 'CruiseCriticPoster25' provoked a supportive post:

> 'Give me a break people! We pay enough for a cruise...and they try to gouge you with every little thing they can. Obviously, if the cruise line really cared about this kind of thing then they would check the cards more carefully! I don't drink soda very often....so i won't bother doing this. But if i did....you bet i would! [CruiseCriticPoster25], Don't let these people make you feel at all guilty about this...The cruise line is not losing....it costs peanuts to make fountain pop' (CruiseCriticPoster30).

Although 'CruiseCriticPoster30's' post indirectly referenced the larger context of cruise line pursuit of even more profits while at sea, many others focused exclusively on individual responsibility, i.e., when consumers willingly exchange money for a cruise vacation, they ought to follow cruise line rules established for consuming pleasure. This sense of individual responsibility becomes even more apparent in an e-discussion thread on tipping seafarers.

To Tip or Not to Tip

'CruiseCriticPoster31' overheard a conversation between cabin stewards about how one of them did not receive any tips from having served a large family who used the tips instead to pay their bills on a seven-day cruise (Cruise Critic, 'Boards' 16 June 2004). She wanted to know from other members whether or not it was true that some seafarers only earned tips, as opposed to wages:

> 'Do you think that the [sic] only pay some of those people get is what we give them? I'm so glad I tipped my people well. I felt really sorry for that man...I know the captain, officers in uniform, spa personell [sic], chefs, and child care professionals are all salaried. The ones I am talking about are the waiters, room stewards and other people who wait on or take care of you. Does anyone have any inside info. on this? I think this is a serious issue that no one has touched on, and I am concerned for these people if all they get is what we give them. That man talked as if all he got was the tips. Is this true?'

When one poster affirmed that servers depend on tips for their living, 'CruiseCriticPoster31' replied by questioning cruise line marketing and sales of 'all-inclusive' cruise vacations while transferring responsibility for some seafarers' wages to passengers:

> '[W]hen we book a cruise and it says paid in full on our credit cards, it makes us think that the whole cruise is paid for. But to the contrary, these room stewards do a tremendous amount of work and rely mainly on our tips for payment. Our cruise is not fully paid for, we still have to pay for our housekeeping. The cruise line should be honest and tell us that. No one normally pays for housekeeping at a hotel, that's included in the cost... In my opinion, this is a serious issue and more people need to know about it. Our cruise is not totally paid for, we need to take tipping into account in our spending budgets'.

'CruiseCriticPoster32' sidestepped 'CruiseCriticPoster31's' critique of this cruise line practice by calculating the possible amount of tips a cabin steward could earn on a 7-day cruise:

'Lets [sic] consider just the 12 rooms with 2 persons per room: each room - $7.00 per day or $49.00 per 7 day cruise, there is [sic] 12 rooms so 12 times the 49 is equal $588.00 per week......no taxes are taken out, food is provided and also place to stay. The dollars earned on the ship have a buying power many times more in the countries that most of the stewards reside in, and living conditions are sometimes a lot worse in their own countries than even in crowded places on the ship'.

'CruiseCriticPoster32', however, did not directly address the issue of what happens when some passengers choose to undertip or even not tip at all on cruise lines that have suggested tipping guidelines as opposed to mandatory service charges. Significantly, 'CruiseCriticPoster32's' rationale is that which is most often invoked to justify this specific cruise line practice, i.e., seafarers are able to earn more and in better work conditions than back in their home countries.

Not wanting to leave the discussion on that point, 'CruiseCriticPoster31' asked the following rhetorical questions:

'Yes, they have potential to make pretty good money. But at what cost? How often do they see their family or their children? How many of us come home and spend time with our spouses and children every day? These people are on that ship for long periods of time and don't always get to see their loved ones. I just wish that the cruise industry would let people know that the tipping makes up most of their salary. Every time they mention tipping, they make it sound like it's just a recommendation but not really necessary'.

Another poster's response echoed the perspective of 'CruiseCriticPoster32':

'I agree with [CruiseCriticPoster32], that the staff is, in most cases, being appropriately compensated for the level of work. Yes, they are limited on 'family time' but this is a choice that they have made. I think that if the service is exceptional, to tip a little extra is not unreasonable. Howver [sic], I see a lot of posting going on that indicates a LOT of tipping in addition to the 'tip' Princess already assesses. I wonder how much of this is really necessary?' (CruiseCriticPoster33).

After reviewing a HAL leaflet titled 'you need to know' (that was distributed before the end of a voyage to passengers explaining the cruise line's rationale for including gratuities in final cruise bills as opposed to having passengers directly tip individual crew members), 'CruiseCriticPoster34' returned the focus back to cruise lines by taking them to task for having passengers pay seafarer wages. First, 'CruiseCriticPoster34' shared an excerpt from the cruise line's leaflet:

'Good service starts with crew members you may never have the opportunity to meet such as our highly trained kitchen staff. They also benefit from the gratuities included with your bill. To ensure the efforts of these crew members and also to discourage solicitation of guests, dining and cabin stewards are required to turn in any tips they receive directly from those guests who have removed or reduced the gratuities on their onboard accounts'.

'CruiseCriticPoster34' then went on to critique HAL's policy on gratuity:

> 'Why am I being asked to ensure the efforts of cooks, night cleaning staff, engineers or ??? Who are these 'behind the scenes' crew? Isn't that the purpose of wages?... I have seen room service waiters look very frightened and shove their hands in their pockets which gave me and my daughter the impression of fear when we offered a tip…A priest, an entertainment staff menber [sic], and a games server all verified that the 'salary' is room and board, medical and dental while on board and a token wage $50-75 US a month…On some lines, the fare home is paid if the crew member stays for the whole term. That is 11 months on a HAL for cabin and wait staff. (Only 4 for bridge, entertainment director) BUT now, I was told, 1/12 of the fare is being deducted from their share of the pooled gratuities…HAL (and most cruise lines) are not registered in the USA, Canada, Britain, Norway etc Instead they are registered in countries where labor and other laws are not as 'strict.'… I have informed my TA [Travel Agent] and HAL that I will never cruise again on a line that forces pooling of tips. WE are our brothers' keepers. I refuse to cooperation [sic] with exploitation of a needy third world people'.

The last sentence of this post elicited several replies that either highlighted the perceived hypocrisy on the part of 'CruiseCriticPoster34', or as a reminder that cruising is about pleasure and not a serious topic such as wage rates:

> 'If you actually feel that way, then you shouldn't cruise any cruise line that doesn't pay its staff a living wage, so basically you're limiting yourself, at this point, to NCL, which actually has a mandatory service charge policy' (CruiseCriticPoster35).

> 'Look at the label on your clothes, see where was it made and think what someone got paid for that. Look at many electronic items as well, look at the cars made in Mexico, Korea........is it better not to buy any of that and have the people starve because they will not have the jobs?' (CruiseCriticPoster32).

> 'You should just TIP at least the minimum $10 pp per day and not worry how the TIP is distributed. Let the Cruiseline work that out. Your job is to board the ship and have a good time. It is not to be a prevailing wage specialist' (CruiseCriticPoster36)

This discussion thread with over 50 replies was concluded by a post from 'CruiseCriticPoster37' whose daughter worked on a cruise ship: 'There were stewards and waiters on their seventh, eighth and ninth contracts which are six months per contract. They must think how things are done, and how they are paid is OK, since they continue to come back year after year'.

The above posts demonstrate consumers' awareness that gratuities are particularly vital for those seafarers employed to clean cabins and serve meals. However, 'CruiseCriticPoster31's intent of sparking a discussion on cruise lines that pay some seafarers fixed salaries while shifting responsibility for the bulk of cabin and dining stewards' wages (monthly base salaries of USD50) to passengers, quickly was recast by many posters. In effect, a potentially negative evaluation of cruise lines' uneven wage practices was transformed into two positive justifications. That is, posters who question this practice should remember that seafarers earn more on cruise ships than back in their home countries, and that seafarers obviously do not to take issue with their conditions of employment because they keep signing new contracts every six months. As rational actors, seafarers have calculated the costs and benefits of working on cruise ships: when the costs outweigh the benefits, then the onus is on them to search for work elsewhere. Conversely, cruise lines have determined appropriate compensation levels as disclosed from suggested gratuity amounts or fixed service charges, hence passengers should just follow cruise lines' instructions and in doing so, will clear their conscience and be able to better enjoy their vacations. Potentially critical focus on cruise line management's relation to seafaring labour is reframed as, or deflected to the microcosm of individual responsibility: seafarers determine the conditions in which they are willing to work. The majority of posts in this e-discussion thread assign to social actors the kind of human agency that is unconstrained by structural forces.

Love and Sex

For some cruisers, the consumption of shipboard pleasure can involve more than getting massages, gambling, golfing, rock-climbing, dancing, shopping, visiting landed sites and so forth: cruise ships also offer the context for experiencing emotional and sexual intimacy among strangers. When cruise line advertisements display pictures of couples hugging each other as they gaze into horizon or having an intimate dinner on their private balcony, what is being promoted is the idea of 'romance' at sea. One Cruise Critic member conducted an informal poll on relationships developed at sea, and of the 108 members who responded to the question 'For those who have had a fling on a cruise, which one applies?', 26 per cent agreed with the answer 'With a crew member—no continuing relationship'; 22 per cent agreed with the answer 'With a crew member—continuing relationship'; 40 per cent agreed with the answer 'With another passenger—no continuing relationship'; and 12 per cent agreed with the answer 'With another passenger—continuing relationship' (Cruise Critic, 'Boards' 17 May 2005). In their posts, several members discussed where relationships could take place on the ship especially since public venues and hallways are covered by closed circuit television. For example:

> 'Although technically crew are not allowed in passenger quarters, it happens every day on every cruise ship…I have heard also of using the dining room after hours, closets, crew quarters, etc' (CruiseCriticPoster38).

> 'I've heard of it happening in crew quarters, passenger rooms, elevators, hot tubs, and pools at 3am, even the disco after hours. [CruiseCriticPoster38's] right, when they're desperate enough, they'll find a place' (CruiseCriticPoster39).

'CruiseCriticPoster 39' added in a later post that '[c]ruise ships seem like people's personal playgrounds for sex'. 'CruiseCriticPoster40' aptly summarized shipboard relationships with the motto: 'well, if you go to cruise..do it...screw it...as much as you can. and leave after a week…that easy…'

Of those who voted, there were roughly equal numbers of relationships (i.e., the total of 'continuing' and 'no-continuing') with a crew member, as those with a fellow passenger. However, the percentage of passenger-passenger relationship that did not continue beyond the cruise was nearly twice that of the passenger-crew relationship. Some posters posited that the higher percentage of passenger-crew relationships may be due to women passengers' search for love, and/or men seafarers desire to obtain 'fiancé visas' in order to reside legally in the US. These rationales also are discernible from e-discussion threads in which women passengers write of their relationships with seafarers. The discussions expose prevailing stereotypes of foreign crew members, and gendered perceptions of intimate relations on board cruise ships.

'CruiseCriticPoster38', in an e-discussion thread a few months earlier, said that she met a Turkish waiter on a cruise and lamented about how much she missed him afterward, 'I actually cried for 3 days straight because I missed seeing him' (Cruise Critic, 'Boards' 12 August 2004). Some posters advised her to let him go because of their own experiences in which foreign men seafarers either were driven by the need for temporary relief of loneliness, or were intent on developing relationships with US women passengers in order to obtain the coveted fiancé visa. 'CruiseCriticPoster41' related the story in which she had developed a relationship with a crew member whom she believed was single until his wife invited her to meet their children:

'She wanted me to meet her sons, I'm guessing she thought that I'd feel so bad for their situation that I'd agree to marry her husband to help him get his green card...I think crew from third world countries are a greater risk since they are so desperate to improve their lives'.

A few months later, 'CruiseCriticPoster38' who had had a very short-lived relationship with the Turkish waiter (he made clear that he had no plans to marry or settle in the US but still wanted to get together with her) initiated another e-discussion thread on the question of why women tended to be more vulnerable (to developing relationships) at sea than on land (Cruise Critic, 'Boards' 9 May 2005). Majority of replies to her question referenced the lull that being on vacation does to one's emotional defences. She was advised by 'CruiseCriticPoster42' that:

'[Y]ou're on a cruise to have fun so you're more open to flirtation and excitement. Here you have these thin, handsome guys with all their hair and teeth and 'sexy' accents waiting on you hand and foot making you feel like a 'goddess'. It's so different from what you find at home. Same thing happens to me when I go to Vegas, beautiful women flirting with me, making me feel like I'm desirable...And just like Vegas, What happens on a cruise should stay on a cruise'.

'CruiseCriticPoster43' who claimed to be a former seafarer, cautioned women passengers that men seafarers will lie about their marital status in order to have a good time:

'For the most part, the crew are married and have wifes [sic] back home so they are mainly looking for booty. They will tell you that they are single though and will give u a line. Please don't trust all seamen. Go in there with an open mind and have fun with them for the week. When I was off with my friends, they would take passengers with them and show them the ports and go to the local restaurants that tourists don't know about. At that time we couldn't take the passengers to our cabins. Otherwise we'd get fired. What I see now is that most of the singles go to the club or the disco at night'.

These two posts reveal gendered perceptions of, and approaches to shipboard relationships. While women posters tend to discuss at greater length their expectations of longer term relationships, men posters are clear that shipboard relationships should be based first and foremost on sexual pleasure with no expectations of commitment or longevity.

The topic of women's vulnerability was discussed again in a thread that asked why women tended to fall for men who would not make longer term commitments (Cruise Critic, 'Boards' 19 August 2005). Among the reasons posited by 'CruiseCriticPoster44' for why her fellow women cruisers develop relationships with 'unavailable, undesirable men aboard a ship' are because 'they [women] are on vacation, defenses are down', 'there are no real world worries to deal with, only fun things', 'being on water is such a good feeling' and 'it's romantic, and women grow up believing fairy tales are based on reality'. 'CruiseCriticPoster44' did not identify the 'unavailable, undesirable men', i.e., to draw a distinction between men from the US and elsewhere. 'CruiseCriticPoster45' however interpreted the phrase as referring to men from other nationalities, hence questioned the sweeping generalization that foreign seafarers are 'undesirable men,' as well as the concomitant traits ascribed to them:

> 'You also cannot assume the crew have nothing at home, are uneducated, etc. Many of them have a college education but find that working on a ship pays much more than the jobs in their own country. I was on the Zuiderdam during one of its first sailings and it had just got some type of xray machine. The medical staff were unfamiliar with this machine and ended up getting one of the dining room waiters to assist them in learning how to operate it. Turns out he was some type of medical technician and had taken medical courses in Indonesia before deciding to take a job on the ship. I was told this by one an American nurse who worked on the ship so I have no reason to doubt what she said. I think it says alot [sic] about their character as well. How many of us would be willing to leave our country, our home, our family for a year at a time? This is a big sacrifice they make. Their family values are also amazing. So many of these people are not just supporting their wives or children; they are supporting brothers, sisters, nieces, nephews and parents. How many Americans work 365 days straight to support the entire family'.

Presented as such, 'CruiseCriticPoster45' created a detailed context for challenging 'CruiseCriticPoster44''s assumptions of foreign men seafarers and further reminded 'CruiseCriticPoster44' that US men may not be much different: 'Sure there are guys just looking for sex or looking for a better way of life…guess what…I've met them right here in the same town too'. 'CruiseCriticPoster41' agreed with the point that the issue is not about foreign men in particular but that of men in general, 'Men don't come on here & post their stories, well because they don't pour out their souls like women do! (Read Men Are From Mars, Women Are From Venus;)) [sic].That's part of what makes life interesting'. 'CruiseCriticPoster46', who later entered the e-discussion thread, supported the Venus-Mars distinction by drawing parallels to that which occur on land, '[T]hey [women] come to the club looking for the same thing you are looking for, and that was Sex...."

'CruiseCriticPoster47,' a former crew member, in seeking to balance the focus after having read many e-discussion threads on why women passengers tend to seek men seafarers, initiated a thread asking for crew members to discuss their relationships with passengers (Cruise Critic, 'Boards' 18 October 2005). The ensuing posts, nevertheless, mostly focused on women passengers. Echoing one of 'CruiseCriticPoster45''s points, 'CruiseCriticPoster48' said that:

> 'I always find it interesting to read posts about what appears to be mostly women trying to 'find' the crew person, then minimizing it that it's 'just a friendship' but the way they carry on it's clear to everyone that they HOPE it will be 'more' than a friendship. Sometimes when a crew doesn't get in touch with them, it's not about them, it's about the reality of the job... Other times if a crew member doesn't get ahold of them, it's the reality that they don't WANT to be found by the passenger who is looking for them'.

Three reasons were put forth by 'CruiseCriticPoster49' for the absence of discussions on women seafarers having relationships with men passengers:

> '1) it's *not* proper for them to do so; 2) there are probably relatively few female flings with male passengers; and 3) female crew members have relationships with male crew members for the most part because the chance of a long-term relationship is much much more probable. This is just my opinion'.

Intimate relationships of different levels of commitment then are yet another kind of extraordinary experience that passengers can get from cruise vacations. In these e-discussion threads, posters clearly approach and interpret such relationships from what they consider distinctly gendered perceptions and expectations, e.g., women passengers are more inclined to develop (or want to do so) longer term relationships with (foreign) men seafarers, than men passengers with women seafarers.

Common Sense at Sea

E-discussion threads painting a world of 'voluntary' shipboard love and sex have been interrupted with allegations of some women and children passengers that they were victims of assault in general or sexual assault in particular either by men passengers or men seafarers. In recent years, cruise lines have had to confront negative publicity of lax security measures and even accusations of case cover-ups involving a variety of shipboard crimes as well as incidences of missing persons. A woman passenger's lawsuit against Carnival in 1999 forced the cruise line to admit that there had been over 100 cases of sexual assaults on passengers and seafarers in five years prior to the lawsuit (Frantz 1999e, 1999f, and 1999g). In some cases, cruise line investigations led to the arrest of seafarers by authorities at ports of call, whereas in other cases cruise lines reportedly removed seafarers from their ships and sent them back to their countries of origin, hence thwarting further investigations.[12]

---

12 In the case of Carnival, Korten reported that, 'In five lawsuits against Carnival reviewed by *New Times*, reporters turned up behavior cruise patrons might find alarming. The company helped at least five employees accused of rape to leave the country; fought to keep a waiter accused of attacking a Minnesota woman from being sued; fired nurse Cathy Wieland after she cooperated with the FBI; and so bungled the gathering of evidence in Mary's case that lawmen had no choice but to cut short their investigation' (2000). See also the website of

The IMO's 1986 Measures to Prevent Unlawful Acts Against Passengers and Crew on Board Ships require cruise lines to report any unlawful act or breach of security procedures against the ship or passengers to the flag state. Further, the US Federal Bureau of Investigation (FBI) and Coast Guard have the right to investigate any criminal act involving US citizens on the high seas. In the wake of the 1999 law suit, the US House of Representatives held hearings on passenger security, following which ICCL standardized reporting procedures for unlawful acts and agreed to immediate referral of cases involving US citizens or within US territorial waters to the FBI (US House of Representatives 1999). Approximately six years later, the US House of Representatives responded again to new allegations of crimes committed on cruise ships as well as criticisms of cruise line reporting procedures by holding the 2005 joint hearing (by the Committee on Government Reform; the Subcommittee on National Security, Emerging Threats and International Relations; and the Subcommittee on Criminal Justice, Drug Policy and Human Resources) on 'International Maritime Security'. J. Michael Crye, then president of ICCL, who testified at the hearing, said that crimes at sea were rare given the statistics, e.g., one case of sexual assault per 100,000 passengers; 13 missing passengers within the past two years (i.e., less than one missing passenger per million); and one case of violent crime per 200,000 passengers.[13]

A poll conducted by Cruise Critic on ship safety demonstrated that members' views were similar to that of the ICCL. Of the 1700 members who voted, 94 per cent believed that cruise ships were safe, and 76 per cent had 'no worries about cruising at all' following negative news media reports. According to Cruise Critic, majority of them also believed that congressional hearings would not lead to mandated changes for cruise line safety partly because some were cynical of lawyers' intent, e.g., 'opportunities for blowhard lawyers to pontificate' or that there were few or even no constructive lessons to be learned from the highly publicized events (Cruise Critic, 'Features' 'Cruise Ship Safety' n.d.). Other members called for heightened passenger awareness of their surroundings, while at least one member reportedly placed responsibility on cruise lines for privileging profits over protecting passengers: 'Although they [cruise lines] will all say that passenger is their primary concern, what they really mean is that customer safety can have a direct effect on their bottom line'. Another member pointedly questioned the uneven handling of land versus sea-based incidences that result in negative depictions of cruise ship

---

Cruise Bruise for detailed description and status of resolved and pending cases, and Du Pont 2004a and 2003c.

13 Critics argue that the statistics are not accurate especially since there have been cases of sexual assault that either were not reported by victims or cruise lines. For more detailed information on testimonies from former passengers, security officers, cruise line executives, and so forth, please see US House of Representatives 2005. During the hearing, HAL's Director of Fleet Security replied to the question 'What types of statistics are kept concerning security incidents on board ships, and how is this data made available to the public?' by stating that 'While Carnival reviews these reports as part of its ongoing efforts to assess and improve upon the effectiveness of vessel security, such sensitive information is not made available to the public in order to protect Carnival's international security procedures' (US House of Representative 2005, 184).

responses: 'Royal Caribbean responded far better than what would be expected of an international resort. What reports has Holiday Inn issued in the case of Natalie Holloway [teenager who went missing in 2005 while on vacation in Aruba]? Is the venue of a potential crime really the accountable source?'

Given that ships operate on the oceans and many fly foreign flags, then the venue of a cruise ship cannot but be an important accountable source especially since there is no stipulated standardized training for shipboard security personnel. It is precisely because, in the words of one Cruise Critic member, 'They [cruise lines] all must deal with the complexities of many various foreign jurisdictions,' that cruise lines ought to be transparent in handling cases of unlawful acts on board their ships.

Passenger safety also was the concern of posters on some e-discussion threads. 'CruiseCriticPoster50' initiated one such thread by sharing what her future father-in-law said to her: '[W]e don't hear about all the things that happen on cruises because they're not actually American ships. He and his wife went on to say that crew workers slip drugs into people's drinks and that cruises are one of the most unsafe types of vacations' (Cruise Critic, 'Boards' 26 November 2005). While a few agreed with 'CruiseCriticPoster10' who said that '[C]ruise lines want to protect their name and so they won't tell you everything that's happened on them if they don't have to'), the majority of replies echoed the industry's position that cruising is safer than other forms of landed activities, and that news media sensationalize cases to increase their audience, e.g.,

> 'Cruising is probably safer than many forms of vacation. No one hides the fact that there are problems…and believe me, the cruise lines do take offenses seriously. I've seen a crewmember hauled off a ship in chains, so I don't doubt that the staff on board take a dim view of bad actors' (CruiseCriticPoster51).

Several posters even raised the issue of passenger 'common sense' or lack thereof as a major contributing factor:

> 'I agree with everyone else. Yes, things do happen on cruises ON OCCASION. But if you check deeper into what took place, you start to realize that maybe someone was drinking too much, or taking too many chances, and so on…The thing is, we're all adults, and if you use common sense, the chances of something bad taking place is [sic] drastically reduced' (CruiseCriticPoster52).

> 'Some scary little-reported things go down, usually involving shady crew members, but it seems to be no more than on land…It's like anywhere else—you have to use common sense. Keep an eye on your drink in public. Never agree to have a crew member take you to any of the crew-only areas. When in port, know the local issues and be aware of those around you, don't wear flashy jewellery, etc. People traveling anywhere on vacation tend to let their guard down, and can make some very stupid decisions' (CruiseCriticPoster53).

These last two posts call attention to the fact that being on vacation while shipboard or shoreside does not mean that passengers can and should be lax about their personal safety. To some extent, posters' exhortation to apply common sense while on dream vacations indirectly challenges an illusion of safety-security elicited and reinforced by the production and consumption of such vacations in a self-contained, gated oceanic community of the cruise ship.

Yet, posters tended not to discuss directly or to critique cruise line security measures and procedures for reporting cases involving US citizens on foreign-flagged ships. Crucially, the total number of shipboard security officers is not proportionate to the total number of passengers on a large cruise ship. According to the testimony of Rivkind, a maritime lawyer, at the 2006 congressional hearing on 'International Maritime Security II':

> My experience is there is a security department onboard the vessel, which may be typically manned by a staff of eight (8) or twelve (12) crewmembers, designated as security. There is usually a Chief of Security, and an Assistant Chief of Security among the eight (8) or twelve (12) crew deemed 'security'. Therefore, the actual number of active security patrols aboard the ship would be less. In addition, the security personnel maintaining rotating shifts, which would leave even a lesser number of security actually patrolling the ship at a given time. It is important to know that the cruise ships are as high as thirteen (13) to fourteen (14) decks, with over 2000 passengers and 800-1000 crewmembers. The current system leaves only a few security personnel assigned specifically to the casino, leaving even less security to patrol the ship (US House of Representatives 2006, 156).

The small size of shipboard security teams also do not convey the fact that there are no industry-wide standardized security training programs for foreign seafarers, presumably because cruise lines employ former police and military officers for these positions. Rivkind testified further at the 2006 congressional hearing that:

> Since we do not have uniform laws addressing the investigation of a crime onboard a cruise ship, nor uniform standards regarding classification of crimes, and we do not have any standards or laws requiring reporting of these crimes, there are currently no uniform laws or standards regarding the investigation of an alleged crime (US House of Representatives 2006, 157).[14]

Even though the FBI has jurisdiction over criminal cases under specific circumstances (e.g., occurrence in US territorial waters, US owned ship despite its foreign flag, or victim is a US citizen), there exists no laws at this time of writing that stipulate mandatory cruise line reporting to US authorities.[15]

---

14 Rivkind also shared with the legislators what Royal Caribbean said as part of its defense against a law suit filed by the family of a missing passenger: 'In a Memorandum of Law filed in court by the cruise line in response to Kendall Carver's claim that the cruise line did not properly investigate the disappearance of his daughter, and intentionally withheld information from him, the cruise line said that it has 'no duty to investigate', and no duty to provide information to any third party' (US House of Representatives 2006, 161).

15 At the 2005 joint hearing before the U.S. House of Representatives' Committee on Government Reform, Subcommittee on National Security, Emerging Threats and International Relations and the Subcommittee on Criminal Justice, Drug Policy and Human Resources, the FBI's Assistant Director of Criminal Investigations Division reiterated in his testimony the 'Special Maritime and Territorial Jurisdiction' (Section 17, Title 18 of US Code) that extends US jurisdiction over crimes committed on a ship under the following conditions: if a ship is

Given the conjuncture of cruise line marketing of romance at sea with cruisers' e-discussion threads on shipboard love and sex, there exists little discursive space encouraging and legitimizing evaluations of cruise line practices especially in relation to preventing and reporting assault incidences. In this kind of milieu, the numerous and lengthy posts seeking advice on how to find/hold on to 'love', or dealing with rejection by shipboard paramours can have an overall effect of minimizing serious allegations particularly of sexual assault. Posters' personal 'testimonies' and hearsay indicate an overwhelming belief and acceptance that intimate relationships, when they occur on the ships essentially are 'voluntary'. Hence, if and when some sexual encounters are alleged not to be voluntary, then the onus falls on accusers to prove that they did exercise common sense despite the violent outcomes. Framed by this perspective, allegations of passenger-on-passenger or crew-on-passenger assaults are less likely to be discussed, and/or evaluated beyond that of individual action and responsibility. It is not that posters are wrong at all to encourage the exercise of 'common sense'. However, when the spotlight is focused only on personal responsibility, then questions relating to the structural dimension (such as how cruise lines produce pleasure for profits that affect the size and training of security teams in relation to the total number of passengers as well as shipboard coverage), are cast away from the view of many who enjoy cruise vacations.

In recent years, nascent alternative virtual communities such as International Cruise Victims Association (ICV) and Cruise Bruise have emerged to increase consumer awareness of cruise line practices via documentation of cases, and identification of resources for victims, researchers and even legislators.[16] They call for more effective regulations of the industry. For example, ICV was founded in early 2006 by relatives of cruise victims. At the 2006 congressional hearing, ICV members testified on cruise line practices of withholding information, covering up incidences and/or delaying reports to the US authorities. Informed partly by such testimonies, US Congressman Christopher Shays who co-chaired the 2005 and 2006 congressional hearings, announced in mid 2006 the introduction of a bipartisan bill (co-sponsored by US Congresswoman Carolyn Maloney): the 'Cruise Line Accurate Safety Statistics Act (CLASS Act) is designed to address issues concerning the reporting of crimes on board cruise ships. Among the measures stipulated by the bill are that cruise lines calling at US ports must report all incidences involving US citizens 'within 4 hours of Captain's knowledge to Dept of Homeland Security'; cruise lines must post quarterly reports of each incidence on the internet; the Department of Homeland Security will participate in security training on cruise ships; and that cruise lines 'make available to any person buying vacation package information concerning crime stats, countries to be visited in itineraries and address of US embassies/consulates'. Cruise lines' failure to comply will incur monetary fines and/or denial of docking rights in the US (Shays 2006).

The individual choice and responsibility perspective held by many posters also can be found on the topic of cruise ship pollution. Notably, this topic did not elicit

---

US-owned despite its foreign flag; the crime occurs in US territorial waters; or the victim is a US citizen (US House of Representatives 2005, 86).

16 For more information, please see the respective websites of ICV and Cruise Bruise.

among posters the frequency and intensity of discussions (e.g., seen in number of threads and concomitant posts) as those of cost-cutting strategies, intimate shipboard relationships and so forth. Between 2004 and 2006, there were two discussion threads that dealt explicitly with cruise ship pollution in the section on general questions (Cruise Critic, 'Boards' 15 September 2005; and Cruise Critic, 'Boards' 24 February 2006).

In the first thread, 'CruiseCriticPoster54' reminisced about the days when passengers could throw streamers signalling the beginning of a voyage. 'CruiseCriticPoster55' replied by informing other members that streamers can be made of recycled paper 'and they disolve [sic] in water anyway, so no pollution problem with them' but added that 'I think that the PC brigade got a bit too far sometimes'. This last point prompted 'CruiseCriticPoster56' to respond in a cynical way by suggesting that cruisers should 'throw them [environmentalists] overboard so they can be closer to nature'.

'CrtuiseCriticPoster57' initiated the second thread of cruise ship sewage by sharing an email that was received from a non-governmental organization describing the volume of garbage and sewage produced by a cruise ship carrying 3,000 passengers, in addition to how cruise ships do not have to comply with local port legislation governing pollution. 'CruiseCriticPoster58' expressed disbelief that cruise ships willingly pollute the oceans because '[i]t is in the cruise ships best interest to make a presentable play ground for you to enjoy and return to. Your source is an off the wall alarmist and worse—total misinformed and wrong'. The implication here is that if and when cases of cruise ship pollution occur then they must be the result of human error.

The human error explanation was invoked explicitly by 'CruiseCriticPoster59' who admitted that '[y]ou will sometimes hear of a cruise line getting fined for discharge of sewage. This is normally as a result of an error by a crew member. The reason it makes the news is that it IS such as rare event'. 'CruiseCriticPoster60' went further to claim that the ocean floor generated more oil and natural decomposition than that of 'garbage ever dumped'. 'CruiseCriticPoster61''s post best articulates the view that 'cruise lines seem fair game for anyone who has some sort of an axe to grind. I call it 'Cruise Ship Envy'.

While some incidences of pollution may result from crew error, this cannot be assumed for all incidences. As discussed in Chapter Three, some incidences were deliberate acts presumably conducted with the implicit consent of cruise line management. The Cruise Junkie Dot Com website publishes and regularly updates a list detailing the type of violation and/or applicable fines ('Pollution and Environmental Violations'), e.g., in 2004 an executive of HAL pled guilty for falsifying environmental audits that had not been performed. He was fined $10,000 and 'ordered to perform 450 hours of community service while on probation for three years'. A year later, NCL America violated its Memorandum of Understanding with Hawai'i when one of its ships discharged tons of treated effluent into the harbour in Honolulu:

On March 12th the Honolulu Advertiser reported that Norwegian Cruise Line America's Pride of Aloha discharged about 70 tons of treated effluent into Honolulu Harbor last month, violating a voluntary agreement with the state. The state's agreement with the cruise ships allows such discharges at least a mile out from shore while traveling at least 6 knots. On March 16th, West Hawaii Today reported it had received numerous calls that Holland America's Statendam discharged what appeared to be 'brown water' into Kailua Bay for about 15 minutes to 20 minutes before it moved further out to sea. Several of the callers reported the discharge left a 'brown mark' on the vessel's side (Cruise Junkie Dot Com, 'Pollution and Environmental Violations' n.d.).[17]

Complexity of Consciousness

Our analysis in the chapter shows how posts on big ships, the Caribbean, private islands, photographs, alcohol and soda cards, seafarers' gratuities, love, sexual assaults and environmental pollution, in the main, echo similar perspectives or positions articulated by cruise lines (especially those in the face of negative publicity). Yet, we also find that some posters can and do express 'flashes' of critical evaluation or understanding of structural forces even though they do not express and pursue it to any great length.

It may be unfair, at the outset, to make the claim that posters only hold flashes of critical evaluation especially since this virtual community is constituted expressly by and for those who are passionate about integrated land-sea vacations. The occurrences of such flashes, nevertheless, expose the complex manner in which this present global era of neoliberal economic restructuring fragments social identities on the one hand, and renders them cohesive on the other. How is this possible?

Increasingly, individuals find themselves as members of overlapping and at times conflicting social networks, hence they can be progressive on some issues and conservative on others (R. Brown 2005; Chin and Mittelman 2000).[18] In the case of cruise tourism, it is posters' social positioning and related privileging of pleasure from extraordinary experiences that encourage a 'preferred' reading/interpretation of dominant meanings encoded by the structure of cruise tourism in particular, and free markets in goods and services in general (Hall 1992). One notable consequence is that posters perceive, explain and reinforce the production-consumption structure,

---

17 Non-governmental organizations such as Oceana and Bluewater Network also have pursued on the internet, their public campaigns against cruise ship pollution. In 2004 and at the end of nearly a year long campaign, Oceana delivered to Royal Caribbean's chief executive officer 10,000 individual pledges 'from citizens across the country who said they would not cruise with Royal Caribbean Cruise Lines until they cleaned up'. One month later, Oceana received a letter from Royal Caribbean stating that the cruise line would upgrade sewage and waste water treatment technology on all its ships, and '[t]he results of third-party audits of Royal Caribbean's wastewater treatment will be made public'. Notably, Royal Caribbean is the first cruise line to make this commitment on a fleet-wide level (Oceana 2004).

18 Brown, in his analysis of changing notions and experiences of American selfhood, wrote that '[p]ostmodern individualism means to *feel* good (Rosen 1984). It implies the pursuit of personal needs or pleasures that are unrelated to civic virtue or attainment' (2005, 158). The bifurcation of personal need and civic virtue is heightened in the case of cruise tourism especially since cruisers purchase vacations to experience pleasure.

processes and contradictions predominantly from the perspective of individual choice, action and responsibility.

Posts on e-discussion threads are illustrative of what has been identified as the 'radical individualism' (Urry 1995, 123) or free market-led individualization (Beck and Beck-Gernsheim 2002; Bourdieu 1984; Giddens 1991) of the new middle classes since the late twentieth century. They are borne from the ashes of an era of welfare states, and armed subsequently with consumption as a key mode of identity construction in national and global contexts. By expanding the horizons and sites from which individuals can select to shape their sense of self and identity, free markets cannot but help naturalize and validate the belief in individuality. This kind of belief, with its corresponding practices and consequences (e.g., personal accountability) increasingly displace social norms that help constitute a viable sense and responsibility to the collectivity: 'Individualism is now expressed through exquisite hedonism and therapeutic searches for the true self' (Brown 2005, 150). An observable phenomenon arising from this is that:

> late capitalist societies have been accompanied by the expansion and exaltation of 'calculating hedonism'... in which the politics of dissent have been displaced by an emphasis on self-identification forged in the process of consumption (Bianchi 2000, 120).

Radical individualism begets and sustains radical subjectivism (Brown 2005, 164), i.e., members of the new middle classes, now more than ever, are 'authors of their own destinies' (Martin 1998, 670). Rising demands for tourism goods and services in general and cruise tourism in particular is indicative of how pleasure culled from extraordinary experiences has become an integral dimension to experiences of 'self-actualization' (Eijck and Mommaas 2004, 376). Even though the centrality of pleasure consumption has not wholly eliminated posters' flashes of critical evaluation, located in a global context of neoliberal economic restructuring however, posters much like other citizen-consumers are expected to resolve free market created contradictions and moral dilemmas by resorting to the perspective of individual choice, action hence responsibility.

It is in this complex manner that mutually constitutive interactions of structural forces and radical individualism-subjectivism are grounded in, and sustain the four principles of efficiency, predictability, calculability and controllability that inform production and consumption in cruise tourism. Although present, structural forces are made to recede by the privileging of individuality and its attendant focus on pleasure. Thus, it becomes increasingly difficult to bring back in any sustained identification and critical discourse on structural forces/constraints (putatively non-existent from this perspective), let alone possible consensus on moral criteria (deemed unnecessary or even self-evident by this manner of conceptualizing individuality) from which to evaluate social conduct and practices. It is not that 'the political' has been eliminated per se, but that it is redefined in a distorted version of feminism's 'the political is personal,' so to speak.

Given this operative adage of 'life is what *you* make of it,' then the next question concerns why and how seafarers from all over the world have come to work on board cruise ships. The cruise ship is not just a large structured leisure site from which cruise passengers experience pleasure. Importantly, it is the work place of migrants from all over the world whose labour makes possible cruise lines' production, and passenger-tourists' consumption of pleasure at sea. The next chapter offers an analysis of seafarer recruitment and employment conditions.

Chapter 5

'Mini-United Nations': Foreign Migrant Labour on Cruise Ships

The bulk of cruise line employees are from countries where employment opportunities are limited and training is scarce. The industry provides the opportunity to travel, free medical care and upward mobility, particularly for women from developing nations.

World Travel and Tourism Council (2002, 14)

Modern cruise ships, indeed, are a testament to human ingenuity. The marriage of shaped metal, glass and wood that house and move thousands of people at once over water cannot but command attention. Cruise ships in the midst of loading and unloading passengers, seafarers, baggage and supplies may be even more awe-inspiring given the logistics involved in coordinating constant movements of cargo, as well as the salient presence of seafarers from so many countries of the world.

At any time during the peak cruising seasons, US home ports and ports of call in the Caribbean, Mexico and Alaska will host two or more cruise ships. For smaller ports of call unable to accommodate more than two at once, the first arriving ships (or those with priority) are berthed directly at the slip to debark passengers and crew, whereas later arriving ones will have to use tenders (small boats that bring passengers from the ship to the dock) to bring passengers and crew shore side. Seafarers who know of their compatriots or friends arriving simultaneously on different ships may look for one another at predesignated hang-outs, after which they can dine or shop together if permitted by the length of shore leave. For retail and wholesale businesses at or near these ports of call, revenue earned from cruise ship crew has become as important as that from passenger expenditure. Seafarers' purchases are significant sources of revenue for shore side businesses (Davidson 2004; Millman 2004). Assuming that two large ships respectively carrying over two thousand persons (passengers and crew) arrive at the same time, and each ship debarks an average of one thousand persons, then the local port community may host at least two thousand passengers and seafarers.

Once passengers have debarked at a port, there will be constant streams of seafarers rushing to use public pay phones and/or waiting to board seafarers' mission-arranged buses (depending on the port of call, some cruise lines also arrange transportation for their crew) to the nearest shopping malls/wholesale outlets. Seafarers may have shore leave ranging from less than an hour to a one-half day depending on their job responsibilities. For many, shore leave is an opportunity to telephone and check-in with their loved ones overseas. Those with longer breaks may opt to go shopping for gifts or to replenish supplies of laundry powder, instant noodles, personal toiletries and snacks sold by seafarers' missions located in the vicinity or by large retail or outlet firms. Even though cruise ships carry some supplies for seafarers, many prefer to buy them elsewhere because of lower shoreside prices.

If one were to observe as I did the debarkation and activities of seafarers, it is quite easy to tell apart seafarers of different nationalities, e.g., senior marine and security officers from specific Western European countries, Bulgarian and Turkish engineers, Filipino waiters, Indonesian cabin stewards, Caribbean bar stewards, El Salvadoran assistant waiters, Canadian and British entertainers, South Asian bar managers and so forth. Many were still in their respective uniforms that identified those who worked in galleys and cabins, from those in the engine room and on the deck. All wore badges bearing their respective names followed by countries of origin. Preferred language of conversation (e.g., Bulgarian, Tagalog, Spanish) further delineated the social boundaries of these small groups as they mingled dockside, queued for access to payphones, shopped or strolled around the area.

As discussed in Chapter 1, the most forthcoming seafarers over the course of interviews were Indonesian and Filipino crew members who kept asking me if I was from their respective homelands. Once I informed them that I originally came from Malaysia, Indonesian seafarers immediately relaxed and engaged me in conversation because it comforted them (*'senang hati'* or 'ease of heart') to interact with someone from the region. Even so, they constantly looked around us as if trying to see if anyone else was listening to our conversation. When I asked Hamid, an Indonesian seafarer who worked as a dishwasher why he kept glancing the perimeter, he answered in *Bahasa Indonesia* that he had to be sure no one made note of his conversation with me namely because they were not supposed to interact with passengers, union representatives and/or newsprint reporters.

Some of the more senior officers tended to keep to themselves. I did not observe them mingling with support staff (the next section will discuss an underlying occupational divide interlaced with nationality and class), and they did not elect to speak with me to any great length during their time on shore. However, I did witness a few instances in which Asian and Eastern European seafarers who worked in the same shipboard department converse together in English about nearby restaurants and/or the cost of supplies. On the whole, seafarers interacted mostly with their compatriots at the port of call. Hence, a walking distance of about 10-20 feet in any direction yielded a variety of different languages being spoken among respective seafarer groups.

When buses returned to the port, seafarers carried large shopping bags filled with personal items and/or gifts back on to the ship. Within a few hours, remaining seafarers all had embarked the ship to prepare for a new itinerary and group of passengers. Those who ran out of time to telephone their loved ones overseas would likely wait until the next port of call (instead of paying the prohibitively expensive rates for using satellite-based shipboard telephone systems).

This brief vignette brings up important questions regarding seafarers on cruise ships. Why and how are migrant workers from so many countries recruited to work as seafarers on these ships? Who does what kind of work, for what level of wages and why? Do women work on cruise ships, and if so from what countries do they come, and in what positions do they work? Finally, how does the presence of so many different nationalities affect intercultural relations and communication at sea?

From Land to Sea

To reiterate, the phenomenon of migration-for-employment is a cause and an effect of labour deregulation or 'flexibilization' processes characterizing the construction and integration of free market economies. On land, labour flexibilization processes generally are observed to have originated in the manufacturing sector toward the end of the twentieth century. 'Core' ('skilled') or permanent workers were asked to perform more tasks and to take on more responsibilities, while 'peripheral' ('semi- and unskilled') workers saw their jobs being contracted out to third parties (and in some cases, eventually off-shored) resulting in lower wages, no job security or benefits (Atkinson 1984; Standing 1999). These respective examples of 'internal' and 'external' flexibilization processes would take on an international (especially with the encouragement of major labour-sending states) and increasingly transnational dimension (the integration of migrants' material and symbolic ties to both sending and receiving countries) as workers migrated across national borders for employment. In major labour-receiving countries, different sectors' secondary and tertiary labour markets of low wage temporary workers began to exhibit unique stratifications. Despite controversial public debates on immigration in major labour-receiving countries of the Global North and South, states are complicit in the stratification processes via immigration rules that directly and indirectly encourage an association of specific occupations with corresponding intersections of migrants' nationality, class, race/ethnicity and gender.

Some scholars of tourism studies, however, assert that labour flexibilization processes in this sector predate that of the manufacturing sector largely because of the former's inherent 'seasonal and spatial' dimensions of employment (see, for example, Shaw and Williams 1994; Urry 2002; Williams and Hall 2000). By the late twentieth century and in the midst of the transnationalization of migration, secondary labour markets of low wage tourism workers evinced similar characteristics as local migrant workers gradually could be and were replaced by foreign workers (see, for example Harris 1995). As a result, tourism employment structures and patterns also gradually became stratified according to different intersections of identity modalities (Shaw and Williams 1994; Sinclair 1997; Urry 2002).

Still, not all low wage workers come from poorer labour-sending countries. There are also young adults from the middle classes of 'post-industrial' societies in the US and the EU who cross borders in search of tourism-related work. What has been observed on land thus is the phenomenon of 'migrant tourist-workers' who seek employment as part of the 'touristic experience', thus obscuring the distinction between work and leisure (Adler and Adler 1999; Bianchi 2000).

Parallel processes and outcomes of deregulating or flexibilizing labour occur out on the high seas as states with open and second ship registries privilege the demands of capital over that of labour. Nonetheless there exists a key difference. While such flag states explicitly (or, at least endeavour to) control and manage the in-migration of landed foreign workers, their open or second registries do not do so. In the main, foreign seafarers are not considered potential economic and social-cultural threats to society because they need never set foot in the country of ship registry. Open registries, by eliminating citizenship requirements for the employment of seafarers (or, relaxing citizenship requirements in the case of second registries) encourage cruise lines to comb the globe for labour: migrant workers are recruited from all over the world after which they travel to designated foreign ports to embark their ships.

Many seafarers sign labour contracts with crewing agencies in their home countries to work for a cruise line in which the holding corporation is registered in one country, while the cruise line is headquartered in another country, and its ships are flagged by a third or a fourth country. From the perspective of a unique maritime regulatory structure in which open registries (and, to a lesser extent second registries) explicitly encourage and legitimize the flexibilization of seafaring labour, it may be appropriate to conceptualize foreign migrant seafarers as 'denationalized' or even 'stateless' migrant workers at sea, rather than that of 'transnational' workers per se.

As we shall see however, even in the absence of flag state immigration regulations, labour flexibilization at sea is not as clear-cut as a simple correlation of 'the lower the labour costs, the higher the profits'. The association of specific intersections of nationality, class, race/ethnicity and gender with specific shipboard positions cannot but expose the extent to which persistent stereotypes inform and are informed by the recruitment and employment of foreign seafarers on modern cruise ships. Seafarers from the Global North who are considered 'white' can be found mostly in higher ranked status and waged positions, while 'others' from the Global South generally are found at the bottom of the hierarchy with concomitantly assigned or denied privileges and benefits. Men, notably, outnumber women even though 'service' is the fulcrum on which rests the business of deep ocean pleasure cruising. In this light, a phenomenon of 'feminizing' men occurs on cruise ships when those from specific nationalities are constituted as better service providers (but not necessarily in higher level positions or wages) than their counterparts elsewhere because of perceived national cultural traits. Cruise lines' employment of foreign seafarers in the production of pleasure on their ships has the effect of resurrecting an uneasy spectre of social stratification reminiscent of colonialism.

Seafarer Recruitment and Terms of Employment

There are early twentieth century records of British seafarers on passenger ships who complained of harsh working conditions (and for some, even the personal expense of paying for their uniforms and/or kitchen knives required to perform their jobs):

> Sightseers who 'swarmed over the ship in hundreds' to admire its grace and beauty 'never saw the glory hole,' which he shared with twenty-four other 'tired-eyed and weary' boys who put in long days scrubbing decks, polishing brass and furniture 'until everything was immaculate' and the ship was ready to 'hold court' with its admiring public (Coons and Varias 2003, 69)

Stewards had some of the most gruelling work cleaning public rooms, serving meals and preparing cabins: 'they worked seven days each week, had little shore leave, and never received overtime'. At that time, men seafarers overwhelmingly dominated employment on passenger ships. In this masculinized maritime workplace, men stewards performed the 'soft work' taking care of passengers (Coons and Varias 2003, 76).

Even though women workers eventually joined their male compatriots on passenger ships, seafarers from other regions of the world gradually would outnumber them. For example, housekeepers on HAL ships mostly were Dutch men and Norwegian women prior to the 1970s. When unionized Dutch stewards began demanding higher wages, HAL abandoned its transatlantic service routes, and focused instead on pleasure cruising particularly in the Caribbean. By reflagging its ships to the Netherlands Antilles, HAL legally could replace European crew members with what was then called the 'Caribbean crew...[an] industry catchword indicating a polyglot of nationalities serving on one vessel' (Maxtone-Graham 1985, 267). HAL eventually recruited the majority of stewards for work in its cruise ships' hotel division from Indonesia and to a lesser extent, the Philippines. The cruise line even established a center in Bandung, Indonesia to train Indonesian seafarers. Since then, it has become the norm to recruit workers globally for all categories of seafaring labour on mass market cruise lines. Variously named by cruise directors as 'multinational', 'diverse' and even 'floating- or mini-UN' crew, these phrases encapsulate, typify and celebrate the presence of seafarers from all over the world.[1] Men, nevertheless, remain the dominant gender employed on cruise ships.

Seafarers and their labour are situated at the intersection of mass market cruise lines' production and passengers' consumption of pleasure at sea. There are over 110,000 seafarers on cruise ships today: 70 per cent in the hotel division, 20 per cent in the marine division and 10 per cent in concessionaires such as spas, health and fitness centres and photography shops (Mather 2002, 11). Unlike cargo ships that have witnessed gradual shrinkages of shipboard work force, mass market cruise lines' growth continues to generate demands for labour, especially in the hotel division of cruise ships. Many in this division are temporary contract workers from the Global South.

It is estimated that only 50 per cent of seafarers are covered by unions. Major cruise lines such as Royal Caribbean and NCL have signed International Transport Workers' Federation (ITF) approved collective bargaining agreements (CBA). Transportation unions in labour-sending countries that are affiliated with the ITF negotiate minimum standards for shipboard employment, e.g., Royal Caribbean workers are covered by a Norwegian Seafarers' Union (NSU) negotiated CBA. NSU also serves as a lead negotiator on behalf of unions elsewhere in the world (Oyen 2005). Royal Caribbean pays their employees' union dues but does not deduct the

---

1 Some cruise directors tend to favour the phrases 'floating UN' or 'mini-UN'. In a 2004 cruise that I took, the cruise director and his assistants invoked them during an emergency drill at the beginning of the voyage, and again during the last night's entertainment program. Researchers who travelled on cruise ships also have written of similar experiences (see especially Garin 2005; R. Klein 2002a; Wood 2000).

contributions from their wages. Carnival, that is known to prohibit their crew from interacting with, or being represented by ITF affiliates, has not signed a CBA at this time of writing.

The mass hiring of seafarers especially from South and Southeast Asia began in earnest during the 1980s, and was extended globally to those from Eastern Europe, Central and East Asia, and Latin America by the early 2000s (ILO 2001; Lane 2001). As 'migrant workers of the oceans', many seafarers are recruited by crewing agencies in their countries of origin (Frantz 1999a). Approximately 74 per cent of cruise lines rely on crewing agents for recruitment. Importantly, ILO conventions prohibit crewing agencies from charging seafarers placement fees (ILO 2001, 44), and cruise lines are expected to bear costs such as seafarers' roundtrip airfares and lodging prior to embarkation. Nonetheless, there have been many reports of crewing agencies that pass the cost to seafarers because, as some of them allege, cruise lines refuse to reimburse them (ICONS 2000, 58-9; Nielsen 2000). Major cruise lines are aware of this illegal practice as they warn prospective applicants on their websites against paying such fees.

Although many cruise lines accept on-line employment applications, in the main they are for specialty and front-line positions, e.g., casino managers, information technology specialists, executive chefs, sous chefs, gift shop sales representative and entertainers. In other words, cruise lines' direct internet recruitment efforts are geared toward what may be considered 'white collar' positions. This discernibly class-based approach then relegates recruitment of 'blue collar positions' mostly to crewing agencies.

In my interviews of active seafarers from the Philippines and Indonesia, home country agency fees ranged from USD500-1250, while the ILO reported fees of USD1200-1500 (ILO 2001, 44). Klein's research identified agency fees that reached upward of USD4000 (R. Klein 2002a, 128). Budi, a seafarer from Indonesia who paid USD850 in agency fees (USD650 for a one-way ticket and USD200 for 'administrative fees') about five years ago, informed me that some of his compatriots paid as much as several thousands of dollars to secure employment on cruise ships. Some seafarers begin work in debt and depending on monthly wages they may have to work several temporary contracts before collapsing the debt (Reynolds and Weikel 2000). However, in interviews with two former seafarers, Felipe from Peru and Irina from Estonia (both left the industry after approximately seven years of cruise ship work) Felipe did not have to pay any agency fees while Irina paid an estimated USD250 for placement. Both said that they were aware of their Asian counterparts having paid substantially higher fees for placement on cruise ships.

Interviews with two former labour brokers based in Kuala Lumpur, Malaysia confirmed the practice of charging prospective seafarers exorbitant placement fees. According to them, the standard fee was US2500 regardless of nationality. Those who could not afford to pay the entire fee upfront either would have to repay it from their monthly wages, or would have to borrow it elsewhere. Workers were recruited from neighbouring countries such as Indonesia, Philippines, Thailand and Burma for cruise lines with Asian and/or European, US, Mexico and Caribbean itineraries. All were expected at least to have rudimentary command of the English language. The seafarers signed contracts with crewing agencies which then arranged for their travel to designated embarkation ports. One broker acknowledged that the profits were 'very good' but that after three years of 'helping' recruit seafarers, he decided to quit because the profits 'came from the blood of these people…I make whether or not they can afford to pay me because they have to pay me, you know, if they want to work. It is not up to me what happens [to them] after I find them the job'.[2]

Of significance also is that unregulated recruitment practices put into question the quality of seafarer background or security checks prior to placement on cruise ships. Recent global media attention implicating seafarers in cases of missing passengers, sexual assault and/or other criminal acts on cruise ships point to the need for industry-wide accreditation of crewing agencies as well as standardized security clearance procedures. One cruise line executive, in his testimony at the 2006 congressional hearing on 'International Maritime Security II", insisted that his company had set in place a three-level vetting process, i.e., from a seafarer's initial interview, followed by the 'C1/D' crew visa application to the US Department of State (for those who will work on ships with US home ports or itineraries) and finally, immigration and customs clearance upon arrival at the first US port of entry. His cruise line's policy 'is not to hire any foreign national if the vetting process uncovers a criminal past' (US House of Representatives 2006, 229-230). A central issue here is not that cruise lines deliberately will hire 'shady' seafarers. Instead, it concerns cruise lines' reliance on non-accredited crewing agencies for the initial recruitment and vetting phases. Depending on the country, there may or may not be clear regulations stipulating licensing requirements for crewing agencies, together with oversight of their practices. As previously discussed, crewing agencies in some sending countries have ignored ILO regulations without impunity.

The internet's global reach, to be sure, has had contradictory effects on seafarer recruitment. On the one hand, many crewing agencies are able to set up websites to recruit seafarers. While some agencies based in North America, for example, recruit seafarers only for white collar positions, others are more diverse in terms of positions and nationalities. Seafarers thus are able to traverse national borders in their cyberspatial search for employment opportunities. On the other hand, seafarers and other licensed crewing agencies are susceptible to the practices of 'fly-by-night' agencies on the internet.

The ITF continues to warn prospective applicants of 'bogus' crewing agency websites that offer 'non-existent employment in exchange for cash up-front' operating out of countries such as Nigeria, Panama and Canada. In 2005, the ITF identified 14 websites under investigation (ITF 2005b). One of the key ways in which these agencies masquerade as legitimate ones is to take information from the latter to publish on their websites. Among them is the website of Sea Cruise Enterprise. It is worthwhile still to examine the website's information on job responsibilities to prospective applicants because such information makes explicit the largely unregulated nature of shipboard work. The website posted a sample contract for the position of second officer:

---

2 Neither of the brokers agreed to disclose names of the crewing agencies, and after much prodding on my part, they insisted that the interconnections were too complicated for me to comprehend.

[The] Employee acknowledges that the scope of his/her duties will require work at irregular hours including weekends and holidays. There will be no set working schedule and Employee working hours will vary in accordance with the necessities of the cruise program.

Aside from varying work hours, the scope of duties also is wide:

Employee shall perform in such shows and assisting such other activities as are deemed necessary or appropriate by the Management or Employer'. S/he will be given opportunities to go on shore 'provided that employee has no other duties aboard the vessel.

Importantly, the employee cannot hold the cruise line liable for quality of medical care ('Employer does not warrant the adequacy of such medical treatment of the vessel's medical facilities and will not be responsible for any claims arising therein') in particular, and overall working conditions in general:

Employee covenant and agree to hold the Employer, its affiliates, agent, servant and employees, harmless from any and all loss and/or damages of property and personal injury sustained, or illness contracted, from whatever cause or causes arising out of, or in connection with Employees services or presence on board the vessel (Sea Cruise Enterprise, 'Sample Contract').

These contract terms are weighted heavily against the prospective employee: the terms, in effect, indemnify the employer even from work-related liabilities. That seafarer-applicants from all over the world paid exorbitant fees to this bogus website (that was taken down by mid 2006) is telling of some of the conditions that elicit demands for paid employment beyond their home countries.

Whether migrant workers need or want to work on cruise ships, the major benefits of being hired to do so are that seafarers' hard work will be offset by unprecedented opportunities to see the world while they earn tax-free wages in a foreign currency such as the US dollar or the Euro, receive shipboard health coverage as well as free board and lodging. Accompanying the allure of tax-free wages for low wage contract seafarers particularly in the hotel division, however, are inordinately long work days, the absence of employer contributions to retirement/pension accounts, paid vacations or even sick pay as delineated by ILO conventions: 'what's different about the cruise industry is you have the same kind of exploitative conditions going on, but they're all lawful' (Nielsen 2000). Such exploitative practices are legitimized by flag state regulations or lack thereof.

In the realm of medical insurance, illnesses contracted and injuries sustained on board are to be treated by the ship's medical doctor and/or nurse. Since international maritime law does not stipulate the presence of shipboard medical personnel nor their accreditation, then there is no guarantee that incidences of shipboard sickness or injury will be diagnosed and treated accurately. There is a long list of litigated cases concerning medical misdiagnosis of passengers and seafarers that in some instances, resulted in deaths (Dickerson 2004). In other documented cases, sick or injured seafarers were prescribed pain medication until the ship reached its next port of call. According to US regulations, ship owners with substantial interests in the US must provide sick pay (regular, overtime and if appropriate, the average amount of expected tips) to seafarers until the end of their contract. Yet, some cruise lines have been reported to provide only base pay to sick or injured crew (Frantz 1999a; Nielsen 2000). There also are reports of seafarers being taken ashore at the next port of call only to be sent back home for further medical treatment: cruise lines' responsibility to them ends once they are taken ashore. Retention of a nineteenth century international maritime law that fails to mandate the provision and quality of medical care on ships, in effect indemnifies ship owners and makes vulnerable the health and welfare of cruise ship passengers and seafarers (Dickerson 2004; Frantz 1999c).

Benefits for seafarers vary according to shipboard positions. Seafarers are divided into two major categories of the marine (deck and engine) and hotel divisions that together are overseen by the ship's captain. The head of each division respectively is the chief officer/mate and hotel manager, followed by junior officers and lastly ratings or support staff who commonly are referred as 'crew': 'A ship is a paramilitary organization, in which officers wear uniforms, and regulations, laws, rank, and discipline play a prominent role in the way things get done' (Dickinson and Vladimir 1997, 73). An ILO study found that cruise ship officers are the highest paid in the global shipping sector as they earn fixed monthly wages and may be awarded bonuses at the end of each voyage, season or year, while some crew positions are among the lowest paid in the sector (ILO 2001, 61). Crew positions come with significantly lower salaries and relatively 'longer' temporary contracts of anywhere from six to 12 months without paid vacations. Succinctly put, 'the more menial the task, the longer the term of the contract' (R. Klein 2002a, 118). These seafarers are required to share cabins and generally are not provided with roundtrip air-fare and overnight hotel room prior to embarking the ship.[3] They also are required to dine in mess halls separate from officers and/or passengers. At the end of their contract, seafarers are expected to return to their home country for a two to three month non-paid break, after which they can reapply to work for the same cruise line or for a new employer.

Within the cruise industry, the average length of employment in the hotel division has declined from three years in 1970, to 18 months in 1990, and eight to ten months in 2000 (ILO-SIRC 2003, 8). Interviews with active seafarers indicate that some cruise lines now offer only temporary contracts that are six months in length. Depending on the cruise line, seafarers who work for concessionaires (e.g., cruise lines contract-out spa, health and fitness, beauty salon services) may be called 'staff' to distinguish them from the crew (see later discussion). Their terms of employment (e.g., wages, tips, rest days and so forth) are determined by the concessionaires and not cruise lines, hence these categories of seafarers earn higher salaries and are given more benefits than seafarers in lower level hotel positions.

---

3 On newer cruise ships, it is an average of two seafarers per cabin. In many of the older ships and even on some new ships, the average may be as high as four persons per cabin. This is the case with NCL ships partly because of the shift to 'freestyle cruising' that requires additional space and service for alternative restaurants that then reduce cabin space to house seafarers.

Table 5.1   Select Cruise Ship Crew Positions

Position	Monthly Salary (tax-free USD)	Work (in months)/ Vacation (in weeks)	A*	H	M	S	C	O/P	V
Captain	$5000-6000	3-4 mths/2-5 wks	X	X	X	X	X	X	X
Chief Officer/ Mate	$3750-4200	3-4 mths/2-5 wks	X	X	X	X	X	X	X
Doctor	$4000-5000 (or free cruise)	3-4 mths/2-4 wks free cruising	X	X	X	X		X	X
Hotel Manager	$3800-4700	3-4 mths/2-5 wks	X	X	X	X	X	X	X
Cruise Staff (entry level position)**	$1000-1300	6 mths/ 4 wks	X	X	X	X	X	X	X
Executive Chef	$4300-4875	3-5 mths/4-8 wks	X	X	X	X	X	X	X
Waiter/Waitress	$50 (plus tips) (average monthly wages = $1500-2200)	6-9 mths/4-8 wks	X	X	X		X		
Busboy	$50 (plus tips) (average monthly wages = $1000-1500)	9-12 mths/8-12 wks	X	X	X		X		
Cabin Steward	$50 (plus tips) (no average given)	9-12 mths/8-12 wks	X	X	X		X		
Laundry Man/Helper	$400-600	9-12 mths/8-10 wks	X	X	X		X		

* A = airfare H = overnight hotel (if deemed necessary) M = medical coverage S = single cabin C = crew mess O = officer mess P = passenger dining V = vacation pay

** Vacation pay given at discretion of cruise lines

Source: Global Ship Services, 'Job Description' (and corresponding sections within this webpage).

Data for Table 5.1 was derived from the website of a Florida-based crewing agency, Global Ship Services that has been in business since the late 1980s. The table illustrates, at a glance, differences in seafarer remuneration, benefits and privileges according to select cruise ship positions.[4] Unlike land-based workers, the length of employment contracts is inversely related to position and wage level. As the table highlights, senior officer positions of the captain and chief mate have shorter work contracts with paid vacations than that of the cabin steward and laundry helper who have longer contract terms without paid vacations. The former group who are given paid vacations may be considered 'company men' or core employees whereas the

---

4 Information from the website was derived in July 2005. At some point after this, Global Ship Services appeared to have been the victim of a bogus crewing agency. Global Ship Services then published an announcement warning applicants that it was *not* affiliated with 'Global Cruise Shipping Services': 'They [Global Cruise Shipping Services] have been defrauding people by using information from this website as well as other legitimate companies'.

latter are peripheral or contract workers who do not have the guarantee of continued employment (assuming they have demonstrated competence) with a cruise line at the end of their contracts.

The director of NSU in Miami confirmed that senior officers generally have job security or long term employment. However, he emphasized that even though many of the hotel staff strictly are contract workers, they often can be and are asked to return to work by their cruise line employers (but not necessarily for the same ship on which they previously sailed): these seafarers have 'fairly secure employment because [the] cost of training is so high'. He also acknowledged that even though the conduct of some cruise lines may have been 'arbitrary' in the past, i.e., 'do as the ship pleased [in response to documented cases of labour exploitation and environmental pollution]', the major cruise lines are 'now, becoming more professional in [their] conduct' because of two intersecting forces, i.e., newsprint reports ('bad press'), in addition to the industry's gradual maturation process ('learning curve') (Oyen 2005).

What often goes unsaid is the fact that future employment opportunities for low wage contract seafarers are not guaranteed after one sailing: their status as contract workers means that jobs do not need to be accompanied by benefits such as long term health care, pensions or paid vacation breaks. Open and second registries permit and legitimize cruise line employment of low wage contract foreign seafarers in the capacity of full-time workers but without the requisite job security, full rest days, vacation pay, pension and/or long term health coverage. Thus, industry adoption of short term seafarer contracts that, ironically are becoming longer in length (in relation to that of ship officers) effectively leads to the legitimate 'recycling' of low wage seafarers today (Petitpas 2005).

Certain shipboard jobs such as those of serving meals and cleaning cabins often receive the lowest monthly base pay of USD50. For these seafarers, the bulk of their income is to be augmented by passenger gratuities/tips or fixed service charges. On cruise lines such as Celebrity, Disney and Royal Caribbean 'suggested' approximate gratuities (that can be prepaid by passengers) range from approximately USD3-3.50 per person, per day for cabin and dining stewards, and USD1-2.00 per day for busboys. Other cruise lines such as NCL, Carnival, Princess and HAL have implemented a mandatory USD10.00 per day service charge to be shared by the crew (Cruise Critic, 'Features' 'Cruise Lines Tipping Policies' n.d.), but it is unknown as to the specific way in which that dollar amount is apportioned. As 'CruiseCriticPoster34' reminded other members in their discussion on tips (see Chapter Four), fixed service charges can be and are shared by even more seafarers, hence reducing the total monthly income for dining room and cabin stewards.

The cruise line practice of augmenting minimal base pay for some categories of seafarers in the hotel division either with passenger gratuities or fixed service charges has the two-pronged objective of reducing total shipboard labour costs (hence making the overall cost of cruise vacations more affordable for consumers), and presumably encouraging seafarers to perform customer service at their very best (especially since passengers can exceed the suggested tipping guidelines or fixed amount of service charges). Yet, if cruise lines are driven to make vacations more affordable for passengers by not paying fixed salaries to some seafarers, then why not extend this practice of giving base monthly wages to other categories of seafaring work in the hotel division that, in turn, can encourage more seafarers to perform at their very best?

The seafarers whom I interviewed expressed a key tension in the relationship between nature of work and related compensation levels. Bakri, an Indonesian 'assistant waiter' said to me while standing in line to use the public pay phone that he had worked in the industry for five years while earning a monthly base income of USD50. When tips were included, his average income rose approximately to USD400-550 per month. He said that the salary allowed him to take care of his spouse, children and extended family members in Indonesia, which then left him with no disposable income. Bakri's friend Raymond (a Christian from one of the outer islands in Indonesia), earned a similar monthly income to support his nuclear family in addition to several nephews and nieces. Raymond laughed as he mentioned that after seven years of employment on cruise ships, he would have been a rich man ('*orang kaya*') if not for the fact that he had to support so many household members.

Budi, their friend and compatriot, did not share Bakri's and Raymond's sentiment on cruise ship employment. Although he also earned a base pay of USD50 in addition to gratuities, Budi insisted that wages were not commensurate with the amount and nature of work required of him as a waiter. He said that he worked at least 15 hour days serving three meals in the main dining rooms, cleaning up after meals as well as other miscellaneous tasks assigned by his supervisor. In his fifth year of work, Budi had applied for a promotion to head waiter but was rejected several times. When I asked him what he believed to be the reason, he touched his arm and said that it was not of the same colour as his supervisor (who was from England). He intended to work for another three years if possible before quitting the industry.

As the four of us spoke, a Filipino cabin steward still in his uniform, rushed toward us only to find long queues at the public pay phones. Jorge paced impatiently and said that he did not have all day to wait and telephone his family in the Philippines. When I asked him why he was in such a rush, he replied by saying that certain categories of staff (he cocked his head toward a group of British and Canadian seafarers who were chatting and laughing as they waited for a bus to take them to a shopping mall) were given many hours of break whereas he only had 20 minutes to debark the ship and make his phone call. He was expected to return to the ship to help set up for the new group of passengers. He had had enough after four years on cruise ships because 'it is very hard work'. Moreover, since the ship had sailed its previous itinerary at slightly above half capacity, Jorge's monthly salary was significantly lower because tips 'depend on the guests'. He kept saying that his total monthly salary 'goes up and down'.

Later in the day, I met Jorge's compatriot Benjamin, a deck attendant who earned a fixed salary of USD1200 per month ensuring supplies (lounge chairs, towels and so forth) were in order for the open decks, cleaning them, and so forth. Benjamin did not hold the same view as Jorge, insisting that his friend had a good opportunity to support his wife and children in the Philippines: 'Hey, my friend [Jorge], you can make money for your family, what's the problem?' When Jorge reminded Benjamin that his friend's fixed monthly salary at least was twice the amount earned by Jorge,

Benjamin nodded, smiled and said that he (Benjamin) was lucky, 'I am blessed by God'. Benjamin easily could dispense such advice to his friend because he believed that he was well compensated for his labour. Jorge, on the other hand, reminded Benjamin that he was responsible for cleaning approximately 13-15 cabins ('I vacuum, I clean shower, I make bed, I wipe furniture'), providing evening turn-down service, room service (meals and other), as well as delivering and removing luggage for each cabin. His labour is evaluated not only by the head housekeeper but importantly it is evaluated and majority-compensated by passengers. Prospects for future contract renewals depend on both kinds of evaluations. Jorge then asked Benjamin, 'Why don't we switch jobs? Then you can tell me if God still bless[es] you'. Benjamin nodded and remained silent.

Shortly thereafter, Belén an assistant bar steward from Honduras who sat on a nearby rock turned around, looked at us and shook his head. He had been working on the ship for nearly two years and was upset about the base pay and low amount of tips. He added that shipboard work stripped 'people of our human-ness…we are expected to smile and be happy all the time, even when some of them [he looked at a group of passengers entering the terminal and then at some men in officer uniforms] are rude'. When I asked Belén if he could explain further his point, he responded by saying that 'You never know who is listening. I still need this job but you know, it is not fair…very tiring'. He turned his attention away from us and gazed at the horizon.

Benny and Francisco, Filipino seafarers who respectively worked as a dining steward and a cabin steward, shared with me that they dreaded the ship's European itinerary because European passengers did not tip as much. Benny, in particular, said that European passengers were 'stingy'. If given the option, both would want to work only on ships that carried US passengers. Benny also said that 'Americans have no problems giving tips. Some are generous'. Francisco added, 'Yes, they follow the instruction card [cruise line's suggested tipping guidelines] and they always say 'Thank you'. They are ordinary people, not [his nose points to the sky connoting what he considered the European ethos of snobbery]'.

An ILO study found that seafarers working primarily on the European and Asian routes tend to get paid relatively higher wages than their counterparts working on the North American and Caribbean routes because tipping is not a cultural practice in many European or Asian countries (ILO 2001, 63). In light of the ease with which many cruise ships can be repositioned for different seasons, there is little guarantee of steady monthly income for those whose cruise ship may spend the summer in Europe and the winter in the Caribbean.

Depending on the cruise line, seafarers employed directly by concessionaires may be considered 'staff' as opposed to 'crew'. 'CruiseCriticPoster62' in her post to an e-discussion thread on crew members, shared with fellow posters that she worked for Carnival. She also informed them that 'spa and fitness staff, casino staff and gift shop staff are actually not staffed by Carnival/the cruise line itself, they each have prospective companies taht [sic] the cruise lines contract out' (Cruise Critic, 'Boards' 26 November 2005). In another reply to a poster's query on looking for shipboard employment, 'CruiseCriticPoster63' who used to work on cruise ships wrote that:

'I have done contract work as part of the entertainment staff. Luckily, since I worked for the CD [cruise director], I had passenger privileges which makes a difference. My shipboard emplyoyees (6 month contracts) did not. I was in a passenger cabin - minimum cateogry [sic] - but it was way better than the crew decks' (Cruise Critic, 'Boards' 8 June 2006).

Although major cruise lines are not known to contract out marine operations, they can and do subcontract with companies or concessionaires specializing in retail goods, health and fitness, and spa services and products. Employees of concessionaires have better terms of work, higher salaries and more benefits. Massage therapists, hairdressers, and physical trainers, for example, are paid monthly salaries and some may even earn a percentage of shipboard generated sales profits. Another poster, 'CruiseCriticPoster64' recounted his conversation with a staff member:

'I was chatting with the girl on Sapphire who did the airbrush tattoos. I noticed she was from Canada which was how we got to talking. She said that since she didn't work for Princess, she wasn't required to do other duties when her tattoo booth wasn't open. She had to wear her name badge at all times in public but was allowed to partake in passenger activities on a space available basis. I don't know where she ate, but I'm sure it was in the crew area. Her cabin, which she had to herself, was on deck 4 at first, then she moved up to deck 5 where the entertainers who came and went through the week stayed' (Cruise Critic, 'Boards' 8 June 2006).

Posters on Cruise Critic's Boards who either were former or active seafarers confirmed the advantages of being considered 'staff' as opposed to 'crew'. In her response to a post on crew quarters, 'CruiseCriticPoster62' compared the benefits respectively given to staff and crew:

'Crew are NOT to be in passenger areas when they are not working. This is very much a no no...these are the hardest working people I've ever seen in my life. I have so much respect for them, I truly don't know how they do it. Their hours are crazy. An example I have (might be a bit off) a food and beverage crew member works 16-18 hour days, 7 days a week straight (ie NO days off for their entire 6-8 month contract..) again, different departments will be different, and I could be totally wrong, but that's to my knowledge. staff-it really varies here too. gift shoppies work crazy hours on sea days (like 14 hour days) but then they are off whenever we're in port (since the shops can't be open) so they can have almost entire days off. They pay for them though on those sea days!... We [staff] honestly have it pretty good' (Cruise Critic, 'Boards' 26 November 2005).

My interviews of concessionaire workers confirmed 'CruiseCriticPoster62's' assertion that staff have better working conditions than crew. For instance, only young women in their early twenties (who referred to themselves as 'spa girls') worked in their cruise ship's spa: one hailed from a Scandinavian country while the rest came from South Africa. One of the South African women, Alexis, said that they applied to work on a cruise ship as 'a good way to see the world and earn some money'. These 'migrant tourist-workers' were sent to London for training, after which they travelled to another European port to board the cruise ship. Their monthly salaries were over USD1000, excluding tips from passengers as well as a percentage of profits from the sale of spa products. The women were housed two to a cabin, and they were allowed to dine with passengers. Julie commented that '[We are] unlike the crew. They eat separately and live on deck #4. They cannot go to the guest public areas'. Thokozile, her friend, chimed in by saying that they enjoyed the shipboard 'good life' when compared to the rest of the crew. Their supervisor gave them four one-half days and one full rest day per month while other crew members worked longer hours without rest days. Despite her youth, Alexis pointedly commented that life on the cruise ship 'is not reality. It is like a dream. No one ever lives like that in their own homes'.

Passengers' 'dream' experience, to be sure, is made possible by the labour of seafarers. An average workday ranges anywhere between 12-16 hours for seafarers especially in the housekeeping, restaurant and galley departments. Cabin stewards are expected to clean staterooms at least twice a day, provide room service, deliver/ remove passenger luggage and any other tasks assigned by the head or assistant housekeeper. Galley and restaurant workers are responsible for breakfast, lunch and dinner service, the latter of which may end late in the evening. Many seafarers then work a seven-day week that can total between 90-100 hours (see especially R. Klein 2002a; Mather 2002; Nielsen 2000).

Nature and length of the workday was partly why former seafarers Felipe and Irina—who met and fell in love on board a cruise ship—decided to quit their jobs. Both had worked for the same cruise line and on the same ships with winter itineraries in the Caribbean and summer itineraries in Europe and the Mediterranean. Irina, who had worked as a cabin steward said that her job was 'very, very tiring'. She and her co-workers were expected to clean between 16-21 cabins twice a day. After each cleaning, the assistant housekeeper would put on white gloves to check for dust. From Irina's perspective, '[We] cleaned not for passengers but for our supervisor'. Some of her co-workers responded to the heavy workload by hiring others to help them. Felipe agreed that his spouse's job was much more strenuous ('She was exploited more than me') than his job as a waiter. Importantly, he shared with me that 'You learn the system. Once you know, then it is not so bad…[it is a] mafia-like system, everything you must pay for and must know people to get things done. It's who you know, one hand washes the other'.

An informal shipboard economy existed in Felipe's and Irina's workplace on various cruise ships as seafarers subcontracted some aspects of their work to co-workers. Especially for those who work in the dining rooms, they also aim to develop good relationships with their supervisors who may assign them choice tasks with regard to time, gratuities and so forth. Newcomers, according to Felipe, had the most difficult time with work assignments either because they were of the 'wrong' nationality, racial/ethnic background, and/or that they were not yet familiar with the existing shipboard work structure and relations.

Active Indonesian and Filipino seafarers appeared to have similar experiences. On occasion, Raymond and Jorge paid others to help them complete certain tasks so that they could get some rest. However, by contracting out some of their responsibilities to other seafarers, Raymond and Jorge earned even lower salaries. As Jorge said, 'there will always be someone who wants to earn more money. Sometimes I do it [pay another seafarer to help him complete his work] but not every time because I won't have enough money each month'. Benny, on the other hand, performed odd jobs as a way to supplement his income. At times, he did so for free especially on behalf of other waiters as well as the restaurant manager in order to develop much needed social capital for favourable table assignments and tasks in the restaurant: 'It is good to build credit. Have credit will travel [taken presumably from his knowledge of the late 1950s US television series]'.

Informal shipboard economies therefore arise as a key seafarer response to the combination of low monthly wages and long labour intensive workdays. Flag state regulations that legalize seafarer labour flexibilization find their expression even within the community of cruise ship crew as seafarers cope with their heavy workload by contracting out some aspects of their work to others.

One major outcome of labour flexibilization is that seafarers in specific support-level positions within the hotel division are expected largely to fend for themselves. It has been reported that a major cruise line even charged its wait staff a deposit of USD50 for restaurant uniforms, and required that they purchase pens to take meal orders (Nielsen 2000; The Sailors' Union of the Pacific 2000). When I asked Felipe whether or not he knew of such cruise line practices or that he was asked to do the same thing, he replied by saying that he and some of his fellow dining room stewards voluntarily purchased 'better wine openers because the ones [supplied by the cruise line were]…no good. If you want good tips, you have to make sure that you can open wine bottles properly'.

Documented exploitative work conditions on cruise ships within the past decade have led some to argue that cruise lines operate 'floating sweatshops' (Coons and Varias 2003, Chapter 4 *passim*) or 'sweatships' (Mather 2002). Among the list of seafarer complaints compiled by the ITF include long hours and low pay, denial of pay and demotions based on passenger complaints (ITF 2005a). Cruise lines are known to deal with worker complaints or organized action by demoting seafarers or terminating their employment. The latter path is especially threatening for seafarers who are designated the status of 'nonimmigrant aliens' or those on 'C1/D' crew visas issued by the US Department of State granting them permission to work on cruise ships based at, or that call at US ports. During the 1980s, Central American crew members engaged in a work strike on board one of Carnival's ships, as did Korean, Jamaican and Haitian crew members on board NCL ships. Both cruise lines declared the strikes illegal, and informed what was then the US Immigration and Naturalization Service (INS) of the seafarers' dismissal. Once notified, the INS required seafarers to be repatriated immediately. In one case, a cruise line made arrangements to have seafarers immediately 'arrested' by private security guards, handcuffed and held until their departure time. This led the INS to announce that it was not necessary to handcuff crew members (Dobbyn 2001). While the practice of handcuffing seafarers may make sense in cases that identify them as alleged perpetrators of sexual or other kinds of assault against passengers or fellow seafarers, it neither is necessary nor appropriate to do so when seafarers engage in non-violent collective action to protest their working conditions. Handcuffing seafarers who protest their work conditions cannot but have an intended effect of criminalizing them.

Increasingly, some seafarers have turned to private US law firms for assistance in addressing work-related disputes.[5] They and their lawyers, however, have to navigate a complex legal environment especially since majority of mass market cruise ships based in the US fly foreign flags while employment contracts are adjudicated in seafarers' home countries. Hence, US courts have no jurisdiction particularly over breach-of-contract cases. The reach of US juridical powers was put to the test in a 2003 law suit against NCL. A Filipina widow sued NCL for negligence after her husband lost his life in a shipboard fire on SS Norway. NCL claimed that the US had no jurisdiction to hear the case, thus shifting it to the Philippines. The Philippines' highest court ultimately ruled that negligence suits could not be handled in the same manner as those concerning salaries. The law suit then could only proceed back in the US. A federal judge in Miami ultimately dismissed the law suit by ruling that seafarers' or survivors' claims must be filed in the Philippines (J. Weaver 2003a and 2003b). On a different issue concerning underpayment of overtime work, Carnival settled two lawsuits in 2006 that were filed by Miami lawyers on behalf of former and active seafarers: the cruise line agreed to pay USD6.25 million to be distributed to over 30,000 seafarers (A. Martinez 2006a).

International maritime law designates flag states as the legal entities responsible for oversight of ships that fly their flags. Although one may assert that it should be in FOC states' interest to strengthen national regulations and to enforce international regulations concerning seafarer recruitment and employment (thereby enhancing their reputations as 'safe' flag states), interstate competition for ship registration fees and tonnage taxes largely mitigates the political will to do so. If cruise ships are reflagged to primary-national registries, then would seafarers' working conditions and responses be much different?

A test case was that of NCL America. In the wake of American Classic Voyages' collapse shortly after 9/11, the Hawai'ian islands were left without a major US flagged cruise line. US Senator Daniel Inouye, in his efforts to address the consequent downturn on Hawai'i's economy, helped NCL win exemption from the Jones Act (Merchant Marine Act of 1920) and the Passenger Services Act of 1886 that barred foreign-built, flagged and crewed ships that transport people from sailing exclusively in US coastal waters without having to call at a foreign port.[6] NCL was

---

5 Oyen asserted that seafarers' complaints were 'a bit of everything' issues ranging from wages to promotion and renewal of contracts. He did, however, point out that 'wage claims' have become a major issue in part because of the involvement of lawyers (i.e., 'they are the ones pushing it and legal costs increase so the company settles') (2005). Martinez identified three well-known lawyers in South Florida who specialize 'in representing injured cruise passengers and crew members'. They are paid on a contingency basis, e.g., '30 percent to 40 percent of settlement'. Cruise lines, on the other hand, have risk management departments staffed by lawyers whose responsibilities include countering these suits. One outcome for seafarers is that 'cruise lines have begun including "arbitration" requirements in their contracts with new crew members in an attempt to curtail filings. The contracts require crew members to go before an arbitration panel to resolve grievances against the cruise line' (A. Martinez 2006b).

6 As stated in the U.S. Passenger Services Act of 1886, 'No foreign vessel shall transport passengers between ports or places in the United States, either directly or by way of a

given permission to do so as long as the cruise line reflagged its ships destined for the islands, promised to build any new ship in the US (such as the *Pride of America* that was built in Northrop Grumman Corporation's Ingalls shipyard in Missisippi, and that went into service in 2005), and abide by US labour regulations.[7] With the creation of NCL America in 2004, the *Norwegian Sky* was reflagged to the US and renamed the *Pride of Aloha* for exclusive sailings around the Hawai'ian waters.

NCL America first looked to US citizens in Hawai'i to work on the *Pride of Aloha*. Inability to attract Hawai'ian workers soon led the cruise line to employ seafarers from the mainland and Guam, in addition to hiring the legal limit of 25 per cent permanent residents. Potential crew members were asked to work ten hour days for a six-day week, which meant that they would earn 40 hours of regular wages and 20 hours of overtime wages (at one and one-half times of base wage). The contract length was six months, of which one month would be considered vacation time (Natarajan 2004). Still, there was a high turnover of seafarers. Major complaints of the US crew were the quasi-military organizational structure's emphasis on discipline, in addition to long work hours and low pay.

One cabin steward complained that she only had a four-hour break in a very long day of cleaning cabins; she had to share a cabin with five other seafarers and that she was given health plan coverage only while she worked on board the ship:

> 'It was awful. It was horrible,' said Brenda Jordan-Ferrari, who moved to Hawai'i from California to take a job with Norwegian and quit after the first week. 'It was definitely one of the hardest weeks of my life. We worked 10 hours a day. When you're not cleaning or working, you're sleeping'.

An NCL representative responded by insisting that US workers on the US-flagged ship ought to be able to do the same kind of work as non-US workers on NCL's foreign flagged ships, 'We have almost no turnover on our international fleet, so I would venture to say without exception [that the US] workers can do it' (Yamanouchi 2004. See also Cruise Critic, 'News' 2004a and 2004b).

In an interview with a former *Pride of Aloha* crew member who left to work for a car rental agency, Cindy recounted her experience with much disdain for the cruise line. She argued that they were interested merely in profits and not the welfare of the crew. She complained of being asked to perform all kinds of 'odd jobs' even though her primary tasks officially were delimited to that of a cabin steward. Cindy said that on the last evening before the conclusion of each voyage, she and her co-workers would spend all night transferring baggage from passenger decks to the storage area, and that on the day of embarkation, she would have to deliver baggage to passenger cabins. She claimed that this was not part of her work contract. She also spoke of 16 hour workdays, cramped cabins, bathrooms with very narrow shower

---

foreign port, under a penalty of $200 for each passenger so transported and landed' (see State Government of Hawaii, n.d.; *New York Times* (n.a.) 16 February 2003).

7 The Fair Labor Standards Act of 1938 that specified among other rights, minimum wage levels, 40-hour week, and over-time pay initially exempted seafarers from such rights. Amendments implemented in 1961 extended coverage to seafarers on US flagged vessels (Nielsen 2000).

stalls ('If you can't even bend a bit in the shower, how can you be clean?'), and crew meals consisting of mostly hot dogs and hamburgers. Cindy alleged that some crew members took amphetamines so that they could stay awake to complete all of their tasks.

From Cindy's perspective, the worst insult occurred when she gave notice to quit. Shortly thereafter, the ship's security personnel escorted her to the cabin and locked her in overnight: 'I am not a criminal. They are the criminals'. After the ship docked at its next port of call, the security personnel checked all of her personal belongings before escorting her off the ramp. She then understood why some seafarers simply walked off the ship without even giving notice. Cindy acknowledged that although 'it is a good vacation for guests [but] they don't know what it is like for us'.

The dominant perception of US seafarers as fussy and arrogant was discussed in an e-discussion thread on Cruise Critic. When a poster inquired about the kind of work he potentially could do on a cruise ship (Cruise Critic, 'Boards' 11 January 2006), 'CruiseCriticPoster65' replied by asking whether or not the poster was a US citizen because:

> 'If you have a US Passport, you may not have too much choice in working for a cruise line company. Most International Cruise Lines will not hire Americans. We have very poor reputation as employees. Cruise Lines have been burned too many times by American Prima Donnas, and generally will not even consider interviewing Americans except as Jugglers, Clowns, Dancers and Singers. NCL America is your best chance—but not recommended'.

Drawing from his experience working on cruise ships and interviewing potential seafarers, 'CruiseCriticPoster65' explained further that '[t]he passport means everything. American Passport means I will consider you for Cruise Staff ONLY'. 'CruiseCriticPoster62' who worked on a cruise ship, concurred with this point and added that:

> 'In my years on ships, I've seen Americans (and Canadians) working as cruise staff (social hosts, dancers, youth programs, musicians, other entertainment) but have also seen many americans in other areas like spa (though yes, that is Steiner), Casino and Gift Shop (again, third party companies but still), photography, Pursers, ShoreEx, Sound and Light tech (which can be placed with other cruise staff), IT techs, shipboard accountants, doctors and nurses, etc etc etc. The only areas I haven't seen americans are [sic] housekeeping, food and beverage and, obviously, Italian officers'.

While there may not be as many US seafarers as those from other nationalities on cruise ships, to note is that when employed, US seafarers are placed in jobs with higher social status and better benefits than those given to other nationalities despite the perception that US seafarers tend to be hired more often than not as entertainers on cruise ships.

The belief that US seafarers such as Cindy are 'too' entitled or spoiled to work hard for their monthly wages was implied by the NCL representative who insisted that US workers ought to be able to do the same kind of work as foreign nationals. To state as such, however, misses the point that work conditions and wages for low level hotel positions on cruise ships are unsatisfactory at best and exploitative, at worst. That non-US seafarers can work longer hours with lower pay and fewer benefits does not justify the continued existence of such work conditions—regardless of seafarer nationality—on a cruise ship's housekeeping, food and beverage, galley and/or laundry departments.

Unlike their predecessors, seafarers in lower level positions of the hotel division today have shorter contract periods of extremely long and hard work days without full rest days and other benefits. However, constant demands for cruise ship workers in the midst of growing competition between states to promote the out-migration of their citizen workers mean that cruise lines easily can and will continue to travel the world in search of low wage workers who are 'willing and able' to perform such work for minimal compensation. It has become a self-perpetuating cycle in the twenty-first century.

Felipe and Irina stated that they had observed within an approximate span of seven years, a gradual decrease in the average length of work contracts, i.e., from one year to six months. Both former seafarers insisted that this was the case mainly because 'so many people want to work [on board cruise ships]'. Felipe later qualified this statement by explaining that his former cruise line employer had a policy of firing any seafarer with an 'attitude'. Profiles of his co-workers had changed over time, i.e., from mostly Central and South Americans in the early-mid 1990s, to Asians and Eastern Europeans by the early 2000s because the former group 'made trouble [for management]'. Cruise lines, in the main, are strategic with regard to the employment of seafarers from various regions of the world. According to the Global Ship Services website, prospective seafarers are to complete an application form detailing the 'Position,' 'Nationality,' 'Languages [spoken by the seafarer],' 'Sex,' 'Age' and so forth ('Crew Member Request Form'). Recruitment for cruise ship work then is not based solely on the criteria of language and skill but importantly it is mediated by identity modalities such as nationality and related national culture, race/ethnicity and gender of the prospective employee.

Manipulating Identities

Large cruise ships today have as many as 80-90 nationalities of seafarers from East, South, Central and Southeast Asia; Western, Southern, Central and Eastern Europe; North, Central and South America; North and South Africa; and Australasia. To reiterate, the diversity of seafarer nationalities encourages cruise directors in charge of entertainment programs to re-present and celebrate their crew as a 'floating' or 'mini-UN'. A Carnival cruise ship crew manifest reflects this kind of national/regional diversity: Italian captain, marine officers and engineers; US hotel manager, cruise director, doctor, and information technology specialists; British food & beverage manager, casino supervisor and staff, hairdressers; Asian, Eastern European, Caribbean and Central American bar staff; Asian, Caribbean and Latin American hotel and cabin stewards; Asian, Central American, Caribbean galley stewards; and Chinese laundrymen (Mather 2002, 12). Depending on one's perspective, the label 'mini-UN' may connote an unprecedented number of nationalities coming together in one workplace or conversely, controversial and unfair relations somewhat reflecting the larger international organization with a small number of powerful and wealthy countries located in the Global North, followed by a large number of less powerful and poorer countries in the Global South.

The uniquely stratified work environment on cruise ships arises from, and is sustained by deliberate recruitment for, and placement of seafarers in specific positions in the context of a traditional shipboard workforce hierarchy. At the apex is the Captain or 'Old Man' or 'Master'. Continued usage of the latter two titles reflects the distinctly gendered leadership at sea, e.g., from 1998-2000, there were only two women captains of cruise ships (ILO-SIRC 2003, 16). The captain is the 'master' of the ship that, in turn and by tradition, is referenced by the feminine noun, e.g., 'her' engine compartment or 'she sails at 20 knots'. International maritime law invests absolute power in the captain to ensure vessel and crew safety while at sea, and he relies on officers to help maintain discipline and order. This structure, even in the early twentieth century, was not always welcomed by the rest of the crew:

> [Although] drawn to the sea because of the adventure, glamour and fantasy lifestyle it promise[d],' [seafarers] resent[ed] the demands and rigors of shipboard employment, the loss of the sense of the individual, and the subordination to an officer hierarchy that seems more powerful and exacting than any authority ashore (Coons and Varias 2003, 65).

Contemporary cruise ship crew hierarchy, to be sure, no longer is delimited identifiably to its predecessor's predominantly single nationality-gender crew.

The recruitment and placement of seafarers on cruise ships today encompasses 'a brave new world with a division of labor that's international' (Seal 1998, 9). Majority of senior officers are recruited from the Global North, e.g., European countries such as those of the United Kingdom, the Netherlands, Greece and Italy, while the rest of the crew are sourced from a multitude of countries particular those in Asia and Eastern Europe: 'With the rare exception, Carnival's senior officers are all Italian; Celebrity's are Greek; NCL's and Royal Caribbean's are Norwegian; Princess's are British; Holland America's are Dutch. Across the board, entertainers and social staff are almost always American or from the UK' (Garin 2005, 197).

Wu's analysis of crew lists collected from three EU ports (Southampton, Amsterdam and Barcelona) that totalled 12,000 seafarers on 37 cruise ships plying the Caribbean, Mediterranean and Western European routes confirm this structure. Cruise ship hierarchies are 'bottom heavy' in that senior officers constituted only three per cent whereas ratings or support staff constituted 59 per cent of the total crew. Italy, Greece, Germany, US and the UK contributed 75 per cent of senior officers, six per cent of junior officers and 50 per cent of petty officers while countries in regions such as Latin America and Asia-Pacific (excluding Japan) contributed 75 per cent of ratings (Wu 2005, 27-33). As discussed in greater detail later, the gender dimension complicates what appears to be a straightforward placement of Global North seafarers in positions of higher status and Global South seafarers in positions of lower status. Men outnumber women in every department except for those seafarers employed by concessionaires; women from some nationalities are placed in higher status and waged positions than men; and men from specific countries are considered better suited than other men and women for providing service to passengers.

The diversity of seafarer nationalities in this shipboard hierarchy has been referred as a 'cultural class system' in which positions are distinguished by intersections of national cultural identity and class (Testa, Mueller and Thomas 2003, 137). This cultural class system has its corresponding spatialized dimension, i.e., while officers have single cabins on upper decks, and can dine with passengers or in their own dining rooms, the majority of the crew share cabins on lower decks, many of them are required to dine in mess halls and are prohibited from being in the public 'guest' areas of the ship.

Crucially, a racialized/ethnicized dimension inheres in this cultural class system because seafarers not only hail from different nationalities with their perceived corresponding cultures but also with corresponding racial/ethnic backgrounds. Culture, race/ethnicity and class then can be and are conflated with, or easily subsumed into the category of nationality. Put in another way, nationality becomes the signifier for culture, race/ethnicity and class. The contemporary cruise ship crew hierarchy resurrects at sea what was previously practiced on land, i.e., a racialized/ ethnicized colonial division of labour with whites at the top of the hierarchy followed by a descending order of different others in subordinate positions. Seafarers from European countries who approximate the physiognomic-cultural expectations of being 'white' tend to have higher level positions and shorter contracts with higher wages and more privileges than seafarers from poorer developing countries. In short, there exists 'significant racial discrimination in the length of crew contracts' (ICONS 2000, 58).

Cruise ships' hierarchical structure and corresponding demarcation and usage of space for seafarers connote much more complexity than is possibly captured by the celebratory phrase 'mini-UN'. Every seafarer on a cruise ship wears a distinct uniform symbolizing his/her occupational position, and a badge inscribed with the seafarer's name and country of origin. As an identification tool, the badge does more than announce the bearer's nationality. Nationality signifies the kind of 'passport' citizenship that is imbued with assumptions of racial/ethnic heritage, class, culture, status of national socioeconomic development and degree of masculinity-femininity. In the galley department of mass market cruise ships for instance, the work of cutting meat, baking pastries, cooking entrees and cleaning dishes are performed mostly by Asian, Latin American and Eastern European men seafarers under the tutelage of Western European head chefs. In some laundry departments, Asian men—especially those from the PRC—are responsible for washing, drying, ironing and folding the entire ship's laundry (Zhao 2002, 14).

In 2002, HAL embarked on an initiative of introducing a fee-based alternative or specialty restaurant throughout its fleet. Beginning with the HAL ship, *ms. Oosterdam*, the restaurant would be 'staffed by a dozen Hungarian waiters, and the line will transition to European service personnel in this specialty venue on other ships'. One of the HAL representatives explained that '[e]mploying European servers is simply a way of further differentiating the Pinnacle Grill from the main dining room' (Garin 2005, 198). In other words, Indonesian seafarers would remain in the main dining room while Hungarian seafarers work in the specialty restaurant, that, conceivably projects a higher social status for its guests as well as offer opportunities for seafarers to earn more tips. Some cruise line brochures, to be sure, make it a point to advertise that their seafarers in the hotel division have trained for many years in Europe.

On board one cruise ship, the majority of servers in its highest fee-based specialty restaurant were from Eastern European countries such as Romania. When I asked Lenka, why she and her compatriot Ana were assigned to the restaurant, she replied by saying that they were better suited for the restaurant, i.e., they were 'more qualified'. The implication here is that they fulfilled expectations of how servers should look and act in the more exclusive restaurants. Other restaurants with lower dining fees were served by seafarers from Thailand, Indonesia and the Philippines. Lenka and Ana acknowledged that they preferred to work in the high-end restaurant because gratuities were substantially greater than if they were to work in the main dining rooms or alternative restaurants with lower fees.

The gradual entry and employment of Eastern Europeans are symbolic of their positioning and concomitant identity in the middle of the nationality-race/ethnic hierarchy. According to a maritime lawyer who represented Eastern European crew members in litigation against Carnival, 'The Eastern Europeans are the new slaves of choice...the cruise industry likes them because they are light skinned, have Romanesque features and will work for peanuts [80-hour work week at USD1.56 an hour]'. A Carnival representative responded to his comments by claiming that, 'People in many developing countries literally line up for cruise ship jobs. They can make much more money than in their own countries' (Torres 2004).[8]

To this end, deliberate recruitment and placement strategies demonstrate that assignations of shipboard responsibilities and privileges are not determined solely by the pursuit of profits per se, for they resurrect and rely on specific intersections of identity modalities. Seen in this way, capital's interest in flexibilized labour at sea is mediated by the resilience of socially constructed, historicized views regarding different peoples from different parts of the world. It is not that capital merely requires low cost labour but that low cost labour comes in the form of specific peoples performing specific jobs to which they are 'entitled' because of their nationality, race/ethnicity and gender.

There are mixed reports on prospects for seafarer promotion in the hotel division. Although Dickinson and Vladimir argue that Carnival's expansion promises not only more opportunities for employment but also opportunities to move out of 'dead end jobs', newsprint articles and scholarly research on seafarer experiences indicate otherwise (Dickinson and Vladimir 1997, 119). Caribbean, Central American, South and Southeast Asian seafarers who work as galley stewards, busboys, cabin stewards, waiters and so forth, generally have not seen opportunities for promotion because of their skin colour (R. Klein 2002a; Mather 2002; Nielsen 2000; Wood 2000 and

---

8 Canadians also have joined the global seafarer labour force, in part, because of favourable currency exchange rates between the US and Canadian dollars. Some cruise lines hire Canadians for specific jobs that involve 'direct interaction with passengers, including pursers, casino dealers and guest relations officers'. This strategy is based on Canadians being 'renowned in industry circles for their hard work and friendly disposition. And it doesn't hurt that most Canadians speak English as their mother tongue and share a lot of the same cultural traits as their American neighbors' (Cassoff 2002).

2004b; Zhao 2002). This does not mean that no seafarers from the Global South are promoted but that it appears not to be the industry norm of promotion to higher level managerial or supervisory positions.

Felipe, in discussing his former career as a waiter or dining room steward, recounted that he once asked his supervisor whether or not he eventually could become a 'hotel director'. He believed it possible because the cruise line already had promoted him from the status of assistant waiter to waiter. Moreover, his new responsibilities included writing reports on behalf of his supervisor as well as keeping track of financial accounts. Felipe said that his supervisor, after much deflection, answered in this way: '[P]robably not because one has to work all the way up [the chain of command]'. When Felipe pressed him further, the supervisor simply shook his head. Felipe then realized that he stood no chance of eventually obtaining the coveted position because 'they [managers] are all Italians. They help themselves, not us Latins'.

Eduardo, a Filipino seafarer, had an experience similar to Felipe. He said that his promotion from cabin steward to butler (assigned to passengers booked in suites) came after the cruise line for which he worked was acquired by one of the major cruise corporations. He was promoted and transferred to another cruise line because of his record of professionalism and that he 'smiled a lot'. Eduardo, however, said that he did not expect to move beyond the position of butler because of his nationality-racial/ethnic origins, i.e., 'Ah, I am not the right kind'. As will be discussed later, the pleasant demeanour of seafarers such as Eduardo is perceived and treated as an indispensable cultural trait.

Women in a Masculinized Oceanic World of Work

> [A] growing number of women across the globe are finding economic opportunities within the cruise industry. The devastating effects of poverty are particularly severe on women in nations struggling with a weak economy and oppressive social and cultural factors beyond their control. Women are relegated to either very low-paying wages or non-employment. Those women who are employed by the cruise industry enjoy personal autonomy from a sustained income that is not matched in their own country. In essence, the cruise industry has provided opportunity for women to achieve increased economic, social and cultural equality.
>
> World Travel and Tourism Council (2002, 48)

The cruise industry's initial difficulties in recruiting low wage seafarers during the 1980s facilitated women's entry into a largely masculinized oceanic world of work on cruise ships. Similar to their earlier twentieth century predecessors as well as their contemporary land-based counterparts in service industries, women seafarers are concentrated mainly in the hotel division of cruise ships performing what Goffman called the 'front stage' work of interacting with passengers and the 'back stage' work of cleaning cabins (1959).[9]

---

9 MacCannell for example, draws from these Goffmanian concepts especially to distinguish between the 'front region' and 'back region' in discussing tourists' search for authenticity (1989).

During the early twentieth century as married, single and widowed women began taking pleasure cruises, shipping lines were compelled to employ women seafarers to better serve women travellers and their children: brochures advertised women seafarers as 'discriminating, feminine, courteous, efficient…possess the valuable quality of human understanding' (Coons and Varias 2003, 112). Socioeconomic necessity thus opened the gangway for women's entry onto shipboard life.

In the contemporary era, that which began from labour shortages is explained as the need to construct a kind of shipboard life that better reflects landed society. Oyen from NSU recounted an early 1990s conversation he had with the Vice-President of Human Resources for Royal Caribbean who said to him that the cruise line had trouble addressing labour shortages. Oyen reminded him that the problem easily could be solved by not 'excluding half of the world's population'. Oyen asserts that since then, Royal Caribbean has practiced a gender-blind employment policy and that cruise line employment of women seafarers 'make [the] ship a better [working] environment…more like normal society' (2005).[10]

Which nationalities of women are hired and under what conditions? An ILO-SIRC study of women seafarers found that women's employment was dependent partly on the criteria of 'attractiveness' (2003, 32). Women are placed in a variety of non-officer positions such as that of receptionists, cabin stewards, waiters, masseuses and hairstylists. This was the case with the 'spa girls' as well as former seafarers Cindy and Irina. The bulk of women's work on cruise lines reflects and affirms the gendered perception that they are born to perform domestic work based on an inherent ability to care, to nurture, to pay attention to detail, and to entertain passengers:

> Women seafarers in the hotel and catering sector of the industry appear to be more readily accepted by their male colleagues than those working in the marine department. This is probably due to the fact that the work women do in this sector often more closely reflects the types of jobs that are traditionally considered 'women's work', for example, cleaning, shop work and employment in the beauty industry (ILO-SIRC 2003, 50).

A cruise ship captain explained it in this way:

> [F]irst of all, in service, I think, girls have better criteria than men, the men are more steady, last more hours, but the women are unique in this thing, they are better, its their nature…For example in the housekeeping you can take the type of the typical British butler like you've seen in the movies, how many of them can you find to make a cabin look luxury [sic] and always with a smile?' (Zhao 2002, 15).

His rationale betrays a worldview in which women's social subordination is inverted and re-presented as being endowed with a unique gift of domesticity unmatched even by the best trained British butler.

As more families purchase cruise vacation packages, cruise lines find themselves having to balance somewhat the ratio of men and women seafarers in order to better

---

10 Oyen, nonetheless acknowledged that shipboard societies '[are] really not 'normal' because it is half a military system…so seafarers are not entirely 'free' to do as they please even during off hours'.

cater to the needs of women and children passengers. Yet women seafarers remain outnumbered by men to a ratio of one to four or five. The ILO-SIRC study on women seafarers also found that 32 per cent of women from OECD countries of North America and Western Europe joined cruise ships to 'see the world', while 69 per cent of their counterparts from developing countries joined cruise ships in order to earn income that would allow them to care for their families (2003, 44). This is glaring in its exposure of the motivation underlying different women's search for employment on cruise ships: migrant tourist-workers from the Global North may 'want' to do so as a way to see the world or explore foreign lands, while those from the Global South 'need' to do so out of economic necessity. As Bianchi noted, however, migrant tourist-workers also are beginning to come from other countries. Although the self-styled 'spa girls' (Julie, Alexis and Thokozile) came from South Africa, their main motivation for cruise ship employment was to be able to visit foreign locales and earn monthly wages in the process. These migrant tourist-workers contrast sharply with Irina who left Estonia because she could not secure employment, or Wiranti, an Indonesian woman who felt that she had no other option but to leave her family for work as a cabin steward.

From Wu's analysis of crew lists, only 19 per cent of the 12,000 cruise ship crew members were women (an approximate ratio of one woman to five men), and out of this merely seven per cent were located in the marine division, while the rest were in the hotel division. Of the top five sending countries for women seafarers, three were in Western Europe (Britain, Italy and Germany), while the other two respectively were the Philippines and Ukraine. Only 20 per cent of women seafarers from advanced economies were employed at the ratings level, whereas:

> 70 to 80 percent of East European and Asian women work aboard cruise vessels as ratings. It is notable that nearly 40 percent of female seafarers from Latin America occupy middle ranking jobs (junior and petty officers), a higher proportion than is found amongst their female colleagues from East Europe and Asia and also their male counterparts from Latin America (Wu 2005, 32).

This is a complex picture of women seafarers' positions demarcated by a hierarchized nexus of region/nationality and race/ethnicity, i.e., Western European, followed by Latin American, Eastern European and Asian women. So, when cruise lines sell dream vacations, in effect they also are selling 'the social composition of the producers, at least those who are serving in the front line, may be part of what is in fact "sold" to the customer…"service" partly consists of a process of production which is infused with particular social characteristics of gender, age, race, education background and so on' (Urry 2002, 61).

Although women seafarers tend to be placed in positions reflecting their ascribed gender traits, there are sharp distinctions between these positions, e.g., as officers or support staff, and as front stage or back stage workers. Some positions require direct interactions with passengers (such as those of the receptionist, cruise entertainer, fitness trainer, *concierge* and so forth). Women from Western Europe mostly are placed at these 'points of sale' and/or in supervisory positions because of management's 'intention to maintain the industry's "classical image" (hence the exclusion of Asians and blacks) or on their concern about the preconceived "lack of smile" of seafarers from Eastern European countries' (Zhao 2002, 16). Majority of women from Southeast Asia and to a lesser extent, Eastern Europe are assigned the work of cleaning cabins and serving meals (Zhao 2002, 17). A cursory review of cruise vacation brochures from the major cruise lines illustrates this very well: women from the Global North generally are photographed in their officer uniforms, and women from the Global South are photographed in their uniforms respectively serving passengers in dining rooms or standing beside neatly made beds.

Women working alongside men on board cruise ships do not come without additional challenges, e.g., allegations of sexual harassment or assaults by men seafarers. As previously discussed in Chapter Four, US citizens have the right and are expected to report such crimes to the FBI. Non-US women seafarers must depend on the cruise line to follow through (i.e., investigate and refer cases to local port authorities and the flag state) on their allegations.

Some seafarers informed me that intimate relationships are quite frequent between seafarers: this is considered 'common knowledge' among the crew. Even though the Indonesian and Filipino seafarers with whom I spoke were aware of shipboard relationships they emphasized that they did not, and had no intentions of developing intimate relationships with fellow seafarers or passengers. Peter, a Filipino who worked as a head cabin steward, tried to explain why seafarers may pursue such relationships by saying that, 'You must understand that it is very lonely at sea'.

Sometimes relationships that develop at sea between seafarers can culminate in marriage, as was the case with Felipe and Irina who, even before they got married, arranged with their cabin mates to swap cabins so that they could be together in their private space.[11] Oyen confirmed this phenomenon and added that he was aware of 'a lot of temporary relationships on ships...in all different ways [heterosexual and homosexual]. In the past, there were not many incidences [especially of gay and lesbian relationships] but today it's more open' (2005).

Shipboard affairs can cause tensions between seafarers and their families. Oyen once received a letter from 'wives of Filipinos' telling him that their husbands were having affairs on the ship. They asked him to cooperate with the cruise line to implement a policy prohibiting affairs between crew members. Although cruise lines prohibit sexual relations between seafarers and passengers, voluntary relations among seafarers fall beyond the scope of management oversight. Indeed, the employment of foreign migrant labour on cruise ships affects not just the workers who spend many months at sea but also family members left behind in their home countries.

Born to Serve: 'Happy' Women and Men from Service Cultures

While the 'mini-UN' moniker may foreground diverse nationalities, it obscures overarching gendered worldviews and related consequences that persist in shipboard employment practices. Given the skewed ratio in which men seafarers outnumber

---

11 Senior officers, on the other hand, are allowed to be accompanied by their spouses in the course of their work. I am not aware, at the time of writing, of available data on the number of married couples (for officers and crew) working on the same ship.

women seafarers several fold, then it is to be expected that the ascribed feminine trait of 'service' on board cruise ships cannot be said to be the exclusive purview or 'natural' endowment of women per se. Rather, it is seen to inhere in certain 'national cultures', hence expectations that some men seafarers also must hold and express it well.

Cruise lines' ability to compete successfully with landed resorts involves not just the provision of many land-based amenities at sea but importantly, that of an unsurpassed quality of service more often than not associated with lifestyle privileges of the wealthy. It is the fulcrum on which hangs passengers' 'dream' vacations in mass market cruising e.g., to have their cabins cleaned twice a day, to be served at their behest, to be graced by constant smiles, to be called 'Sir' or 'Ma'am', and to be delighted upon discovering little mementoes left by cabin stewards after evening turn-down service.[12] As Urry puts it succinctly, in tourism '[t]he quality of the social interaction is itself part of the service purchased' (2002, 60). Consequently, 'employees'' speech, appearance and personality may all be treated as legitimate areas of intervention and control by management' (Urry 2002, 60-1), i.e., seafarers 'perform' their jobs on the 'stage' of the cruise ship and with the instructions of supervisor- or manager- 'directors' (see also Crang 1997).

Men and women cabin stewards are encouraged to personalize their work in the hope that passengers may remember to tip them well at the end of the cruise itinerary. In this way, cruise lines shift a large part of the task for evaluating the conduct of, and financially compensating these seafarers on to passengers while encouraging seafarer self-surveillance.[13] Given the centrality of service on cruise ships, passenger complaints can and have resulted in termination of employment for some seafarers.

Tracy, who worked as an assistant cruise director while conducting her field research, noted the importance of 'comment cards' that passengers are asked to fill-in at the end of their cruise:

> Our cruise director kept a detailed record of the number of passenger comments each employee received, subtracting negative ones from positive ones, and used this as a basis for cruise staff evaluation and promotion. No one complained to the cruise director about this evaluation method---or the somewhat strange effects it had on our behavior (2000, 108-9).

---

12 Take, for example, one of Carnival's 2005 television advertisements in the US. It begins with a cabin steward making an origami dog out of bath towels, after which it is placed gently on the bed. The next frame shows the cabin's occupants who delight in discovering the item. The frame then shifts from one of the passengers holding the item to thousands of pictures that come together in the form of a Carnival cruise ship.

13 Wiranti and her Filipino coworker Cesar who were responsible for cleaning my cabin in addition to 14 others throughout the voyage, left different mementoes such as mint chocolates, flowers, and miniature animal-shaped origami items on the bed after every evening turn-down service. When I asked them if they did the same for other passengers, they replied in the affirmative stating that they hoped passengers would remember them at the end of the voyage.

For cabin stewards such as Wiranti and Cesar, passenger comment cards with positive evaluations of their work were of the utmost importance to their continued employment with the cruise line. Wiranti, in particular, mentioned that even if passengers were stingy (*'kedekut'*) with dispensing gratuities at the end of a voyage, their positive comments went a long way to helping her keep the position.

Irina, the former seafarer who had worked as a cabin steward, said that 'if one passenger mentions your name [on the comment card] then you are good. But if they don't mention your name, then you get "extra duties"'. She remembered that some of her co-workers felt compelled to plead with passengers to 'mention' their names at the end of each itinerary. Irina, who found the act of pleading with passengers to have been quite 'very demeaning' made it a point to ask only one passenger per voyage to record her name on the card. Even so, 'I was never comfortable begging. It's so hard, no person should be asked to do it'.

Comment cards are seafarers' tool of self-surveillance in the name of income and employment longevity. Cruise lines' dependence on comment cards encourage an oceanic version of Urry's 'interiorization of the gaze' in which landed workers and communities of the more popular foreign tourist locales gradually find themselves behaving according to tourists' expectations:

> Those living in tourist 'honeyports' may believe that they are always about to be gazed upon, even if they are not. They may therefore feel 'under the gaze,' even if no tourist is actually about to capture them in his or her mind's eye…they may not venture out or may only do so in ways appropriate for the gaze, even if no tourist is actually present (Urry 1992, 177-8).

Seafarers' expression of their perceived 'happy' personalities is indispensable to obtaining and continuing employment on cruise ships. According to an executive of Barber International (that is one of the world's largest recruiters of cruise ship crew via its unit, Barber Marine Team), 'One important criteria is attitude; the whole thing is about a service and if you feel a person is not service minded, he or she has nothing to do on board a cruise vessel'(International Cruise & Ferry Review 2002). Hotel staff on board cruise ships are expected and further trained specifically to project a happy, amiable personality. A server described her training session in this way:

> He [trainer] was talking about like we are a friendly crew, we are a happy crew. I mean it's like you don't have to talk with passengers about your problems like you are not happy. It's like…most of the time you have to smile, talk about something nice, to show you are happy (Zhao 2002, 10-11).

The commodification of seafarers' emotional labour, hence, has become an integral dimension of their employment. Similar to other customer-service based industries, seafarers are recruited, employed, evaluated and compensated for their physical *and* emotional labour (see, for example, Hochschild 1983; Taylor 1998).

To reiterate, although the major cruise lines employ seafarers from all over the world, they do exhibit preference for some nationalities over others. While some hotel divisions (e.g., HAL and Royal Caribbean) hire mostly Indonesians for work in cabins and restaurants, others (e.g., Carnival) appear to prefer seafarers mainly from the Philippines and Eastern Europe. Cruise lines' preference for Southeast Asian seafarers in general is not based merely on wage levels (i.e., Southeast Asian seafarers can be hired for lower wage levels than those from other regions) and proficiency in the English language, but also on management's experience with, and/ or stereotypes of different nationalities. For some, Philippine nationals are perceived to come from what can be called 'service' cultures:

> 'They seem to have been born with a wonderful service culture. They always greet the guests and always smile. And, they do it so naturally. We get very good feedback from our guests about these seafarers'. Managers compare them with Eastern Europeans who are unable 'to smile...always so rigid' (Zhao 2002, 11).

Seafarers from other Southeast Asian countries such as Indonesia and Thailand also are considered better service providers in these positions than their counterparts from the Global North. Notably, the physical and emotional work of nurturing passengers is not restricted to women from the above countries. Men nationals recruited to work in cabins and restaurants expectedly share in this 'trait' when compared to the conceivably more masculinized, i.e., Western and Eastern European officers employed in the deck and engine departments.

The constructed 'service culture' on cruise ships thus is replete with racialized-feminized undertones in which the 'happy' personalities of Southeast Asian women and men seafarers are considered vital to shipboard service, yet disqualifies them for more prestigious, higher-paying jobs. They are back stage workers located primarily in support positions of restaurants, galleys and cabins in the hotel division. The front stage work of managers, receptionists, *concierge* and *maître d'* are performed by those who, in the main, look more 'European' or 'Western' (read: white) than others.

Cruise ships' uniquely stratified work environments cannot but also affect intercultural relations among seafarers. One of the 'spa girls' Julia noted that intercultural relations are 'generally harmonious' and that 'Filipinos and Indonesians are happy people, easy to get along with'. As she made this comment, her compatriot Alexis added that '[They] are 'calm people...always smiling'. Alexis then turned her head in the direction of a group of Bulgarian engine room crew members (who stood behind us at the port of call while complaining loudly of being cheated by their telephone calling cards), implicitly compared the verbal and nonverbal communication styles of the three nationalities and then concluded verbally that the Bulgarians were crass.

Julia further emphasized that she was uncomfortable around the ship's senior marine officers (from a specific Western European country) because they were status conscious in their interactions with the rest of the crew. She deemed them to be 'rude' and 'arrogant' in their overall interactions with lower ranked seafarers, and they especially made her feel as if she did not deserve to be in their presence. Differences in verbal and nonverbal communication styles within a shipboard environment stratified according to nationality, national culture, race/ethnicity, class and gender led her to make the comment that 'they [senior officers] are snobs'.

The two South African women's views of Filipinos and Indonesians were not shared by Alfonso, a Filipino seafarer. He said to me during our dockside conversation that he, unlike his compatriots, preferred interacting with seafarers of other nationalities because the interactions gave him opportunities to 'learn different languages' even though he also pointed out that differences in 'values' could cause 'misunderstandings'. He offered the example of speech patterns and tones, i.e., while seafarers of other nationalities spoke softly and slowly, Filipinos and Indonesians tended to speak loudly and quickly amongst themselves leading some to think that 'we have no manners'. While management and even fellow seafarers perceive Indonesians and Filipinos as friendly, polite and service-oriented workers, Alfonso saw his compatriots in the exact opposite manner hence he preferred to interact with seafarers from other regions.

Sampson and Zhao ascertained similar trends on other kinds of oceanic vessels and posited that the transfer of existing regional and national cultural prejudices by seafarers to their workplace at sea has led some to be less courteous to their compatriots, preferring instead to work with seafarers from other regions (2003). Irina and Felipe, in recollecting some of their more salient memories of intercultural shipboard relations, agreed that 'Asians' were more friendly and quiet in comparison to seafarers from the Caribbean and Latin America whom they considered to be naturally more animated in social interactions. However, when directed at shipboard work conditions, the 'boisterous' characteristic manifested in very vocal complaints about workers' lack of rights on cruise ships. Felipe added, 'It is good that they [seafarers from the Caribbean and Latin America] make noise because sometimes management is wrong, discriminate against us. But they [the seafarers] cause trouble [by 'making noise']..[For example] they [cruise line management] don't want to hire Jamaicans anymore'. From Felipe's standpoint then, this cultural-linguistic 'trait' becomes a distinct disadvantage when its expression causes repercussions affecting the future employability of all its speakers.

Irina, on the other hand, experienced difficulties in negotiating gender relations within a multicultural context: 'I learned a lot from so many nationalities on board. As a young girl from Europe, it was hard because Latins [tended to] whistle at me. Every time they see me, they whistled and said 'Mama Sita'. I was very angry and tired all the time [from being verbally harassed]'. She also challenged a common stereotype among Western European seafarers that 'Eastern European girls are easy. We, I, am not easy'. Felipe built on her point that Western Europeans have a tendency of stereotyping other nationalities by adding that, 'They think Latins are all alike. Europeans put us all in the same box: Central Americans. They see no difference. We are all the same to them. But to us, there are differences. Central Americans are less educated and more rude than South Americans'.

Cruise lines' employment of seafarers from all over the world and the latter's unique placement in shipboard positions cannot but transfer existing gender, racial-ethnic, class, national and regional cultural stereotypes and prejudices from land to sea. Given the nature of shipboard hierarchy in a self-contained environment at sea, seafarers' preconceptions of the 'other' then will be confirmed or challenged, but they cannot be ignored.[14]

---

14 Relations among cruise ship crew deserve greater attention by intercultural communication researchers because they potentially can reveal in greater detail how shipboard

The Sisyphean Challenge

Dickinson and Vladimir offer the cruise industry's rationale for placing specific nationalities of seafarers in specific positions by shifting responsibility to seafarers. First, they collapse the distinction between what seafarers of the Global South 'need' and 'want' from cruise ship employment:

> On mass market ships the executive maitre chefs and some other key personnel are Europeans, as are the food and beverage managers, but the larger fleets have found that these jobs are more enthusiastically filled by people from the Far East, the Caribbean, and South America, where the wages paid are very high by the standards at home. These employees are willing and capable of learning, and they enjoy the lifestyle and economic opportunities a cruise ship offers (1997, 63).

Seafarers are seen to need-want relatively higher wages, and they also appear to welcome the accompanying work conditions. Seafarers from the Global North, on the other hand, are perceived as being acutely aware of the relationship between shipboard position, wage level and work conditions. In their discussion of why US seafarers are concentrated in certain positions, the authors assert that '[t]he egalitarian nature and heritage of Americans tend to work against their ability to be motivated to serve others' (1997, 67), and that, '[o]n the major lines, the Purser's staff are often Americans because these jobs appeal to them and aren't regarded as servile' (1997, 86).

Instead of addressing the shipboard work and compensation structure as key to shaping US seafarers' rejection of lower level positions, Dickinson and Vladimir reveal the pervasiveness of a 'developmental' continuum on which to locate seafarers, and from which to justify their shipboard placement. Seafarers from the Global South and North are constituted and positioned respectively at the 'low' and 'high' end of a continuum constructed from a concatenation of culture, nationality, state of national economic development, race/ethnicity, gender and class. The process of infantilizing contract seafarers from the Global South then becomes complete once the wage factor is accompanied by the belief that the seafarers 'are willing and capable of learning' what others may and do consider 'servile' jobs. Taken to its logical conclusion, the overall rationale is damning in its presumption that not only should seafarers from the Global South *be grateful* for being gainfully employed but that they are *culturally* suited for the terms and conditions of work rejected by others. As a Thai headwaiter explained to Zhao:

> It's a very hard job. I always feel exhausted when I finish it and come down to my cabin. You may not know the nature of hospitality industry. The restaurant is a stage, a show. You are an actor. Believe me, you can be totally drained just by greeting people, chatting with them, smiling to them, and things like that. As an Asian, I have to work harder, I have to make more efforts to please the passengers (Zhao 2002, 10-11).

At the outset, the earlier experiences of NCL America's *Pride of Aloha* involving rapid turnovers of US seafarers may appear to affirm Dickinson and Vladimir's

---

identities are affected by, and affect, land-based identities and interactions.

point that US seafarers are not culturally suited for harsh working conditions in hierarchized workplaces. What remains unsaid is that US workers are resistant to 'serving others' under less than acceptable conditions: they come from a political economic context in which, historically, they have had certain rights as workers and that they can articulate such rights without the kind of legal and economic ramifications that were and continue to be confronted by many of their counterparts in the Global South. Hence, to argue that some are culturally better suited to serve others under conditions of low pay, few benefits and long hours is to relegate them to a permanent status of relative servility that, somehow, absolves cruise lines and flag states from the responsibility of improving terms and conditions of work for all seafarers.

Cruise lines' employment of flexibilized foreign migrant workers do not operate according to a generic formula as seafarers are placed in positions that help construct the larger context to best maximize profits even if such positions reproduce national cultural, gender, class and racial/ethnic stereotypes with their accompanying inequities at sea. That this is occurring presently should be of concern especially since foreign flagged cruise ships are able to operate in a manner likened to that of 'sovereign islands' (Frantz 1999a). Emerging from these floating chunks of capital is the kind of employment segregation in place and space reminiscent of a bygone era in which white colonialists were situated at the apex of colonies, followed by middlemen brokers and lastly, indigenous peoples.

The causes and consequences of changing seafarer profiles are much more nuanced than a simple observation that cruise lines have gone global in their labour recruitment and employment practices. Cruise lines sell to consumers affordable all-inclusive vacations at sea revolving on being pampered and entertained throughout the voyage. Not immediately apparent to many passengers are the mutually constitutive processes of flexibilizing labour and manipulating identities at sea, i.e., terms of recruitment, work and relations that make possible extraordinary experiences.

From a free market perspective, seafarers willingly exchange their labour for wages. Missing from this picture however are structural forces that encourage their search for employment, as well as the terms of recruitment and ensuing work on cruise ships. Particularly for seafarers whose monthly wages depend inordinately on passenger tips or service charges, the ability to earn income is accompanied often by extremely long work hours, job insecurity and the absence of labour rights/benefits that are justified by and justify distinct cultural traits ascribed to them. It is in this way that cruise lines' pursuit of profits at sea cannot but give to, while taking away from seafarers at the same time.

Chapter 6

Navigating Morality in and for the Twenty-First Century

It is no less ancient than a pestilent error wherewith many men (but they chiefly who abound in power and riches) persuade themselves, or (as I think more truly) go about to persuade, that right and wrong are distinguished not according to their own nature but by a certain vain opinion and custom of men. These men therefore think that both laws and show of equity were invented for this purpose: that their dissensions and tumults might be restrained who are born in the condition of obeying; but unto such as are placed in the height of fortune they say that all right is to be measured by the will and the will by profits.

Hugo Grotius, 1609 (trans. by Hakluyt 2004, 5)

Hence, neoliberal policies that promote the cutthroat downsizing of the workforce, the bleeding of social services, the reduction of state governments to police precincts, the ongoing liquidation of job security, the increasing elimination of a decent social wage, the creation of a society of low-skilled workers, and the emergence of a culture of permanent insecurity and fear hide behind appeals to common sense and allegedly immutable laws of nature.

Henry Giroux (2005, 10)

Cruise tourism in the contemporary era has emerged from, and continues to expand within changing national and global political economies that explicitly validate free market competition and exchange. Flag states create open or second ship registries to compete against one another in the exchange of minimal regulatory power for cruise ship registration fees and tonnage taxes. Port communities compete with one another in the exchange of infrastructural services and port taxes for cruise line, passenger and seafarer expenditures. Cruise lines compete with one another and with landed firms for revenue from passenger-tourists, and the latter in turn, exchange monies for the opportunity to consume integrated sea-land experiences of pleasure. Seafarers (in some cases, with the help of labour sending states) compete to exchange labour in return for wages.

A key operative assumption informing these transactions between willing buyers and sellers is that they are void of structural constraints precisely because they occur within free markets for products and services. This assumption is powerful in spite of, and some might even argue because of the fact that a host of inequities have arisen from the historical development of national and global political economies. Despite the most noble of intentions, while on-going efforts to construct and integrate free markets will address some forms of disparities but at the same time can and do strengthen others or even create new ones. Although free market exchange relations are 'voluntary' between buyers and sellers, structural forces shape the conditions in which they occur (e.g., state creation of open registries to flag foreign-owned ships) giving rise to various kinds of contradictions (e.g., effects on health of the oceans as well as land-based tourism firms). Of importance is that contradictions are not *sui generis* phenomena or aberrations; they inhere in free markets constructed and maintained by social actors in a world that continues to be differentiated by, or stratified according to nationality, status of economic development, class, gender and so forth.

From the free market perspective however, cruise lines' relationships with flag states, port communities, passengers and seafarers appear as separate and distinct dyads. Nonetheless, we have seen why and how each set is linked to one another, i.e., they are intertwined in complicated ways as structural forces shape the conditions in which buyers and sellers come together that, in turn, directly and indirectly affect other dyads.

Persistent dismissal of, or inability to ascertain structural forces and ensuing constraints elicits two related consequences. At the very least, it leads to tacit acceptance of the loss, pain and servility underside that accompanies the profits-pleasure-work at sea connection. This is discerned especially from explanations of the contradictions as cruise tourism's growing pains or as outcomes of human error. As such, evaluatory criteria for what is and should be good or right conduct cannot but be left decisively to the free market. Market competition *sans* state intervention, for example, is and should be good because it generates 'fair' prices, encourages transactions between willing buyers and sellers, and so forth. So long as actors in the market are free to make decisions based on their self-interest, then as they prosper so too eventually will the economy and society. The relationship between morality and the free market thus is given an unambiguously positive outcome since the end justifies the means. What happens in the process (e.g., people's experiences and understandings of the world around them; social norms that help give sense and order life), is deemed tangential at best. Succinctly put, it is the condition of self-interested materiality that ultimately delineates morality not vice versa or even in concert with one another. The net effect is unconditional validation of free market institutions and related conduct that circumscribes critical questions while normalizing outcomes as worthy of being moral because of material benefits to the collective.

Cast in this way, social actors in the free market are absolved from any serious considerations of morality. For example, in the exchange of minimal regulatory power, open registries flag ships but seldom investigate the conduct of ships at sea or at ports of call (e.g., environmental pollution, and seafarer exploitation). Cruise ships call at ports but can and do frequently reject tax increases that help finance projects addressing infrastructural stress. Cruise lines produce and sell pleasure on gated vacation communities at sea but on the whole see no further need to better protect passengers against shipboard crimes beyond hiring disproportionately small teams of shipboard security personnel. Middle class consumers exchange monies to consume pleasure at sea but are not concerned overall with how cruise lines compensate their employees or some of the latter's working conditions.

Conduct within each dyad is framed by contractual relations between willing buyers and sellers. Free market transactions that are encapsulated and affirmed by legal contracts, also are severely delimited by them. There is little to no room for examining larger contexts, let alone pose the question of whether or not such relations are or should be informed by moral principles. The changing form of the state today only seems to accentuate this point. Given the commercialization of sovereignty, not only are states retreating from direct intervention in the economy but they are abdicating also their historical role as the highest juridically empowered moral agent within geopolitical borders. States, instead, are modelling conduct commensurate with free market competition and exchange as their open or second registries help transform the foundation on which to base, guide and evaluate maritime commercial activities and life in the twenty-first century.

In the political, policy and academic arenas, proponents and supporters of free markets today readily call on the eighteenth century Scottish scholar Adam Smith and his text *An Inquiry into the Nature and Causes of the Wealth of Nations* (published in 1776, hereafter called WN) to demonstrate an historical inevitability of the free market route to improving the human condition.[1] Even lay persons are familiar with the Smithian metaphor of 'the invisible hand': it is expected to bring about overall economic growth despite selfish motivations of actors in the free market.

Overwhelmingly absent from arguments and blueprints for constructing free markets, is recognition of Smith's other well-known text, *The Theory of Moral Sentiments* (first published in 1759, hereafter called TMS) that examines morality in society. This omission implies that morality has no role in the free market.[2] In the rest of this chapter, then, we will draw from TMS to delineate Smith's astute identification of the moral voice in social interactions as well as his observation of a moral dilemma that confronted the emerging commercial society of his time. Over two hundred years later, the moral dilemma persists and promises to remain as long as morality continues to be marginalized from evaluations of free market practices.

---

1 Wight offers a quantitative analysis of academic publishing on Smith, focusing specifically on the pre- and post-bicentennial period of WN. Among his findings are that references to Smith increased significantly in economic and interdisciplinary journals during the 1990s (2002).

2 TMS was published initially in 1759 followed by successive editions, the last of which was published in 1790, just before Smith's death. Some insist that WN and TMS are incommensurate because there are two distinctly different Smiths with their respective authorial intents (Evensky 1987; Hirschmann 1977), or that Smith had devised a hierarchy of morality applicable respectively in different realms of life (Brown 1994). The existence of separate volumes on each topic does not mean, however, that Smith's understanding of social life was segmented or that he would agree to differential applications of morality in the different dimensions of life. Even though he published separate volumes on different topics that allowed him to offer detailed analysis of each, we cannot assume that his understanding of social life was segmented (Dickey 1986; Lamb 1974; Raphael and Macfie 1982; and Winch 1978). Resistance to the juxtaposition of TMS and WN then keeps hidden Smith's warning of the moral dilemma from contemporary understandings and efforts to implement free markets (see especially the different perspectives taken by V. Brown 1994 and Werhane 1991).

The Moral Dilemma

Adam Smith, similar to some of his contemporaries in the eighteenth century such as John Locke, grappled with reconciling individual and societal interests, .e.g., the construction of individual identity, the articulation/negotiation of interests in relation to others, and the related effects on maintenance and transformation of society. Although in WN, Smith focused on self-interest (among other more detailed topics such as trade and taxation) in the free market, he began TMS with this sentence:

> How selfish soever man may be supposed, there are evidently some principles in his nature, which interest him in the fortune of others, and render their happiness necessary to him, though he derives nothing from it except the pleasure of seeing it (1982b, I.i.1.1).

The above quote stresses that individuals are not simply driven by self-interest for they can and have the capacity to hold, and concomitantly act from genuine concern for others.

Individuals learn at an early age that they are not alone in the world nor are they the most important persons, i.e., they rely on one another for their sense of physical and emotional well-being. Given that each person can fully know only her/his experiences, according to Smith, the way in which it is possible to know the experiences of others is via the 'imagination' that elicits 'sympathy': 'By the imagination we place ourselves in his situation, we conceive ourselves enduring all the same torments, we enter as it were into his body, and become in some measure the same person with him, and thence form some idea of his sensations' (Smith 1982b, I.i.2). The perfection of human nature is realized when 'it is, that to feel much for others and little for ourselves, that to restrain our selfish, and to indulge our benevolent affections…can alone produce among mankind that harmony of sentiments and passion in which consists their whole grace and propriety' (Smith 1982b, I.i.5.5).

Smith, to be sure, understood the fallibility of human beings in society. He did not discount the power of individual self-interest in this text on morality: 'Every man is, no doubt, by nature, first and principally recommended to his own care; as he is fitter to take care of himself than of any other person, it is fit and right that it should be so' (Smith 1982b, II.ii.2.1). From Smith's perspective however, since individuals are social beings endowed with imagination and sympathy, they also will seek 'approbation' (and avoid disapprobation) from one another:

> Nature, when she formed man for society, endowed him with an original desire to please, and an original aversion to offend his brethren. She taught him to feel pleasure in their favourable, and pain in their unfavourable regard. She rendered their approbation most flattering and most agreeable to him for its own sake; and their disapprobation most mortifying and most offensive (1982b, III.2.6).

Tempering the pursuit of self-interest in society then are individuals' need for approbation from one another. To note is that approbation is not subsumable under the umbrella of self-interest.[3] Individuals care about each other beyond what they can gain manifestly in material life and social status.

Crucially, individuals not only seek approbation but that they seek what *ought* to be approved or disapproved in the course of social interactions: 'Nature, accordingly has endowed him, not only with a desire of being approved of, but with a desire of being what ought to be approved of; or of being what he himself approves of in other men' (Smith 1982b, III.2.7). Smith qualified approbation as moral approbation, i.e., over time, individuals in society develop rules of morality from which to evaluate social conduct in the marketplace, the home, the school and so forth.[4] How does this occur, and what about the challenge involved in balancing interest for self and for others?

Smith was quick to caution against listening to those who insist that individuals either care for themselves, or for others. He rejected this 'either-or' schema when he took to task philosophers who did so: 'Two different sets of philosophers have attempted to teach us this hardest of all the lessons of morality. One set have laboured to increase our sensibility to the interests of others; another, to diminish that to our own' (Smith 1982b, III.3.8). Thus, he was sharply aware of tensions between interests of self and other in the conduct of everyday life. Smith did not agree with exclusive privileging of the self or the other because the outcome would be biased in favour of either side.

It is the 'eyes of a third person' or the 'impartial spectator' existing within the self who counteracts and qualifies approbation as *moral* approbation. The impartial spectator works by prompting individuals to view themselves as fair-minded objective spectators would view them. Variously named by Smith as 'inhabitant of the breast', 'conscience' and 'the great judge and arbiter of our conduct':

> It is he, who, whenever we are about to act so as to affect the happiness of others, calls to us, with a voice capable of astonishing the most presumptuous of our passions, that we are but one of the multitude, in no respect better than any other in it; and that when we prefer ourselves so shamefully and so blindly to others, we become the proper objects of resentment, abhorrence, and execration. It is from him only that we learn the real littleness of ourselves, and of whatever relates to ourselves, and the natural misrepresentations of self-love can be corrected only by the eye of this impartial spectator. It is he who shows us

---

3 Smith rejected the subsumption of approbation in self-interest when he discussed Bernard Mandeville's 'licentious system' in which the latter claimed that all human actions and interactions are driven by, and could be understood as, individual self-interest. Mandeville included 'love' and 'benevolence' as originating from self-interest because they were seen to enhance the individual's sense of vanity. Smith wrote: 'I shall only endeavour to show that the desire of doing what is honourable and noble, of rendering ourselves the proper objects of esteem and approbation, cannot with any propriety be called vanity' (1982b, VII.ii.4.8).

4 'It is thus that the general rules of morality are formed. They are ultimately founded upon experience of what, in particular instances, our moral faculties, our natural sense of merit and propriety, approve, or disapprove of…When these general rules, indeed, have been formed…we frequently appeal to them as the "standards of judgment," in debating concerning the degree of praise or blame that is due to certain actions of a complicated and dubious nature. They are upon these occasions commonly cited as the ultimate foundations of what is just and unjust in human conduct' (Smith 1982b, III.4.8-11).

the propriety of generosity and the deformity of justice…It is not the love of our neighbour, it is not the love of mankind, which upon occasions prompts us to the practice of those divine virtues. It is a stronger love, a more powerful affection, which generally takes place upon such occasions; the love of what is honourable and noble, of the grandeur, and dignity, and superiority of our own characters' (1982b, III.3.5).

Since sociality is a key characteristic of being a member of society, then it follows that the impartial spectator's guiding voice should apply even in free market exchange relations. Smith wrote in WN that buyers ought to appeal to the self-love as opposed to the benevolence of the 'butcher, the brewer, or the baker' (1981, I.ii.2). It follows that so long as the butcher, brewer or baker's actions are filtered through the impartial spectator, then s/he will not cheat or harm buyers with regard to the quality and price of the product. There is no need to appeal to the humanity of the seller: the impartial spectator is integral to the seller's self-command, so to speak, shaping the necessity of, and morality in, interacting with others in the course of making a living. As Smith wrote in TMS, 'Those general rules of conduct, when they have been fixed in our mind by habitual reflection, are of great use in correcting misrepresentations of self-love concerning what is fit and proper to be done in our particular situation' (1982b, III.4.12).[5]

From Smith's perspective, moral approbation/disapprobation should not be suspended even in situations that, conceivably, inflict little harm. In his discussion of the intent of a poor man to defraud a rich man, he wrote: 'One individual must never

---

5 Smith's writings should be of great interest to researchers of international/intercultural communication. For Smith, communication in human interaction takes on a meaning deeper than that of utility evinced by the common definition and practice of communication as the transmission of information to achieve utilitarian purposes. In TMS, and to a greater extent in WN, Smith traced social stratification to the division of labour that arose from human dispositions to 'truck, barter and exchange'. The respective dispositions, in turn, were premised on and correlated to different kinds of persuasive styles (see Smith 1982a and 1985). At the outset, the meaning of communication that informs and is expressed from exchange relations in the market is epitomized by the sentence, 'Give me that which I want and you shall have this which you want' (Smith 1981, I.ii.2). Thus, communication here can be defined as the transmission of information to achieve utilitarian purposes. Nonetheless as Smith implied in his discussion on morality, communication cannot be narrowly and exclusively bounded by utility in self-interest. Rather, its meaning emerges from and encompasses realization of the self in and for human collectivities because of his premise that peoples seek moral approbation. Even though individuals cannot fully know others except by way of 'imagination' or 'fellow feeling', the desire to do so in ways that affirm one's existence as a social being is that which builds and maintains communities and societies. Discourse on free markets today privileges communication as the transmission or exchange of information. Although necessary to the conduct of business, when accepted and practiced unconditionally and uncritically, this definition marginalizes communication as the realization of the moral self in and for community and society. It can be said then that when free markets are disembedded from society, concomitant shifts in the meaning of communication (from a moral dimension related to building and maintaining communities, to that of transmitting information for the utility of self-interest) furthers not only the processes of legislative deregulation but that of 'moral deregulation' as well.

prefer himself so much even to any other individual, as to hurt or injure that other, in order to benefit himself, *though the benefit to the one should be much greater than the hurt or injury to the other* [emphasis mine]' (Smith 1982b, III.3.6). Evaluations of right and wrong conduct transcend even conditions that may not appear to cause visible harm.

It is appropriate here to bring up a related point. In his discussion, Smith offers a gendered impartial spectator: 'he' (not 'she') guides the self. However, if we follow Smith's point of never hurting or injuring 'the other in order to benefit himself', then it is possible to argue that inequities in gender roles and relations emerge from, and are affirmed by, the inability/unwillingness to consider the guidance of one's impartial spectator who 'whenever we are about to act so as to affect the happiness of others' informs us that 'we are but one of the multitude, in no respect better than any other in it'.[6]

Smith, nonetheless, was aware of the difficulties involved in inflicting as little harm as possible on fellow humans. His subsequent acknowledgment of the imperfectability of human nature is affirmed in discussions of institutional contexts (in TMS, WN as well as *Lectures on Jurisprudence*) required to ensure justice within and beyond the marketplace: 'justice, on the contrary, is the main pillar that holds up the whole edifice...as the great safe-guards of the association of mankind, to protect the weak, to curb the violent, and to chastise the guilty' (Smith 1982b, II.ii.3.4). Smith acknowledged that a key function of states was to ensure commutative, legal and other types of justice.

---

6 Smith did appear to argue that women were better suited for a moral life because of their location in the private-domestic domain. After all, he reflected and affirmed the dominant perspective of his time in which there clearly were delimited and unequal gendered spheres and roles: the public sphere for men and the private-domestic sphere for women (Smith 1981,V. i.f.47). From his perspective, since women lived in the private-domestic domain, they had the better capability to hold and express 'exquisite fellow feeling' than men who dominated the public domain: 'Humanity is the virtue of a woman, generosity of a man' (Smith 1982b, IV.2.10). Yet, his critique of the public-private distinction was evident when he observed men to be generous only when they heeded the advice of the impartial spectator. Even though women had achieved some inheritance rights in his time, they were educated predominantly at home and they, in turn, held the important role of being the primary socializers of children. That boys eventually were educated outside the home and became active consumers in the emerging commercial society, the challenge befell upon them to obey consistently the impartial spectator who would try to lessen the crude utility of their actions: 'We are never generous except when in some respect we prefer some other person to ourselves, and sacrifice some great and important interest of our own to an equal interest of a friend or of a superior' (Smith 1982b, IV.2.10.). Applied to the present day, some might still argue that this supports the demand for women's return to the private-domestic sphere as a key way to protect moral life. This is a fallacious argument, I contend, because it neither resolves persistent problems of inequities in gender roles and relations (e.g., that range from the 'benign' expression of ascribing to women work reminiscent of domesticity, to the more horrific expressions in domestic violence, as well as the continued legitimation of rape as a tool of conflict between communities and nation-states) nor Smith's contention that utility in self-interest dominates the public sphere. For a specific discussion of Smith and gendered citizenship, see Rendall 1987.

Even though Smith celebrated the material advantages accorded by the emerging commercial society of his time, he also identified its moral dilemma. He understood that economic growth via the free market path was driven in part by the poor's emulation of the rich and their ability to demand and consume a variety of goods and services. He observed over the course of time that free markets could and did improve the human condition in specific ways: the more individuals engaged in exchange relations with strangers in the market, the more such interactions facilitated the establishment of economic and political institutions that were comparatively more just and transparent than their predecessors (Smith 1981, 1982a, and 1982b).

Yet, he also identified a key moral dilemma, i.e., corruption of the impartial spectator. Despite material advantages of his emerging commercial society, Smith realized in TMS and WN that this kind of society with its more complex divisions of labour encouraged mental stupor and moral ills that had negative repercussions for social life (1981, V.i.f.50; 1982b, IV.I.6-10). One of his major critiques of commercial society was that participation in the free market had failed to promote critical inquiry and/or self-reflexivity. That which accompanied the emergence of commercial society was a gradual divorce or reworking of the moral foundations for social life. Heightened emphasis on material consumption and wealth made possible by the free market elicited a contradictory effect of corrupting the impartial spectator's ability to guide individuals. Material consumption and the accumulation of wealth had come to assume a central role in informing people's sense of self-worth and their interactions with others.

Smith explicitly warned of the consequences in an increasingly consumption oriented way of life offered by the free market as moral approbation gradually was conflated with materialist criteria in which the rich used their wealth to accumulate and display 'baubles and trinkets' while the poor continued to emulate them. He provided the example of a poor man's son who strove to attain all of the symbols of material wealth and status:

> With the most unrelenting industry he labours night and day to acquire talents superior to all his competitors. He endeavours next to bring those talents into public view, and with equal assiduity solicits every opportunity of employment. For this purpose he makes his court to all mankind ... (Smith 1982b, IV.I.8).

At the end of this man's life, however, he will find that '[p]ower and riches...keep off the summer shower, not the winter storm, but leave him always as much, and sometimes more exposed than before, to anxiety, to fear, and to sorrow; to diseases, to danger, and to death' (Smith 1982b, IV.I.8).

In the sixth and last edition of TMS, revised and published in 1790 nearly two decades after publication of WN, Smith made distinct changes amongst which he identified and discussed the two different paths respectively of the wise and virtuous, and the rich and great: 'Two different roads are presented to us, equally leading to the attainment of this so much desired object; the one, by the study of wisdom and the practice of virtue; the other, by the acquisition of wealth and greatness'. He concluded that:

They are the wise and the virtuous chiefly, a select, though, I am afraid, but a small party, who are the real and steady admirers of wisdom and virtue. The great mob of mankind are the admirers and worshippers, and, what may seem more extraordinary, most frequently the disinterested admirers and worshippers, of wealth and greatness (Smith 1982b I.iii.3.2).

The latter path of 'wealth and greatness' was becoming the norm as the 'great mob of mankind' conflated commercial society's customs and fashions with moral approbation from the impartial spectator (see also TMS, Part IV on virtue).

Thus, Smith highlighted a key contradiction and concomitant moral dilemma emerging from the 'system of natural liberty' brought about by changing economic practices and institutions. While people's pursuit of self-interest in the free market inadvertently had facilitated economic growth and a more just social order than that of the past, emphasis placed on the pursuit of wealth and material consumption in the process had had an adverse effect on the development of the moral self in society (see especially Dickey 1986). Smith died in the same year as publication of TMS' sixth edition.

The moral dilemma has not dissipated since the late eighteenth century. In fact, it is becoming even more resilient and salient with the adoption of free market exchange relations in nearly all dimensions of life, and throughout all regions of the world in the twenty-first century. So long as Smith continues to be invoked in political and economic discourse to help justify the construction and integration of free markets globally, then it is incumbent on us to punctuate this kind of discourse with his thoughts on the 'impartial spectator' and the relationship between morality, economy and society. Now as then, individuals come together to form families, neighbourhoods, cities, firms, and so forth, and they also must grapple with the tensions between self-interest and moral approbation. Living and working increasingly in an integrated global political economy means that identifying the impartial spectator to help navigate morality represents one of the biggest challenges for the foreseeable future.

Four major points arise from our discussion on Smith's understanding of morality. Individuals in collectivities have the capacity for, and are driven by self-interest and approbation. The pursuit of one does not have to entail an exclusion of the other. The impartial spectator that exists within the self is critical to reconciliation of self-interest and approbation by way of moral approbation: it is the barometer that assesses conduct within and beyond the free market. Corruption of the impartial spectator occurs when individuals fail to exercise 'habitual reflection' hence allow substitution of its moral criteria with materialist ones (Smith 1982b, III.4.12).

Applied to our examination of cruise tourism, the issue does not concern open and second registries' right to flag cruise ships but whether or not they should be made to assume the responsibility such as to enforce regulations governing seafarers on ships flying their flags, to help protect ports to which ships call and/or to care for the oceans on which ships sail. It also is not an issue of cruise lines' right to engage in profit seeking activities per se. Rather it is how cruise lines produce pleasure for profits together with the different kinds of costs to port communities, the environment, passengers and seafarers. In this light, institutional and individual investors of cruise corporation stocks can assist possibly by revisiting expectations of corporate earnings and dividends, and by reevaluating corporate conduct to help encourage cruise line practices that mitigate the underside loss, pain and servility.

Indeed, the issue is not one of foreign migrant workers' right to be gainfully employed on cruise ships but the ways in which they are recruited, employed and compensated differentially for their labour. In this light, there also ought to be discussions on accreditation standards for crewing agencies. Nor is it even a question of consumers' right to purchase dream vacations of their choice. Instead, it concerns cruise passengers' understandings of why and how women and men from different countries have come to work in the production of dream vacations, as well as consumers' willingness or not to hold cruise lines accountable for their shipboard security, labour and environmental practices.

To insist that the overall outcome of free market practices is moral without prior discussions of what can and ought to be considered moral conduct today for individuals, firms, communities and states, is to relinquish the right of exercising what free markets continue to promise, i.e., unprecedented choice-making opportunities. Until then, the conclusion to our story of profits, pleasure and work at sea rightly should remain unwritten.

Bibliography

Adler, P.A. and Adler, P. (1999), 'Transience and the postmodern self: The geographic mobility of resort workers', *Sociological Quarterly* 40:1, 31-58.

Ahmed, Z.U., Johnson, J.P., Ling, C.R., Fang, T.W. and Hui, A.K. (2002), 'Country-of-origin and brand effects on consumers' evaluations of cruise lines', *International Marketing Review* 19:3, 279-303.

Aitchison, C. (1999), 'New Cultural Geographies: The Spatiality of Leisure, Gender and Sexuality', *Leisure Studies* 18, 19-39.

Alderton, T. and Winchester, N. (2002), 'Globalisation and de-regulation in the maritime industry', *Marine Policy* 26:1 35-43.

Arakawa, L. (2005), 'Cruise Company violated accord', *The Honolulu Advertiser*, 12 March <http://the.honoluluadvertiser.com/article/2005/Mar/12/bz/bz03p. html> accessed 20 July 2005.

Arshad, L. (2003), 'Star Cruises Spends US $50 Mln and US $100 Mln per annum in Malaysia', *Bernama* (Malaysia), 21 July.

Arya, S. and Roy, A. (eds) (2006), *Poverty, Gender and Migration* (London: Sage).

Ateljevic, I. (2000), 'Circuits of Tourism: stepping beyond the "production/ consumption" dichotomy', *Tourism Geographies* 2:4, 369-88.

Atkinson, J. (1984), 'Manpower strategies for flexible organizations', *Personnel Management* August, 28-31.

Axtmann, R. (2004), 'The state of the state: the model of the modern state and its contemporary transformation', *International Political Science Review* 25:3, 259-79.

Azarya, V. (2004), 'Globalization and International Tourism in Developing Countries: Marginality as a Commercial Commodity', *Current Sociology* 52:6, 949-67.

Bahamas Maritime Authority (n.d.) <http://www.bahamasmaritime.com> (home page).

Ball, R. (1997), 'The role of the state in the globalisation of labour markets: the case of the Philippines', *Environment and Planning A* 29:9, 1603-28.

Barthes, R. (1973), *Mythologies* (Boston: Hill & Wang).

Bauman, Z. (1998), *Globalization: The Human Consequences* (New York: Columbia University Press).

Bax, E.H. (1996), 'Globalization and the Flexibility of Labour: A New Challenge to Human Resource Management. SOM theme A: Structure, Control and Organization of Primary Processes', Research Report number 96A41. Research Institute SOM (Systems, Organisations and Management) University of Groningen, The Netherlands <http://www.som.eldoc.ub.rug.nl/reports/1996/96A41/> accessed 29 September 2005.

Beck, U. (2000), *What is Globalization?* (Cambridge: Polity Press).

Beck, U. and Beck-Gernsheim, E. (2002), *Individualization: Institutionalized Individualism and its Social and Political Consequences* (London: Sage).

Bei, L.T., Chen, E.Y.L. and Widdows, R. (2004), 'Consumers' Online Information Search Behavior and the Phenomenon of Search vs. Experience Products', *Journal of Family and Economic Issues* 25:4, 449-67.

Berger, A.A. (2004), *Ocean Travel and Cruising: A Cultural Analysis* (New York: Haworth Hospitality Press).

Bianchi, R.V. (2000), 'Migrant Tourist-Workers: Exploring the "Contact Zones" of Post-industrial Tourism', *Current Issues in Tourism* 3:2, 107-37.

Bloor, M., Pentsov D., Levi, M., and Horlick-Jones, T. (2004), *Problems of Global Governance of Seafarers' Health and Safety* (Seafarers International Research Centre, Cardiff University, Cardiff, Wales) <http://www.sirc.cf.ac.uk/pdf/ ProblemsGlobalGovernance.pdf> accessed 10 March 2006.

Bluewater Network (2005), 'Safeguarding the Seas' <http://www.bluewaternetwork. org/campaign_ss_cruises.shtml> accessed 11 December 2005.

Bluewater Network (2004a), 'New Cruise Ship Pollution Bill Prohibits Coastal Dumping', *Bluewater Network*, 1 April <http://www.bluewaternetwork.org/press-releases/pr2004apr1_cv_durbinbill.pdf> accessed 7 July 2005.

Bluewater Network (2004b), 'California Cruise Ship Pollution Bills Pass', *Bluewater Network*, 26 August <http://www.bluewaternetwork.org/press-releases/ pr2004aug26_cv_billpass.pdf> accessed 7 July 2005.

Blum, R.H. (1984), *Offshore Haven Banks, Trusts and Companies: The Business of Crime in the Euromarket* (New York: Praeger).

Boczek, B.A. (1962), *Flags of Convenience: An International Legal Study* (Cambridge: Harvard University Press).

Boggs, C. (2000), *The End of Politics: Corporate Power and the Decline of the Public Sphere* (New York: The Guilford Press).

Borgese, E.M. (1998), *The Oceanic Circle: Governing the Seas as a Global Resource* (Tokyo: University Nations University Press).

Bourdieu, P. (1984), *Distinction: A Social Critique of the Judgment of Taste*. Trans. by R. Nice (London: Routledge).

Braudel, F. (1987), *A History of Civilizations*. Trans. by R. Mayne (New York: Penguin).

Britt, J. (2003), 'Netherlands Antilles: A Kind of its Own', *The Maritime Advocate. com*, 22 April <http://www.maritimeadvocate.com/i22_neth.php> accessed 5 August 2005.

Britton, S. (1991), 'Tourism, Capital and Place: Towards a Critical Geography of Tourism', *Environment and Planning D: Society and Space* 9:4, 451-78.

Brown, E. Jr. (2002), 'Cruise Ship Industry: San Pedro's Piece of the Pie?', *Ambergris Today*, 24 January <http://www.ambergristoday.com/archives/24-1-02/> accessed 29 September 2005.

Brown, R.H. (2005), *Culture, Capitalism, and Democracy in the New America* (New Haven: Yale University Press).

Brown, V. (1994), *Adam Smith Discourse: Canonicity, Commerce and Conscience* (London: Routledge).

Bruner, M. (1991), 'Transformation of Self in Tourism', *Annals of Tourism Research* 18:2, 238-50.

Buhalis, D. (1998) 'Strategic use of information technologies in the tourism industry', *Tourism Management* 19:5, 409-21.

Business Research & Economic Advisors (BREA) (2006), *The Contribution of the North American Cruise Industry to the U.S Economy in 2005*. Prepared for the International Council of Cruise Lines, 2006 <http://www.cruising.org/Press/research/Ecoimpact/2005%20Econ%20Impact%20detail.pdf> accessed 30 January 2007.

Business Times (Malaysia) (2004), 'Star Cruises gets China Approval', 14 August.

Caribbean Tourism Organization (CTO) (2004), *Caribbean Tourism Statistical Tables 2003-2004* (Christchurch, Barbados: Caribbean Tourism Organization).

Carlisle, R. (1981), *Sovereignty for Sale: The Origins and Evolution of the Panamanian and Liberian Flags of Convenience* (Annapolis: Naval Institute Press).

Carnival Corporation & plc. (CCL) (2006a), *Form 10-K Annual Report*. SEC EDGAR Filing Information <http://www.sec.gov/Archives/edgar/data/815097/000116923206000521/d66078_10k.txt> (9 February), accessed 9 October 2006.

Carnival Corporation & plc. (CCL) (2006b), *Exhibit 21* of *Form 10-K Annual Report*. SEC EDGAR Filing Information <http://www.sec.gov/Archives/edgar/data/815097/000116923206000521/d66078_ex21.txt> (9 February) accessed 9 October 2006.

Carnival Cruise Lines (n.d.), <http://www.carnival.com> (home page).

Cartwright, R. and Baird, C. (1999), *The Development and Growth of the Cruise Industry* (Oxford: Butterworth Heinemann).

Cassoff, D. (2002), 'Canadians see the world staffing cruise ship crews', *South Florida Business Journal*, 15 November.

Castells, M. (2000), *The Rise of the Network Society* (Malden: Blackwell Publishers).

Cerny, P.G. (1997), 'Paradoxes of the Competition State: The Dynamics of Political Globalisation', *Government and Opposition* 32:2, 251-74.

Chase, G.L. (2001), 'The Economic Impact of Cruise Ships in the 1990s: Some Evidence from the Caribbean', unpublished PhD Dissertation, Kent State University, Ohio.

Chin, C.B.N. (1998), *In Service and Servitude: Foreign Female Domestic Workers and the Malaysian 'Modernity' Project* (New York: Columbia University Press).

Chin, C.B.N. and Mittleman, J.H (2000), 'Conceptualizing Resistance to Globalization', in B.K. Gills (ed.) *Globalization and the Politics of Resistance* (Houndmills: Macmillan).

Chua, B.H. (2000), *Consumption in Asia: Lifestyle and Identity* (London: Routledge).

Chung, Y. (2001), 'Look who's Cruisin'': Star plays for the Asian family in search of a cheap holiday thrill', *Asiaweek*, 2 February, 1.

Churchill, R.R. (2000), 'The Meaning of The "Genuine Link" Requirement in Relation to the Nationality of Ships', Study prepared for the International Transport Workers' Federation <http://www.itfglobal.org/seafarers/icons-site/images/ITF-Oct2000.pdf> accessed 15 April 2005

Clegg, C.A. (2004), *The Price of Liberty: African-Americans and the Making of Liberia* (Chapel Hill: University of North Carolina).

Cohen, E. (1988), 'Authenticity and commoditization in tourism', *Annals of Tourism Research* 15:3, 1-32.

Cohen, M. (2004), 'Wave of the Future', *Far Eastern Economic Review* 23 September, 46-9.

Conroy, M. (2004), 'Upbeat Developments in the State of the Cruise Industry', *Business Briefings: Global Cruise 2004*, 12-14.

Coons, L. and Varias, A. (2003), *Tourist Third Cabin: Steamship Travel in the Interwar Years* (New York: Palgrave Macmillan).

Cordle, I.P. (2002), 'Three Women Sue Royal Caribbean Cruises Ltd. for Alleged Sexual Assault', *Miami Herald*, 5 June.

Cordle, I.P. (2001), 'Fort Lauderdale, Fla.-Based Renaissance Cruises Shuts Down', *Miami Herald*, 26 September.

Courtman, S. (ed.) (2004), *Beyond the Blood, the Beach and the Banana* (Jamaica: Ian Randle).

Crang, P. (1997), 'Performing the Tourist Product', in C. Rojek and J. Urry (eds) *Touring Cultures: Transformations of Travel and Theory* (London: Routledge).

Crawshaw, C. and Urry, J. (1997), 'Tourism and the Photographic Eye,' in C. Rojek and J. Urry (eds) *Touring Cultures: Transformations of Travel and Theory* (London: Routledge).

Crick, M. (1989), 'Representations of International Tourism in the Social Sciences: Sun, Sex, Sights, Savings, and Servility', *Annual Review of Anthropology* 18, 307-44.

Cruise Bruise (n.d.), <http://www.cruisebruise.com> (home page).

Cruise Critic (n.d.), 'About Us' <http://www.cruisecritic.com/aboutus/demographics. cfm> accessed 10 April 2006.

Cruise Critic, Boards (n.d.), <http://boards.cruisecritic.com/> accessed April-June 2006.

Cruise Critic (n.d.), 'Community' <http://www.cruisecritic.com/community> accessed 10 April 2006.

Cruise Critic, Features (n.d.), 'Cruise Line Tipping Policies: Big-Ship Lines' <http:// www.cruisecritic.com./features/articles.cfm?ID=266> accessed 3 April 2006.

Cruise Critic, Features (n.d.), 'Members Speak Out: Cruise Ship Safety', <http:// www.cruisecritic.com/features/articles.cfm?ID=241> accessed 18 June 2006.

Cruise Critic, Features (n.d.),'Members Speak Out: How Big Is Too Big?' <http:// www.cruisecritic.com/features/articles.cfm?ID=246> accessed 3 April 2006.

Cruise Critic, (n.d.), 'Group Cruises' <http://www.cruisecritic.com/interests/ groupleader.cfm> accessed April 25, 2006.

Cruise Critic, News (2006), 'Royal Caribbean Orders New 220,000-Ton Ship!', 6 February <http://www.cruisecritic.com/news/news.cfm?ID=1506> accessed 10 May 2006.

Cruise Critic, News (2004a), 'NCL Alters Pride of Aloha Policies', 6 October <http:// www.cruisecritic.com/news/news.cfm?ID=1131> accessed 11 July 2005.

Cruise Critic, News (2004b), 'NCL Cancels Pride of Aloha Voyage; 'Crew Exhausted', 18 June <http://www.cruisecritic.com/news/news.cfm?ID=1131> accessed July 11 2005.

Cruise Junkie Dot Com (n.d.), <http://www.cruisejunkie.com> (home page).

Cruise Junkie Dot Com (n.d.), 'Pollution and Environmental Violations and Fines, 1995-2005 (Only those reported in the media or public documents)' <http://www.cruisejunkie.com/envirofines.html> accessed 25 May 2006.

Cruise Lines International Association (CLIA). (n.d), <http://www.cruising.org> (home page).

Cruise Lines International Association (CLIA) (2006a), 'Cruise Industry Associations, CLIA and ICCL, To Merge' <http://www.cruising.org/press/press-kits.news.news.cfm?NID=252> accessed 29 June 2006.

Cruise Lines International Association (CLIA) (2006b), *The 2006 Overview* <http://www.cruising.org/press/overview%202006/ind_overview.cfm> accessed 12 December 2006.

Dahl, R. (1971), *Polyarchy, Participation, and Opposition* (New Haven: Yale University Press).

Davidson, L. (2004), 'Cashing in on Cruisegoers', *Mobile Register* 12 December.

Davis, D.E. (1978), 'Development and Tourism in Third World Countries', *Sociology of Leisure* 1: 301-22.

De Pauw, L.G. (1982) *Seafaring Women* (Boston: Houghton Mifflin).

Devraj, R. (2001), 'Rights-Taiwan: Recession puts squeeze on Asian migrant workers', *Interpress* 11 December.

Dewailly, J.M. (1999), 'Sustainable Tourist Space: From Reality to Virtual Reality', *Tourism Geographies* 1:1, 41-55.

Diamond, W.H. and D.B. Diamond (1998), *Tax Havens of the World* (New York: Matthew Bender).

Dickerson, T.A. (2004), 'The Cruise Passenger's Dilemma: Twenty-First-Century Ships, Nineteenth-Century Rights', *Tulane Maritime Law Journal* 28:2, 447-517.

Dickey, L. (1986), 'Historicizing the Adam Smith Problem: Conceptual, Historiographical, and Textual Issues', *Journal of Modern History* 58:3, 579-609.

Dickinson, B. and Vladimir, A. (2004), 'Cruise Line Marketing', in B. Dickinson and A. Vladimir (eds) *The Complete 21st Century Travel and Hospitality* (New Jersey: Pearson).

Dickinson, B. and Vladimir, A. (1997), *Selling the Sea: An Inside Look at the Cruise Industry* (New York: John Wiley & Sons).

Dobbyn, P. (2001), 'Cruises cited in INS crackdown', *Scripps Howard News Service*, 29 August.

Domhoff, G.W. (1979), *The Powers That Be* (New York: The Guilford Press).

Donn, C. (2002) 'Two-tiered Employment in the Global Economy: The World Maritime Industry. Working Paper Series', Working Paper WP2002-002. Management Division, Le Moyne College, Syracuse, New York <http://www.lemoyne.edu/library/mgmt_wp/wp2002-002.pdf> accessed 29 September 2005.

Douglas, W.A. (2000) 'Labor Market Flexibility Versus Job Security – Why Versus?', 1 November <http://www.newecon.org/LaborFlexibility_Douglas.html> accessed 7 October 2005.

Du Gay, P. (1997), *Production of Culture/Cultures of Production* (London: Sage).

Duménil, G. and Lévy, D. (2004), *Capital Resurgent: Roots of the Neoliberal Revolution*. Trans. by D. Jeffers (Cambridge: Harvard University Press).

DuPont, D.K. (2004a), 'Former Security Officer Sues Royal Caribbean Cruises', *Miami Herald*, 9 June.

DuPont, D.K. (2004b), 'Royal Caribbean May Switch Cruise Ship Flags from Norway to Bahamas', *Miami Herald*, 26 May.

DuPont, D.K. (2004c), 'Royal Olympic Cruises Files for Bankruptcy, Idling Miami Ship, Fleet Carnival', *Miami Herald*, 29 January.

DuPont, D.K. (2003a), 'Carnival Corp. Executive Talks about Jump to Global Business', *Miami Herald*, 29 September.

DuPont, D.K. (2003b), 'Carnival Cruise Lines Promotes Payroll-Deduction Installment Plan', *Miami Herald*, 6 September.

DuPont, D.K. (2003c), 'Woman Sues Norwegian Cruise Line Claiming Assault by Wine Steward', *Miami Herald*, 10 June.

Duval, D. (ed.) (2004), *Tourism in the Caribbean: Trends, Developments, Prospects* (London: Routledge).

Eijck, K.v. and Mommaas, H. (2004), 'Leisure, Lifestyle and the New Middle Class', *Leisure Sciences* 26:4, 373-92.

Enloe, C. (2001), *Bananas, Beaches and Bases: Making Feminist Sense of International Politics* (Berkeley: University of California Press).

Ensign, P.C. (1998), 'Interrelationships and horizontal strategy to achieve synergy and competitive advantage in the diversified firm', *Management Decision* 36:1, 657-68.

Evensky, J. (1987), 'The Two Voices of Adam Smith: Moral Philosopher and Social Critic', *History of Political Economy* 19:3, 447-68.

Fan, J.P.H. and Goyal, V.K. (2006), 'On the Patterns and Wealth Effects of Vertical Mergers', *The Journal of Business* 79:2, 877-902.

Farrell, M., Hettne, B. and Van Langenhove, L. (2005), *Global Politics of Regionalism: Theory and Practice* (London: Pluto Press).

Figueroa, A. (2002), 'Coming to a port near you', *Newsweek*, 15 July, 50.

Fineman, M. (1998), 'Tax on Passengers Is a Lot of Garbage, Cruise Lines Say', *Los Angeles Times*, 20 March.

Florida-Caribbean Cruise Association (FCCA) (n.d.), <http://www.f-cca.com> (home page).

Forman-Barzilai, F. (2003), 'Adam Smith as globalization theorist', *Critical Review* 14:4, 391-419.

Franklin, A. and Crang, M. (2001), 'The trouble with tourism and travel theory?', *Tourist Studies* 1:1, 5-22.

Frantz, D. (1999a), 'SOVEREIGN ISLANDS: A special report; For Cruise Ships' Workers, Much Toil, Little Protection', *New York Times*, 24 December.

Frantz, D. (1999b), 'SOVEREIGN ISLANDS: A Question of Regulation; Alaskans Choose Sides in Battle Over Cruise Ships', *New York Times*, 29 November.

Frantz, D. (1999c), 'A Closer Look at the High Seas and the Fine Print', *New York Times*, 31 October.

Frantz, D. (1999d), 'Language Barrier Cited in Inquiry into Ship Fire', *New York Times*, 8 October.

Frantz, D. (1999e), 'Carnival Cruises Raises its Tally of Sexual Misconduct Reports', *New York Times*, 29 July.

Frantz, D. (1999f), 'Cruise Officials to Report Accusations of Crimes at Sea', *New York Times*, 27 July.

Frantz, D. (1999g), 'Cruise Line Reports 62 Alleged Sex Assaults Since '93', *New York Times*, 14 July.

Frantz, D. (1999h), 'Cruise Line Pleads Guilty in Dumping', *New York Times*, 23 March.

Frantz, D. (1999i), 'Cruise Line Is Indicted in Dumping.' *New York Times*, 26 February.

Frantz, D. (1999j), 'SOVEREIGN ISLANDS: A special report; Cruise Lines Reap Profit From Favors in Law', *New York Times*, 19 February.

Frantz, D. (1999k,) 'SOVEREIGN ISLANDS: A special report; Gaps in Sea Laws Shield Pollution by Cruise Lines', *New York Times*, 3 January.

Frantz, D. (1999l), 'Lawmakers Want I.R.S. Help on Cruise Ships and Tax Laws', *New York Times*, 3 January.

Fraser, H. (2003), 'Common Sense & Evidence: Big Bullies in Paradise', *Daily Nation*, 26 October.

Gardner, M. (2003), 'Nakano, others seek tough controls on cruise lines', *Copley News Service*, 11 April.

Garin, K. (2005), *Devils on the Deep Blue Sea: The Dreams, Schemes and Showdowns That Built American's Cruise-Ship Empires* (New York: Viking).

Genting Group (n.d.), <http://www.genting.com> (home page).

George, S. (1999), 'A Short History of Neo-liberalism: Twenty Years of Elite Economics and Emerging Opportunities for Structural Change', Conference on Economic Sovereignty in a Globalizing World, Bangkok, Thailand, 24-26 March <http://www.globalexchange.org/campaigns/econ101/neoliberalism.html> accessed 3 March 2004.

Gershman, S. (1997), *Born to Shop: Caribbean Ports of Call* (New York: Praeger).

Gershuny, J. and Miles, I. (1983), *The New Service Economy* (London: Praeger).

Giddens, A. (1991), *Modernity and Self-Identity: Self and Society in the Late Modern Age* (Cambridge: Polity Press).

Gilmore, W.C. (ed.) (1992), *International Efforts to Combat Money Laundering* (Cambridge: Grotius in association with the Commonwealth Secretariat, London).

Giroux, H.A. (2005), 'The Terror of Neoliberalism: Rethinking the Significance of Cultural Politics', *College Literature* 32:1, 1-19.

Global Ship Services (n.d.), <http://www.globalshipservices.com> (home page).

Global Ship Services (n.d.), 'Crew Member Request Form' <http://www. globalshipservices.com/GSWeb/CrewMemberRequest.htm> accessed 29 July 2005.

Global Ship Services (n.d.) 'Job Description' <http://www.globalshipservices.com/ GSWeb/JobDesc/jobdescTop.htm> accessed 29 July 2005.

Goffman, I. (1959), *The Presentation of Self in Everyday Life* (Garden City: Doubleday).

Goldberg, D.T. (2002), *The Racial State* (Malden: Blackwell).

Goshal, S. and Patton, L. (2002), 'Integrating the Enterprise', *MIT Sloan Management Review* 44:1, 31-41.

Gottdiener, M. (ed.) (2000), *New Forms of Consumption: Consumers, Culture, and Commodification* (Boston: Rowman & Littlefield).

Gramsci, A. (1971), *Selections from Prison Notebooks*. Ed. and trans. by Q. Hoare and G.N. Smith (New York: International Publishers).

Grieder, William (1997), *One World, Ready or Not: The Manic Logic of Global Capitalism* (New York: Touchstone).

Grotius, H. (2004), *The Free Sea*. Trans. by R. Hakluyt with W. Welwod's critique and Grotius' reply; ed. with an introduction by D. Armitage (Indianapolis: Liberty Fund).

Hall, S. (1992), 'Encoding/Decoding', in S. Hall, D. Hobson, A. Lowe and P. Willis (eds) *Culture Media and Language* (London: Routledge).

Hanks III, D. (2002), 'Norwegian Cruise Line to Pay $ 1.5 Million for Polluting Miami-Area Waters', *Miami Herald*, 1 August.

Hannam, K. (2002), 'Tourism and development I: globalization and power', *Progress in Development Studies* 2:3, 227-34.

Harvey, D. (1989), *The Condition of Postmodernity* (Oxford: Blackwell).

Harris, N. (1995), *The New Untouchables: Immigration and the New World Worker* (London: I.B. Tauris).

Hawai'i, State Government of (n.d.) 'The U.S. Passenger Services Act' <http://www. hawaii.gov/dbedt/hecon/he7-99/psa.html> accessed 19 February 2005.

Heilbroner, R.L. (1982), 'The socialization of the individual in Adam Smith', *History of Political Economy* 14:3, 427-39.

Hekimoglu, L. (2001), 'Globalization, Coastal States, and the Turkish Straits', Paper presented at the Conference on 'The Impact of Caspian Oil and Gas Development on Turkey and Challenges Facing the Turkish Straits', organized by The Istanbul Bilgi University Maritime Law Research Centre, Istanbul, Turkey, 9 November.

Hesse, H.G. (2003), 'Maritime Security in a Multilateral Context: IMO Activities to Enhance Maritime Security', *International Journal of Marine and Coastal Law* 18:3, 327-40.

Hirschmann, A.O. (1977), *The Passions and the Interests* (Princeton: Princeton University Press).

Hirst, P. and Thompson, G. (1999), *Globalization in Question: The International Economy and the Possibilities of Governance*, 2nd Edn (Cambridge: Polity Press).

Hochschild, A.R. (1983), *The Managed Heart: Commercialization of Human Feelings* (Berkeley: University of California Press).

Holland America Line (HAL) (n.d.), <http://www.hollandamerica.com> (home page).

Honolulu Star Bulletin (2001), 'Renaissance Cruises halts operations', 26 September <http://starbulletin.com/2001/09/26/business/story5.html> accessed 12 September 2006.

Horck, J. (2004), 'An analysis of decision-making processes in multicultural maritime scenarios', *Maritime Policy and Management* 31:1, 15-29.

Ignacio, L.V.O. (2005), 'Is the POEA Standard Employment Contract Inviolable?', *Tinig Ng Marino*, January-February 2005 <http://www.ufs.ph/tinig/ janfeb05/01020509.html> accessed 12 September 2006.

International Commission on Shipping (ICONS) (2000), *Ships, Slaves and Competition* (Charlestown, Australia: ICONS).

International Council of Cruise Lines (ICCL) (n.d.), 'ICCL Shipboard Workplace Code of Conduct', Cruise Industry Policies <http://www.iccl.org/policies.conduct. cfm> accessed 29 September 2005.

International Council of Cruise Lines (ICCL) (2005), *The Cruise Industry: 2005 Economic Summary* (Arlington, VA: ICCL) <http://www.cruising.org/Press/ research/Ecoimpact/2005%20Econ%20Impact%20Summary.pdf> accessed June 8, 2006.

International Council of Cruise Lines (ICCL) (2001), 'New Mandatory Environmental Standards for Cruiseships', Press Release, 11 June 2001 <http://www.iccl.org/ pressroom/press55.cfm> accessed 12 September 2005.

International Cruise & Ferry Review (2002), 'Manning the decks', Autumn: 122.

International Cruise Victims Association (n.d.) <http://www.internationalcruisevictims. org> (home page).

International Labour Organization (ILO) (2001), *The impact on seafarers' living and working conditions of changes in the structure of the shipping industry*. Report for discussion at the 29th Session of the Joint Maritime Commission, Geneva, Switzerland (Geneva: ILO).

International Labour Organization (ILO) in collaboration with the Seafarers International Research Centre (SIRC) (contributing authors P. Belcher, H. Sampson, M. Thomas, J. Veiga and M. Zhao) (2003), *Women Seafarers: Global employment policies and practices* (Geneva: ILO).

International Maritime Organization (IMO) (n.d.), <http://www.imo.org> (home page).

International Maritime Organization (IMO) (2002), 'Port State Control', <http:// www.imo.org/Safety/mainframe.asp?topic_id=159> accessed 2 August 2005.

International Marketing Strategies (n.d.), <http://www.guidetoshipregistries.com> (home page).

International Transport Workers' Federation (ITF) (n.d.), 'FOC Countries' <http:// www.itfglobal.org/flags-convenience/flags-convenien-183.cfm> accessed 2 May 2006.

International Transport Workers' Federation (ITF) (2005a), *Campaign Against Flags of Convenience and Substandard Shipping: FOC Annual Report 2004* (London: ITF) <http://www.itfglobal.org/infocentre/pubs.cfm/detail/1324> accessed 24 April 2006.

International Transport Worker's Federation (ITF) (2005b), *ITF Seafarers' Bulletin* 19, April.

Ioannides, D. and Debbage, K. (1997), 'Post-Fordism and Flexibility: the travel industry polyglot', *Tourism Management* 18:4, 229-41.

Jaakson, R. (2004), 'Beyond the Tourist Bubble? Cruiseship Passengers in Port', *Annals of Tourism Research* 31:1, 44-60.

Jansson, A. (2002), 'Spatial Phantasmagoria: The Mediatization of Tourism Experience', *European Journal of Communication* 17:4, 429-43.

Jensen, P. (2004), 'Advanced satellite communications for cruise and ferry fleets', *International Cruise & Ferry Review* Spring, 120.

Jones, C.T. (1995), 'The Practical Effects on Labor of Repealing American Cabotage Laws', *Transportation Law Journal* 22:3 403-48.

Kahler, M. and Lake, D.A. (eds) (2003), *Governance in a Global Economy: Political Authority in Transition* (Princeton: Princeton University Press).

Keck, M.E. and Sikkink, K. (1998), *Activists Beyond Borders: Advocacy Networks in International Politics* (Ithaca: Cornell University Press).

Klein, L.R. (1998), 'Evaluating the potential of interactive media through a new lens: Search versus experience goods', *Journal of Business Research* 41:3, 195-203.

Klein, R.A. (2005), *Cruise Ship Squeeze: The New Pirates of the Seven Seas*. (Gabriola Island: New Society Publishers).

Klein, R.A. (2003a), 'The Cruise Industry and Environmental History and Practice: Is a Memorandum of Understanding Effective for Protecting the Environment?' (CA: Blue Water Network) <http://www.bluewaternetwork.org/reports/rep_ss_ kleinrep.pdf> accessed 4 October 2005.

Klein, R.A. (2003b), *Cruising–Out of Control: The Cruise Industry, The Environment, Workers and the Maritimes* (Ottawa: Canadian Centre for Policy Alternatives).

Klein, R.A. (2002a), *Cruise Ship Blues* (Gabriola Island, CA: New Society Publishers).

Klein, R.A. (2002b), 'Left in its wake', *Alternatives Journal* 28:4, 22-7.

Klikauer T. and Morris, R. (2002), 'Into murky waters: Globalisation and deregulation in German's shipping employee relations', *Employee Relations* 24:1-2, 12-28.

Korten, T. (2000), 'Carnival? Try Criminal', *Miami New Times*, 3 February.

Kroll, L. (2004), 'Cruise Control', *Forbes* 174:4, 96.

Laidman, D. (2004), 'Monterey, Calif., City Council Bans Cruise Line for 15 Years after Incident', *Monterey County Herald*, 26 May.

Lamb, R.B. (1974), 'Adam Smith's System: Sympathy not Self-Interest', *Journal of History of Ideas* 35:4, 671-82.

Lane, A.D. (1999), 'Flags of Convenience: Is It Time to Redress the Balance?', *Maritime Review* <http://www.sirc.cf.ac.uk/pdf/Flagcon.pdf> accessed 30 June 2005.

Lane, T. (2001), 'Study looks at mixed nationality crews', first appeared in *The Sea* published by The Mission to Seafarers, Issue 150 March/April <http://www.sirc. cf.ac.uk/The%20Sea/150.pdf> accessed 30 June 2005.

Langewiesche, W. (2004), *The Outlaw Sea: A World of Freedom, Chaos, and Crime* (New York: North Point Press).

Lao Tzu (1997), *The Complete Works of Lao Tzu: Tao Te Ching and Hua Hu Ching*. Translation and Elucidation by H.C. Ni (Santa Monica: Seven Star).

Lebowitz, L. (2003), 'Three Norwegian Cruise Line Engineers Indicted for Concealing Dumping Scheme', *Miami Herald*, 19 December.

Leggate, H. (2004), 'The future shortage of seafarers: will it become a reality?', *Maritime Policy and Management* 31:1, 3-13.

Leyco, N.A. (2004), 'Shipowners Return to RP Shores', *Tinig ng Marino* July-August <http://www.ufs.ph/tinig/julaug04/07080401.html> accessed 29 September 2005.

Li, K.X. and Wonham, J. (1999), 'Who mans the world fleet? A follow-up to the BIMCO/ISF manpower survey', *Maritime Policy and Management* 26:3, 295-303.

Liberian International Ship & Corporate Registry (n.d.), <http://www.liscr.com> (home page).

MacCannell, D. (2001), 'Tourist Agency', *Tourist Studies* 1:1, 23-37.

MacCannell, D. (1989) *The Tourist: A New Theory of the Leisure Class* (New York: Schocken).

MacKinnon, C. 1991. *Toward a Feminist Theory of the State* (Cambridge: Harvard University Press).

Mancini, M. (2000), *Cruising: A Guide to the Cruise Line Industry* (Albany, NY: Delmar).

Mancke, E. (1999), 'Early Modern Experience and the Politicization of Oceanic Space', *Geographical Review* 89:1, 225-36.

Martin, B. (1998), 'Knowledge, identity and the middle class: from collective to individualised class formation?', *The Sociological Review* 4646:4, 653-86.

Martinez, A. (2006a), 'Carnival agrees to settle lawsuit for $6.25 million', *Miami Herald*, 3 May.

Martinez, A. (2006b), 'Miami Center for Litigation Against Cruise Lines', *Miami Herald*, 20 March.

Martinez, M. (2004), 'Cruises that promise something in common', *Seattle Times*, 17 October.

Massey, D.S., Arango J., Hugo G., Kouaouci, A., Pellegrino A. and Taylor J.E. (1998), *Worlds in Motion: Understanding International Migration at the End of the Millennium* (Oxford: Oxford University Press).

Mather, C. (2002), *Sweatships: What It's Really Like to Work on Board Cruise Ships* (London: ITF) <http://www.waronwant.org/Research%20for%20Download%20 3%205472.twl> accessed 2 August 2004.

Mathisen, O. (2005) 'Full Steam Ahead', *Cruise Industry News*. 15 March <http:// www.cruiseindustrynews.com/index.php?option=com_content&task=view&id= 43&Itemid=42> accessed 29 September 2005.

Mathisen, O. (2004a), 'Bigger is Better', *Cruise Industry News*, 16 October <http:// www.cruiseindustrynews.com/index.php?option=com_content&task=view&id= 32&Itemid=42> accessed 29 September 2005.

Mathisen, O. (2004b), 'New Wave of Orders', *Cruise Industry News*, 16 October <http://www.cruiseindustrynews.com/index.php?option=com_content&task=vie w&id=31&Itemid=42> accessed 29 September 2005.

Maxtone-Graham, J. (1985), *Liners to the Sun* (New York: Macmillan).

McDougall, D. (2004), 'Extra hands on deck: Gentlemen hosts and butlers offer personal luxury', *National Post* (Canada), 10 January.

Meethan, K. (2001), *Tourism in Global Society: Place, Culture, Consumption* (Basingstoke: Palgrave).

Messina, A.M. and Lahav, G. (2005), *The Migration Reader: Exploring Politics and Policies* (Boulder: Lynne Rienner).

Miliband, R. (1983), *Class Power and State Power* (London: Verso).

Miliband, R. (1969), *The State in Capitalist Society: An Analysis of the Western System of Power* (New York: Basic Books).

Miller, A.R. and Grazer, W.F. (2002), 'The North American cruise market and Australian tourism', *Journal of Vacation Marketing* 8:3, 221-34.

Millman, J. (2004), 'Enterprise: Cruise Ships Also Bring Crews' Appetite to Port', *Wall Street Journal*, 20 April.

Mitroussi, K. (2003), 'Third party ship management: the case of separation of ownership and management in the shipping context', *Maritime Policy Management* 30:1, 77-90.

Molz, J.G. (2004), 'Playing online and between the lines: round-the-world websites as virtual places to play' in M. Sheller and J. Urry (eds) *Tourism Mobilities: Places to Play and Places in Play* (London: Routledge).

Momsen, J.H. (2005), 'Uncertain Images: Tourism development and seascapes of the Caribbean' in C. Cartier and A.A. Lew (eds) *Seductions of Place: Geographical Perspectives on Globalization and Touristed Landscapes* (London: Routledge).

Morris, J. (1996), 'Lost at sea: 'Flags of Convenience' give owners a paper refuge; Banners don't always represent a nation – and they can mean a way around shipping regulations', *The Houston Chronicle* 22 August.

Morris R. and Klikauer T. (2001), 'Crews of Convenience from the South West Pacific: The 'German' Sailors of Kiribati', *New Zealand Journal of Industrial Relations* 26:2, 185-98.

Mott, D. (2004), 'Are big ships the way forward for the cruise industry?', *International Cruise & Ferry Review* Spring, 94-5.

Mowforth, M. and Munt, L. (1998), *Tourism and Sustainability: New Tourism in the Third World* (London: Routledge).

Munro, E. (2004), Interview by author. Baltimore, MD, 20 September.

Nash, D. (1996), *Anthropology of Tourism* (Oxford: Pergamon Press).

Nash, D. (1978), 'Tourism as a form of imperialism', in V. Smith (ed.) *Hosts and Guests: The Anthropology of Tourism* (Oxford: Blackwell).

Natarajan, P. (2004), 'Cruise line looks to Guam for recruitment', *Pacific Business News*, 3 September.

Nevins, B. (1989), 'Cruise liners no luxury for crew as long hours, low wages prevail', *The Sun-Sentinel*, 2 July.

New York Times (2003), 'In Hawaii, Ship Line Gets Exclusive Rights', 16 February.

Ng, D. (2002), 'Star Cruises outlines US$1b expansion in mainland, US markets', *The Standard*, 19 August.

Nicholson, P.Y. (2001), *Who Do We Think We Are?: Race and Nation in the Modern World* (New York: M.E. Sharpe).

Nielsen, K. (2000), 'The Perfect Scam: For the workers life is no carnival, believe it or not', *Miami New Times*, 3 February.

Norwegian Cruise Line (NCL) (n.d.) <http://www.ncl.com> (home page).

Oakley, A. (1994), *Classical Economic Man: Human Agency and Methodology in the Political Economy of Adam Smith and J.S. Mill* (Aldershot: Edward Elgar).

Oceana (2004), 'Royal Caribbean Campaign Victory', 4 May <http://www.oceana.org/index.php?id=801> accessed 3 April 2006.

Oceans Blue Foundation (2002), 'Blowing the Whistle and the Case for Cruise Certification', October <http://www.kahea.org/ocean/pdf/blowing_whistle_10-02.pdf> accessed 29 September 2005.

Opello, W.C. and Rosow, S.J. (1999), *The Nation-State and Global Order: A Historical Introduction to Contemporary Politics* (Boulder: Lynne Rienner).

Otteson, J.R. (2002), *Adam Smith's Marketplace of Life* (Cambridge: Cambridge University Press).

Oude Elferink, A. G. (1999), 'The Genuine Link Concept: Time for a *Post-Mortem*?', (Netherlands Institute for the Law of the Sea (NILOS), Utrecht University, The Netherlands) <http://www.uu.nl/content/genuine%20link.pdf> accessed 15 June 2005.

Oyen, J. (2005), Telephone interview by author. Miami, FL. 3 August.

Pabico, A.S. (2003), 'Despite the Risks, Filipino Seafarers Toil in the World's Oceans', Philippines Center for Investigative Journalism <http://www.pcij.org/stories/print/seafarers.html> accessed 5 January 2005.

Palan, R. (2003), *The Offshore World: Sovereign Markets, Visual Places and Nomad Millionaires* (Ithaca: Cornell University Press).

Palan, R. (2002), 'Tax Havens and the Commercialization of State Sovereignty', *International Organization* 56:1, 151-176.

Palmeri, C. (2004), 'Carnival: Plenty of Ports in a Storm', *Business Week*, 15 November.

Panama, Consulate in New York (n.d.) 'Maritime Section', <http://www.nyconsul.com> (home page).

Panitch, L. (1996), 'Rethinking the Role of the State', in J. H. Mittelman (ed.) *Globalization: Critical Reflections* (Boulder: Lynne Rienner).

Pattullo, P, (2005) *Last Resorts: The Cost of Tourism in the Caribbean*, 2nd edn, updated and revised (London: Latin American Bureau).

Pattullo, P. (1996), *Last Resorts: The Cost of Tourism in the Caribbean*. Kingston (Jamaica: Ian Randle).

Pearce, D. (1999), *Tourism Development* (Harlow: Longman).

Persaud, R.B. and Walker, R.B.J. (eds) (2001), Special Issue 'Apertura: Race in International Relations', *Alternatives: Global, Local, Political* 26:4.

Petitpas, A. (2005), Interview by author. Baltimore, MD. 21 July.

Philippine Overseas Employment Administration (POEA) (2003), *Annual Report 2003*. (Mandaluyong City, Philippines: Department of Labor and Employment, Government of Philippines) <http://www.poea.gov.ph> (home page), accessed 29 September 2005.

Philippine Seafarers Assistance Programme (1999), 'Rough sailing for Filipino sailors', *Philippines International Review* 1:4, n.p <http://www.philsol.nl/pir/Seafarers-99a.htm> accessed 28 July 2004.

Picard, M. and Wood, R.E. (eds) (1997), *Tourism, Ethnicity and the State in Asian and Pacific Societies* (Honolulu: University of Hawaii Press).

Pijl, K.v.d. (2004), 'Two faces of the transnational cadre under neoliberalism', *Journal of International Relations and Development* 7:2, 177-207.

Polanyi, K. (1944), *The Great Transformation: The Political and Economic Origins of Our Time* (Boston: Beacon Press).

Poon, A. (1993), *Tourism, Technology and Competitive Strategies* (Wallingford: CAB International).

Poon, A. (1990), 'Flexible specialization and small size: the case of Caribbean tourism', *World Development* 18:1, 109-23.

Poulantzas, N. (1973), *Political Power and Social Classes* (London: New Left Books).

Pred, A. (1996), 'Interfusions: Consumption, Identity and the Practices and Power Relations of Everyday Life', *Environment and Planning A* 28, 11-24.

Preece, J. (2000), *Online Communities: Designing usability, supporting sociability* (New York: John Wiley).

Prentice, R. (2001), 'Tourism in the Information Society', *International Journal of Tourism Research* 3:1 62-4.

Princess Cruises (n.d.), <http://www.princess.com> (home page).

Raphael, D.D. and Macfie, A.L. (eds) (1982), 'Introduction', in A. Smith *The Theory of Moral Sentiments* (Indianapolis: Liberty).

Rapley, J. (2004), *Globalization and Inequality: Neoliberalism's Downward Spiral* (Boulder: Lynne Rienner).

Rendall, J. (1987), 'Virtue and Commerce: Women in the Making of Adam Smith's Political Economy', in E. Kennedy and S. Mendus (eds) *Women in Western Political Philosophy: Kant to Nietzche* (New York: St. Martin's Press).

Reynolds, C. and Weikel, D. (2000), 'For Cruise Ship Workers: Voyages Are No Vacations', *Los Angeles Times*, 30 May.

Ritzer, G. (2005), *Enchanting a Disenchanted World: Revolutionizing the Means of Consumption* (Thousand Oaks: Pine Forge Press).

Ritzer, G. (2003), 'Rethinking Globalization: Glocalization/Grobalization and Something/Nothing', *Sociological Theory* 21:3, 193-209.

Ritzer, G. and Liska, A. (1997). 'McDisneyization and "Post-Tourism": Complementary perspectives on contemporary tourism', in C. Rojek and J. Urry (eds) *Touring Cultures: Transformations of Travel and Theory* (London: Routledge).

Ritzer, G. and Stillman, T. (2001), 'The Modern Las Vegas Casino-Hotel: The Paradigmatic New Means of Consumption', *M@n@gement* 4:3, 83-99.

Robinson, W. I. (2003), 'Review Article: The Debate on Globalization', *Science and Society* 67:3, 353-60.

Rojek, C. (2000), 'Mass Tourism or the Re-Enchantment of the World/Issues and Contradictions in the Study of Travel', in M. Gottdiener (ed.) *New Forms of Consumption* (Lanham, Rowman & Littlefield).

Rojek, C. (1995), *Decentring Leisure: Rethinking Leisure Theory* (London: Sage).

Rojek, C. and Urry, J. (eds) (1997), *Touring Cultures: Transformations of Travel and Theory* (London: Routledge).

Romero, M. (1992), *Maid in the U.S.A.* (London: Routledge).

Royal Caribbean International (n.d.), <http://www.royalcaribbean.com> (home page).

Royal Caribbean Cruises Limited (RCL) (2006a), *Form 10-K Annual Report*. SEC EDGAR Filing Information <http://www.sec.gov/Archives/edgar/data/884887/00 0088488706000003/form10k2005.htm> (24 February) accessed 9 October 2006.

Royal Caribbean Cruises Limited (RCL) (2006b), *Exhibit 21.1 of Form 10-K Annual Report*. SEC EDGAR Filing Information <http://www.sec.gov/Archives/edgar/data/884887/000088488706000003/ex21_1.htm> (24 February) accessed 9 October 2006.

Said, E.W. (1993), *Culture and Imperialism* (New York: Knopf).

Sampson, H. (2003), 'Transnational drifters or hyperspace dwellers: an exploration of the lives of Filipino seafarers aboard and ashore', *Ethnic and Racial Studies* 26:2, 253-77.

Sampson, H. and Zhao, M. (2003), 'Multilingual crews: communication and the operation of ships', *World Englishes* 22:1, 31-43.

Sassen, S. (2001), *Globalization and Its Discontents* (New York: The New Press).

Scholte, J.A. (2000), *Globalization: A Critical Introduction* (Basingstoke: Palgrave).

Schubert, W.G. (2002), 'Vessel Operations under 'Flags of Convenience' and National Security Implications', House Armed Services Committee Special Oversight Panel on the Merchant Marine, 13 June <http://www.house.gov/hasc/openingstatementsandpressreleases/107> accessed 2 May 2006.

Sea Cruises Enterprise (n.d.), 'Sample of Employment Contract' <http://www.seacruiseent.com/scesite/samplecontract.html> accessed 18 November 2004.

Seafarers International Research Centre (n.d.) <http://www.sirc.ac.uk> (home page).

Seal, K. (1998), 'Cruise ships draw new crews', *Hotel and Motel Management* 213: 4, 9.

Seamen's Church Institute of New York and New Jersey (n.d.) <http://www.seamenschurch.org> (home page).

Selwyn, T. (1996), *The Tourist Image: Myths and Myth Making in Tourism* (Chichester: Wiley).

Sen, K. and Stivens, M. (ed.) (1998), *Gender and Power in Affluent Asia* (London: Routledge).

Shakespeare, W. (2005), *Merchant of Venice* (New York: Pearson Longman).

Sharpe, P. (ed.) (2001), *Women, Gender and Labour Migration: Historical and Global Perspectives* (London: Routledge).

Shaw, G. and Williams, A.M. (eds) (1994), *Critical Issues in Tourism: A Geographical Perspective* (Oxford: Blackwell).

Shays, C. (2006), 'International Cruise Victims announce Bipartisan Cruise Line Accurate Safety Statistics Act' <http://www.house.gov/shays/news/2006/june/junecruise.htm> accessed 28 June 2006.

Sheller, M. (2004a), 'Demobilizing and remobilizing Caribbean paradise', in M. Sheller and J. Urry (eds) *Tourism Mobilities: Places to Play and Places in Play* (London: Routledge).

Sheller, M. (2004b), 'Natural Hedonism: The Invention of Caribbean Islands as Tropical Playgrounds', in S. Courtman (ed.) *Beyond the Blood, the Beach and the Banana* (Kingston: Ian Randle).

Sheller, M. and Urry, J. (2004), 'Places to Play, Places in Play', in M. Sheller and J. Urry (eds) *Tourism Mobilities: Places to Play, Places in Play* (London: Routledge).

Shick, T.W. (1980), *Behold the Promised Land: A History of African-American Settler Society in Nineteenth Century Liberia* (Baltimore: Johns Hopkins University).

Shie, T.R. (2004), 'Ports in a Storm? The Nexus Between Counterterrorism, Counterproliferation, and Maritime Security in Southeast Asia', *Pacific Forum CSIS (Honolulu) Issues & Insights* 4:4, 1-68.

Showalter, G.R. (1994), 'Cruise Ships and Private Islands in the Caribbean', *Journal of Travel and Tourism Marketing* 3:4, 107-18.

Sinclair, T. (ed). (1997), *Gender Work and Tourism* (London: Routledge).

Singh, A. (2000), 'Growth and Development of the Cruise Line Industry in Southeast Asia', in K.S. Chon (ed.), *Tourism in Southeast Asia: A New Direction* (New York: Haworth Hospitality Press).

Smith, A. (1985), *Lectures on Rhetoric and Belles Lettres* Ed. by J.C. Bryce (Indianapolis: Liberty Fund).

Smith, A. (1982a), *Lectures on Jurisprudence*. Ed. by R.L. Meek, D.D. Raphael, and P.G. Stein (Indianapolis: Liberty Fund).

Smith, A. (1982b), *The Theory of Moral Sentiments*. Ed. by D.D. Raphael and A.L. Macfie (Indianapolis: Liberty Fund).

Smith, A. (1981), *An Inquiry into the Nature and Causes of the Wealth of Nations* (WN) vols. I and II, general ed. by R.H. Campbell and A.S. Skinner, textual ed. by W.B. Todd (Indianapolis: Liberty Fund).

Smith, M.A. and Kollock, P. (1999), *Communities in Cyberspace* (New York: Routledge).

Sottili, C. (2004), 'Baltimore Cruises Cut Back: Only One Major Line Plans to Sail From Md. Port in 2005', *Washington Post*, 3 October.

Standing, G. (1999), *Global Labor Flexibility: Seeking Distributive Justice* (New York: St. Martin's Press).

Star Cruises (n.d.), <http://www.starcruises.com> (home page).

Star Cruises Limited (SCL) (2005), *2005 Annual Report* <http://info.sgx.com/listprosp.nsf/4f925e50089e98bf48256dad001425f5/f4c4d23cc47dff0b48257147000811a2?OpenDocument> (31 December 2005), accessed 10 October 2006.

Stevenson, D.B. (2005), Interview by author. New York, NY. 24 March.

Stevenson, D.B. (n.d.), 'POEA Approves New Standard Agreement', Center for Seafarers' Rights of the Seamen's Church Institute of New York and New Jersey <http://www.seamenschurch.org/CSR%20Website/POEA's%20New%20Agreement.htm> accessed 1 August 2004.

Stevenson D. B. (n.d.), 'Illegal Contracts', Center for Seafarers' Rights of the Seamen's Church Institute of New York and New Jersey <http://www.seamenschurch.org/CSR%20Website/Illegal%20Contracts.htm> accessed 1 August 2004.

Stopford, M. (1988), *Maritime Economics* (London: Unwin Hyman).

Strachan, I.G. (2002), *Paradise and Plantation: Tourism and Culture in the Anglophone Caribbean* (Charlottesville: University of Virginia).

Strange, S. (1996), *The Retreat of the State: The Diffusion of Power in the World Economy* (Cambridge: Cambridge University Press).

Strange, S. (1976), 'Who Runs World Shipping?', *International Affairs* 52:3, 346-67.

Stratton, S. (2000), 'Marxist Theory, the Globalisation of Port Development, and the Role of Labour', *JoSCCI* (Journal of Social Change and Critical Inquiry) No. 2 <http://www.uow.edu.au/arts/joscci/stratton.html> accessed 29 September 2005.

Stubbs, R. and Underhill, G. (2005), *Political Economy and the Changing Global Order* (Oxford: Oxford University Press).

Tang, E. (2001), 'Home away from home for Myanmar migrants', *The Straits Times*, 26 May.

Taylor, S. (1998), 'Emotional Labour and the New Workplace', in P. Thompson and C. Warhurst (eds) *Workplaces of the Future* (New York: Palgrave Macmillan).

Testa, M., Mueller, S.L. and Thomas, A.S. (2003), 'Cultural Fit and Job Satisfaction in a Global Service Environment', *Management International Review* 43:2, 129-48.

The Sailors' Union of the Pacific (2000), *West Coast Sailors* LXIII: 9, 22 September.

The San Pedro Sun (2004), 'Cruise Ship Contracts Spout Controversy', 7 October <http://www.sanpedrosun.net/old/04-342.html> accessed 6 June 2005.

Tickner, J.A. (2001), *Gendering World Politics* (New York: Columbia University Press).

Tisdell, C. (ed.) (1999), *The Economics of Tourism* vol. 2 (Cheltenham: Edward Elgar).

Torres, J.A. (2004), 'Immigrants are dominant work force on cruise ships', *USA Today*, 10 March <http://www.usatoday.com/travel/news/2004-03-10-workers-cruise_x.htm> accessed 13 November 2004.

Tracy, S.J. (2000), 'Becoming a Character for Commerce: Emotional Labor, Self-Subordination, and Discursive Construction of Identity in a Total Institution', *Management Communication Quarterly* 14:1, 90-128.

Turner, G. (2004a), 'Cruise lines choosing to book private islands', *The Vancouver Sun*, 24 January.

Turner, G. (2004b), 'Your own private island: Between ports of call, cruise lines discover the secret to satisfaction', *National Post* (Canada), 10 January.

United Nations (n.d.) 'Convention on the Law of the Seas of 10 December 1982: Article 91', <http://www.un.org/Depts/los/convention_agreements/texts/unclos/closindx.htm> accessed 1 August 2005.

United Press International (2004), 'Cruise liners prepare to stop in India', 31 March.

Urry, J. (2002), *The Tourist Gaze*, 2nd Edition. (London: Sage).

Urry, J. (1995), *Consuming Places* (London: Routledge).

Urry, J. (1992), 'The Tourist Gaze '"Revisited"', *American Behavioral Scientist* 36:2, 172-86.

Urry, J. (1990), 'The Consumption of Tourism', *Sociology* 24:1, 23-35.

US Department of the Navy, Military Sealift Command (2006), 'Strategic Sealift Inventory As of 1 January 2006', <http://www.msc.navy.mil/n35/quarterly.htm> accessed 20 May 2006.

US House of Representatives. Committee on Government Reform, Subcommittee on National Security, Emerging Threats and International Relations (2006), Hearing on *International Maritime Security II.* 7 March <http://a257.g.akamaitech.net/7/257/2422/16aug20061200/www.access.gpo.gov/congress/house/pdf/109hrg/28532.pdf> accessed 20 August 2006.

US House of Representatives. Committee on Government Reform, Subcommittee on National Security, Emerging Threats and International Relations, and the

Subcommittee on Criminal Justice, Drug Policy and Human Resource (2005), Joint Hearing on *International Maritime Security.* 13 December <http://a257. g.akamaitech.net/7/257/2422/12jul20061200/www.access.gpo.gov/congress/ house/pdf/109hrg/27923.pdf> accessed 20 August 2006.

US House of Representatives, Subcommittee on Coast Guard and Maritime Transportation, of the Committee on Transportation and Infrastructure (1999), *Hearing on Cruise Ship Safety* (1999), 7 October <http://www.commdocs. house.gov/committees/trans/hpw106-45.000/hpw106-45_0.HTM> accessed 8 September 2006.

US Joint Chiefs of Staff (2005), 'Sealift Support to Joint Operations', Joint Publication 4-01.2. 31 August <http://www.dtic.mil/doctrine/jel/new_pubs/jp4_ 01_2.pdf> accessed 7 September 2006.

Veseth, M. (2005), *Globaloney: Unraveling the Myths of Globalization* (Lanham, MD: Rowman & Littlefield).

Vidas, D. and Ostreng, W. (eds) (1999), *Order for the Oceans at the Turn of the Century* (The Hague: Kluwer Law International).

Von Dreele, J.D. (2004), Interview by author. Philadelphia, PA. 28 September.

Wackermann, G. (1997), 'Transport, trade, tourism and the world economic system', *International Social Science Journal* 49:1, 3-9.

Walsh, D. (2000), 'Huge Ships, High Tech, and High Value', *Sea Power* 43:5, 41-3.

Wang, Y., Yu, Q., and Fesenmaier, D.R. (2002), 'Defining the virtual tourist community: implications for tourism marketing', *Tourism Management* 23:4, 407-17.

Watson, H.A. (2004), 'Liberalism and Neo-liberal Capitalist Globalization: Contradictions of the Liberal Democratic State', *GeoJournal* 60:1, 43-59.

Weaver, A. (2005a), 'Representation and Obfuscation: Cruise Travel and the Mystification of Production', *Tourism Culture & Communication* 5:3 165-76.

Weaver, A. (2005b), 'Spaces of Containment and Revenue Capture: "Super-Sized" Cruise Ships as Mobile Tourism Enclaves', *Tourism Geographies* 7:2, 165-84.

Weaver, J. (2003a), 'Norwegian Cruise Line's Crewmen, Kin Want U.S. Trials', *Miami Herald*, 23 September.

Weaver, J. (2003b), 'U.S. Judge Rejects SS Norway Crew's Lawsuit against Norwegian Cruise Line', *Miami Herald*, 13 October.

Webber, D. (ed) (2005), *Regional Integration in Europe and East Asia: Convergence or Divergence* (London: Routledge).

Werhane, P.H. (1991), *Adam Smith and His Legacy for Modern Capitalism* (New York: Oxford University Press).

Wight, J.B. (2002), 'The Rise of Adam Smith: Articles and Citations, 1970-1997', *History of Political Economy* 34:2, 55-82.

Wilkinson, P.F. (1999), 'Caribbean cruise tourism: delusion? illusion?', *Tourism Geographies* 1:3, 261-82.

Williams, A.M. and Hall, C.M. (2000), 'Tourism and migration: new relationships between production and consumption', *Tourism Geographies* 2:1, 5-27.

Wilson, D. and Sherwood, D. (eds) (2000), *Oceans Governance and Maritime Strategy* (Australia: Allen & Unwin).

Wilson, T. and Suraya, R.M.Y. (2004), 'The tourist gaze goes on-line: Rojak (hybrid) reception theory structures of ludic looking at/from Malaysia', *Tourist Studies* 4:1, 69-92.

Wilthagen, T. (2002), 'The Flexibility-Security Nexus: New approaches to regulating employment and labour markets', OSA Working Paper WP2002-18, OSA/Institute for Labour Studies, Tilburg University, The Netherlands. September (Also written for the *British Journal of Industrial Relations* 'The Politics of Employment Relations' Conference, 16-17 September 2002, Cumberland Lodge, The Great Park, Windsor, UK.).

Winch, D. (1978), *Adam Smith's Politics: An Essay in Historiographic Revision* (Cambridge: Cambridge University Press).

Wise, J. (1999), 'How cruise ships shortchange the Caribbean', *Fortune* 139:6, 44-5.

Wiseman, J. (2005), 'USD236 million Cruise Ship Deal Criticized', *Washington Post*, 28 September.

Wood, R.E. (2004a), 'Caribbean of the East? Global Interconnections and the Southeast Asian Cruise Industry', *Asian Journal of Social Science* 30:2, 420-40.

Wood, R.E. (2004b), 'Global Currents: Cruise Ships in the Caribbean Sea', in David Duval (ed.) *Tourism in the Caribbean: Trends, Developments, Prospects* (London: Routledge.

Wood, R.E. (2000), 'Caribbean Cruise Tourism: Globalization at Sea', *Annals of Tourism Research* 27:2, 345-70.

World Tourism Organization (WTO) (2003), *Worldwide Cruise Ship Activity* (Madrid, Spain: World Tourism Organization).

World Travel and Tourism Council (WTTC) (2004), *The Caribbean: The Impact of Travel & Tourism on Jobs and the Economy* (London: WTTC).

World Travel and Tourism Council (WTTC) (2002), International Hotel & Restaurant Association (IH&RA), International Federation of Tour Operators (IFTO) , International Council of Cruise Lines (ICCL), and The United Nations Environment Programme, *Industry as a partner for sustainable development: Tourism* (UK: Beacon Press).

Wu, B. (2005), *The World Cruise Industry: A Profile of the Global Labour Market* (Cardiff Seafarers International Research Centre, Cardiff University) <http://www.sirc.cf.ac.uk/pdf/WorldCruiseIndustry.pdf> accessed 3 February 2006.

Wu, B. (2004), 'Participation in the global labour market: experience and responses of Chinese seafarers', *Maritime Policy and Management* 31:1, 69-82.

Yamanouchi, K. (2004), 'Cruise Lines Job Not What Some Thought', *The Honolulu Advertiser*, 18 April <http://the.honoluluadvertiser.com/article/2004/Apr/18/bz/bz04a.html> accessed 29 September 2005.

Young, R. (1977), 'The Structural Context of the Caribbean Tourist Industry: A Comparative Study', *Economic Development and Cultural Change* 25:4, 657-72.

Zhao, M. (2002), 'Emotional Labour in a Globalised Labour Market: Seafarers on Cruise Ships', Cardiff School of Social Sciences, Seafarers International Research Centre, Working Paper Series No. 27, Cardiff, Wales, May <http://www.sirc.cf.ac.uk/pdf/MZwrkgpaper27%5B1%5D.pdf> accessed 10 May 2005.

Zhao, M. (2001), 'The Impact of Enterprise Reform on Chinese Seafarers', Cardiff University, Cardiff School of Social Sciences, Seafarers International Research

Centre, Working Paper Series No. 14, Cardiff, Wales, September <http://www.cardiff.ac.uk/socsi/resources/wrkgpaper14.pdf> accessed 10 May 2005.

Zhao, M. (2000), 'Women seafarers on cruiseships', first appeared in *The Sea* published by The Mission to Seafarers). Issue 145, May/June <http://www.sirc.cf.ac.uk/pubssea.htm> accessed 30 July 2004.

Index

THE INTERNATIONAL POLITICAL ECONOMY OF NEW REGIONALISMS SERIES

Full series list

Governing Regional Integration
for Development
Monitoring Experiences, Methods and
Prospects
*Edited by Philippe De Lombaerde,
Antoni Estevadeordal and Kati Suominen*

Beyond Regionalism?
Regional Cooperation, Regionalism and
Regionalization in the Middle East
*Edited by Cilja Harders
and Matteo Legrenzi*

The EU–Russian Energy Dialogue
Europe's Future Energy Security
Edited by Pami Aalto

Regionalism, Globalisation and
International Order
Europe and Southeast Asia
Jens-Uwe Wunderlich

EU Development Policy and
Poverty Reduction
Enhancing Effectiveness
Edited by Wil Hout

An East Asian Model for Latin
American Success
The New Path
Anil Hira

European Union and New Regionalism
Regional Actors and Global Governance in
a Post-Hegemonic Era
Edited by Mario Telò

Regionalism, Globalisation and
International Order
Europe and Southeast Asia
Jens-Uwe Wunderlich

The Limits of Regionalism
NAFTA's Labour Accord
Robert G. Finbow

Regional Integration and Poverty
*Edited by Dirk Willem te Velde and the
Overseas Development Institute*

Redefining the Pacific?
Regionalism Past, Present and Future
*Edited by Jenny Bryant-Tokalau and
Ian Frazer*

Globalization and Antiglobalization
Dynamics of Change in the
New World Order
Edited by Henry Veltmeyer

Latin America's Quest for Globalization
The Role of Spanish Firms
*Edited by Félix E. Martín and
Pablo Toral*

Exchange Rate Crises in
Developing Countries
The Political Role of the Banking Sector
Michael G. Hall

Persistent Permeability?
Regionalism, Localism, and Globalization
in the Middle East
*Edited by Bassel F. Salloukh and
Rex Brynen*

Reforging the Weakest Link
Global Political Economy and Post-Soviet
Change in Russia, Ukraine and Belarus
Edited by Neil Robinson

Twisting Arms and Flexing Muscles
Humanitarian Intervention and
Peacebuilding in Perspective
*Edited by Natalie Mychajlyszyn and
Timothy M. Shaw*